Weekend Utopia

modern living in the hamptons

ALASTAIR GORDON

PRINCETON ARCHITECTURAL PRESS *NEW YORK*

PUBLISHED BY

Princeton Architectural Press

37 East Seventh Street

New York, NY 10003

For a catalog of books published by Princeton Architectural
Press, call toll free 800.722.6657 or visit www.papress.com.

EDITOR: Mark Lamster

BOOK AND JACKET DESIGN: Sara E. Stemen

INDEX: Judith Koppenberg

SPECIAL THANKS: Nettie Aljian, Ann Alter, Amanda Atkins,
Janet Behning, Jan Cigliano, Jane Garvie, Clare Jacobson,
Nancy Later, Anne Nitschke, Lottchen Shivers, Jennifer
Thompson, and Deb Wood of Princeton Architectural Press
—Kevin C. Lippert, publisher

LIBRARY OF CONGRESS CATALOGING-IN-PUBLICATIONS DATA

Gordon, Alastair.

    Weekend utopia : modern living in the Hamptons / by

    Alastair Gordon.— 1st ed.

      p. cm.

    Includes bibliographical references and index.

    ISBN 1-56898-272-0

      1. Seaside architecture—New York (State)—Hamptons.

    2. Vacation homes—New York (State)—Hamptons.

    3. Architect-designed houses—New York (State)—

    Hamptons. 4. Artists—Homes and haunts—New York

    (State)—Hamptons. 5. Lifestyles—New York (State)—

    Hamptons—History—20th century I. Title.

    NA7575 .G67 2001

    728.7'2'0974721—DC21   2001000160

PRINTED IN CHINA

for Helen and Ernest Gordon

CONTENTS

Acknowledgments   ix

Introduction   1

CHAPTER ONE   The Fresh Green Breast   4

CHAPTER TWO   Bauhaus on the Beach   24

CHAPTER THREE   Convergence   40

CHAPTER FOUR   Laboratories of Leisure   68

CHAPTER FIVE   The Anticube   100

CHAPTER SIX   Twist and Shout   124

EPILOGUE   Past Perfect   162

Notes   169

Selected Bibliography   173

Index   175

Image Credits   181

SPECIAL THANKS GO to the Graham Foundation for Advanced Study in the Fine Arts for its generous support of the research and writing of this book. I am grateful to Kevin Lippert of Princeton Architectural Press for having faith in this project, and to my editor, Mark Lamster, who worked tirelessly toward its realization. Sara Stemen is to be commended for her thoughtful design.

Many individuals provided invaluable information and insight along the way. Some were kind enough to lend photographs, drawings, and other artifacts for reproduction in this book. I wish to acknowledge and thank Anneli Arms, John Arms, Sarah Auld, Fred Baker, Joan Banach, Robert Barnes, Richard Bender, Fernanda Bennett, Peter Blake, Keith Boyce, John Cays, Alan Chimacoff, Karen Cooper, Chris Coy, Diana Dayton, Alfredo De Vido, Dallas Ernst, Paul Domzal, Kate Evarts, Eliot Fischman, Harry Fischman, B. H. Friedman, Jonathan Friedman, Andrew Geller, Shirley Geller, David Giovannitti, John Githens, David Goldstein, Jake Gorst, Peter Gluck, Naomi Goodman, Percival Goodman, Vera Graaf, Lisa Green, Richard Grimes, Charles Gwathmey, Ingeborg ten Haeff, Helen Harrison, Jeff Heatley, Peter Hendrickson, David Hirsch, Jay Hoops, Norman Jaffe, Sarah Jaffe, Carlton Kelsey, Lillian Kiesler, Dorothy King, Eric Kuhn, Marvin Kuhn, Jack Lenor Larsen, Roland Legiardi-Laura, Stephen Lesser, Bernard Marson, Richard Meier, Joseph Montezinos, Robert Motherwell, William Muschenheim, Hans Namuth, Peter Namuth, Jacqueline Nelson, Barbara Neski, Julian Neski, Costantino Nivola, Ruth Nivola, Preston Philips, Ron Pisano, Edward Pospisil, Jeffrey Potter, Rameshwar Das, David Rattray, Helen Rattray, Carol Rifkin, Jaquelin T. Robertson, Julie Rosenberg, Barney Rosset, Bret Sanders, Susan Scanlon, Max Scott, Constance Schwartz, Julie Maris Semel, Beatrice Simpson, Mike Solomon, Jane Smith, Frederick Stelle, Robert A. M. Stern, Erica Stoller, Ezra Stoller, Hattie Strongin, Peter Turino, and Robert Venturi.

Those institutions, publications, and archives that deserve my gratitude include the Avery Library Special Collections at Columbia University, Condé Nast Publications, the Chrysler Museum, the Dedalus Foundation, the *East Hampton Star*, Friends of the Motherwell House, the Geraldine R. Dodge Foundation, the Guild Hall Museum in East Hampton, the Long Island Collection at the East Hampton Library, the Macdowell Colony, the Museum of Modern Art in New York, the Hans Namuth Estate, the Nassau County Museum of Art, the New York State Council on the Arts, the *New York Times*, the Ossorio Foundation, the Pollock-Krasner House and Study Center, the Tony Smith Estate, the Society for the Preservation of Long Island Antiquities, and the Paul Lester Wiener Collection at the University of Oregon Library.

Most of all, I want to thank my wife, Barbara, for her patience and never-ending support, and my children, Iain, Iona, Kiki, and Leila, for allowing me the time to write. Finally, I give thanks to my parents, Helen and Ernest Gordon, for building such an inspired beach house. It is to them that this book is lovingly dedicated.

OPPOSITE:
Andrew Geller, Jossel House, Fire Island, 1959.

ABOVE:

Photograph of a Techbuilt house from an advertisement in *Life* magazine.

OPPOSITE:

Shapshots of the author's family, friends, and beach house, Amagansett, 1958–1964. The author sits with his sister and mother in the top right photo.

The very openness of this region is its best defense against conformity.

—William K. Zinnser, 1963[1]

IT MUST HAVE been around 1962 when I saw the photograph in *Life* magazine. It was a full-page advertisement for a new kind of vacation house. What I remember best about that photograph was the way the house hung out over the dune, challenging the elements as if it were about to leap into the water and take a swim. I never imagined that a house could look so free-spirited. Alone on the beach, it looked like an updated version of Henry Thoreau's shack at Walden. It made me want to run outside and take my clothes off even though it was the middle of winter. I learned from the blurb that it was a product of Techbuilt, a company that specialized in prefabricated housing kits: "The perfect answer to anyone wanting a vacation house in a hurry."[2] The house could be ordered directly from a factory, shipped in sections to the site of your choice, and erected in a matter of days.

I was only ten years old, but the photograph in the magazine made a deep impression, and I ripped it out to show my parents. A couple of months later they bought a waterfront lot in Amagansett and decided to build one of these prefab units.

As the roof was entirely supported by the outer walls of the structure, the client had complete freedom in arranging interior spaces. You could put rooms anywhere you wanted or, alternatively, leave the house completely open. (I remember my mother playing around with a book of floor plans that arrived one day in the mail.) Best of all was the price. The house was designed for the middle class, and even a Presbyterian minister like my father could afford to build one.

When the house was finished (it took about a month to build) we started to have second thoughts. It was a rude looking thing-not quite the image I had seen in *Life*. It stood out too prominently on the dune. It was not a normal house, not like the kind of houses our friends lived in. My sister and I walked down the beach and looked back with a cringing sense of embarrassment.

"It's ugly," I said.

"It's so ugly," said my sister.

Our parents had obviously made a terrible mistake. What would people think? What would our friends say? We shook our heads and wandered back up the beach.

The actual thing was impossibly small. My bedroom measured about 10 feet by 10 feet, with the kind of double-decker bunk bed that every beach house had in those days. There were two tiny bathrooms. The kitchen was little more than a cubby hole. How could anyone live in such a house? We began to long for our old house with its spacious rooms, but it had already been sold to another family. We were stuck.

Ever so gradually, our feelings began to change. The deck was large and the views were wide, and this helped us to forget how small the house really was. The upper level was surrounded by floor-to-ceiling glass. Interior spaces spilled outside. The long, sweeping curve of Gardiner's Bay appeared to bend right through our living room. We were right there, riding the crest of a dune with steps leading down to our very own beach. On some days it felt as if we had reached a state of complete unity with nature. We would never again have to pack a picnic basket and carry coolers, umbrellas, or wonky aluminum chairs over burning tar.

My sister and I were surprised to learn that other kids were envious of our brash little beach house.

Rather than setting us apart, or being an embarrassment, it made us more popular. The house was all about freedom. Freedom from the confining rooms and corridors of the past. Freedom for my mother, who would no longer have to cook in a gloomy kitchen. At our old summer house there had been several extra bedrooms and they were often filled-my mother used to say that "guests, like fish, begin to smell after three days." At the new house there was only a single room designated for guests, so most of the time we had the place to ourselves.

A family trip through Scandinavia in 1963 determined the decorating theme for our beach house, condemning us to a future of Norwegian wood and blindingly bright fabrics. My mother collected orange ashtrays with gaping mouths, fuzzy rugs, and Marimekko tablecloths with bold geometric patterns. Curtains were made from a kind of space-age synthetic woven with wide gaps. I once touched the burning end of a cigarette against the astronaut fabric, and a patch of it exploded into stringy black ferrules of smoke.

We gradually learned to adapt to the small spaces of our new house—to live neatly, as if on board a boat. On rainy days the spatial intimacy made everyone slightly insane, but when the sun shone everything was perfect. It felt as though we possessed our own little utopian world, at least until Labor Day, when the house was boarded up for winter.

The modern beach house offered a utopian promise. This promise was centered on the self, physical health, and beauty, but nonetheless suggested a radiant future that would combine the best of the city (power and cultural sophistication) with the best of the country (nature and peace). It's hard to look back at this period and not feel a twinge of nostalgia mixed with a sense of unfulfilled promise. As in my own case, the beach house was a means of release and self-discovery, much like the music and subculture of the sixties. It was the smallness and simplicity of those houses that forced one to experience nature first hand, to learn tolerance, and even to become closer knit as a family.

Those were the true rewards. The landscape of Eastern Long Island invited reverie with its empty beaches and meadows of scrub and pine: "bird-haunted, ocean-haunted-land of youth…and desired return," as poet John Hall Wheelock described it.[3] It was also a nurturing environment for some of the most innovative art and architecture of the past century.

OVER THE COURSE of this book, I use the term "the Hamptons" to denote the region at the eastern end of Long Island that includes the villages of Amagansett, Bridgehampton, East Hampton, Southampton, the Springs, Montauk and several other neighboring hamlets. "The Hamptons" has the sound of an event (or a marketing ploy) compared to the more prosaic "Eastern Long Island" or "South Fork," which long-suffering locals tend to prefer. As a general designation, "the Hamptons" dates back at least as far as the nineteenth century. In a promotional brochure published in 1879, the different villages were already being lumped together as a single destination: "These Hamptons are no hackneyed watering-places, and people who want the glitter and excitement of Long Branch or Saratoga are solemnly warned away from here."[4]

Sigfried Giedion once wrote that "architecture reflects the inner tendencies of the time and therefore may properly serve as a general index."[5] This has been especially true in the Hamptons, where so many different levels of reality coexist in a relatively small area. Some see a quiet retreat from the city. There are even a few who still see it as a place to harvest potatoes. Others see an extension of the Manhattan media vortex or a launching pad for celebrity. Houses in the Hamptons stand out prominently against the sea and sky. Their sense of scale is magnified by the flatness of the landscape, and their significance is magnified by the inordinate amount of coverage that the area receives in the press. Architecture has been the most visible indicator of the area's change, and I use it here to trace the Hamptons' transformation from rural outpost to high-powered resort.

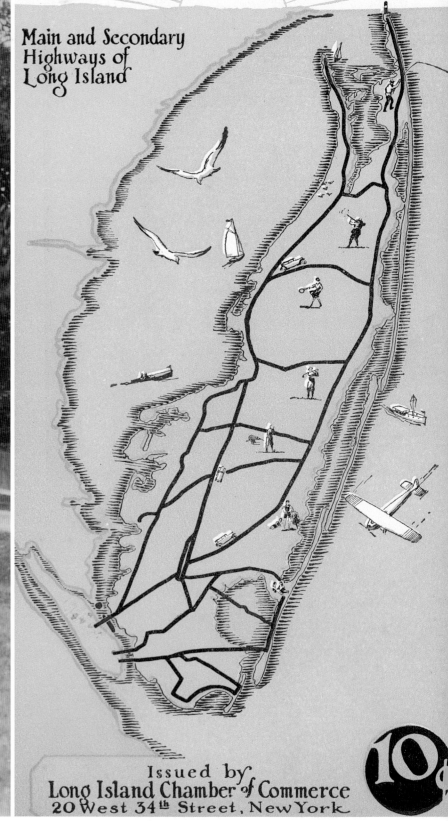

Long Island
Sunrise Trails
to
MONTAUK BEACH
"The Miami Beach of the North"

Main and Secondary
Highways of
Long Island

10¢

Issued by
Long Island Chamber of Commerce
20 West 34th Street, New York

the fresh green breast

Our tourists came out upon a scene of freshness
and uncontaminated splendor such as they had
no idea existed a hundred miles from New York.
—William Mackay Laffan and
Edward Strahan, 1879[1]

TO MANY, THE landscape of Long Island seemed an open template, a blank sheet of paper. It has always been subject to interpretation. It was Walt Whitman's "Fish-Shaped Paumonok" and F. Scott Fitzgerald's "fresh green breast of the New World," a place of global discovery and self discovery where the sea-reflected light created a sense of heightened expectation.[2] A landscape of extremes, it nevertheless has a neutral, passive quality that outsiders tend to read in their own willful ways. With few natural barriers or breaks, it is all too ready for exploitation and misplaced intentions, for visionary schemes and utopian dreams. Stretching roughly one hundred miles from New York City, this glacial deposit, scoured by time and tide, represents the perfect convergence of capital, media, and geography. How can anyone resist?

Early accounts of Eastern Long Island do not provide much detail about the area, and if they do, it usually isn't flattering. There is certainly nothing to compare to the gushing prose generated by Niagara Falls or the Hudson River Valley. Certain villages were thought to possess varying degrees of the picturesque, with their quaint windmills, old churches, and saltbox houses. But the surrounding beachscape was seen as something of a void, and was often described as a "sandy waste," or an "empty expanse." The rolling white beaches, strewn with the skeletons of wrecked ships, appeared forlorn to early visitors. In many accounts, these stretches didn't even rate a mention.

One early nineteenth-century visitor described the area as a "wild, desolate country, infested by mosquitoes and snakes." Another traveler, visiting in 1835, described the area west of Montauk as a "low, sandy, desolate tract, which seems to have been recently formed." Richard M. Bayles, who came in 1874, recorded a similar set of impressions: "Proceeding eastward from Amagansett," he wrote, "we enter immediately upon the dreary waste of Napeague Beach, weary where this part of the Island is narrowed down to a width of about one mile by an abrupt advance of the water upon the north side." A poet who passed through a few years later wrote of "a misty light and wastes of sandy gray."[3]

As sensibilities changed, the landscape of Eastern Long Island was seen in a more positive light. A younger generation of writers and artists helped change the general perception. William Cullen Bryant, poet of American nature, was one of the first to recognize a distinct beauty. In *Picturesque America* (1874), he described the "peculiar charm" of the sandy landscape that stretched eastward from Southampton to Montauk.[4] Walt Whitman had grown up on Long Island and had a deep affection for the place: "Sea-beauty! stretch'd and basking!" In 1888, as a late addition to *Leaves of Grass*, Whitman wrote "From Montauk Point":

> *I stand as on some mighty eagle's beak,*
> *Eastward the sea absorbing, viewing, (nothing but sea*
> *   and sky),*
> *The tossing waves, the foam, the ships in the*
> *   distance.*[5]

While there had been summer visitors before the Civil War, the first real influx came in the 1870s. The Tile Club was an informal association of like-minded artists, architects, and journalists who met on a regular basis to exchange ideas, paint ceramic tiles, and organize summer sketching expeditions. Its more distinguished members included Winslow Homer, William Merrit Chase, Augustus Saint-Gaudens, and Stanford White.

TOP LEFT:
William Merrit Chase,
A Subtle Device, 1880.

TOP RIGHT:
**Arthur Quartley, *Girl on
Beach, East Hampton***
(painted tile), 1878.

BOTTOM:
**Edward Lamson Henry, *East
Hampton Beach*, 1881.**

On 19 June 1878, eleven members of the club ventured out to Eastern Long Island. They went by train to Babylon, sailed in a sloop to Captree Island, rode a stagecoach on the next leg of their trip, and went the rest of the way by train. The artists disembarked in Brideghampton—at the time, the eastern terminus of the Long Island Rail Road—and sketched the town's windmill and a few other local sites. Transportation for the group was organized by William Mackay Laffan, a Tile Club member who also happened to be an agent for the LIRR, so the tickets for all eleven "Tilers" were free.[6]

From Bridgehampton, the group continued on to East Hampton, where they settled into boarding rooms and began to work in earnest. Inspired by the local scenery, they ventured out in search of new subject matter. They set up their easels in the fields and along the ocean dunes. They sat on folding stools and sheltered themselves from the sun with folding umbrellas.[7] Wherever they turned there was another scene worthy of attention. The New York art world was just beginning to break free from the gloomy tones of academic genre painting, to look at nature firsthand and to work in the new European style of *plein air* painting. One writer suggested Eastern Long Island was now the "American Barbison [sic]"—a reference to Barbizon, the village outside Paris where painters like Camille Corot and Jean François Millet had gone to paint the rural scenery. The Tilers came out to capture the essence of the place—"its whirling mills, its silvery, silent beaches, its watery marshes and bays." The bright light, the low-lying landscape, and the expansiveness of the ocean horizon all fostered an ideal state of mind for this kind of artistic production.[8]

Arthur Quartley, one of the founding members of the Tile Club, painted *Seascape*, a canvas that depicted a sublime crashing of waves against the shoreline. He also sketched a girl staring out to sea in thoughtful introspection. The beach appeared tranquil and inviting. White sails pricked the horizon. Sea gulls reeled overhead. William Trost Richards

painted a seascape in which the light of a rising sun transformed the ocean breakers into curling whisps of angelic hair. Others, like Bruce Crane and Henry Ferguson, captured the rustic simplicity of hay harvesting and cows being driven to pasture. In Howard Russell Butler's *View of Georgica Pond*, a woman with a red parasol strolls dreamily along the water's edge.

After a few days in East Hampton, the "artistic argonauts" from New York continued on by carriage. As they passed the lonely stretch of Napeague and approached the hills of Montauk they were thrilled by the sublime landscape that lay before them:

> The woods rolled gloriously over the hills, wild as those around the Scotch lakes; noble amphitheaters of tree-tufted mountains, raked by roaring winds, caught the changing light from a cloud-swept heaven; all was pure nature, fresh from creation. The beach they skirted was wild and stern, with magnificent precipices.[9]

As these artists demonstrated, Eastern Long Island wasn't a dreary wasteland, but a "painter's gold-mine, all bits and nuggets." They recognized something timeless about the place. They could see a raw beauty where previous visitors had seen a kind of emptiness. To them, the landscape offered a multitude of choices—from wild ocean scenery to saltwater marshes and tranquil ponds. The local architecture was also ideal for their pur-

poses, with so many tumbledown colonial houses, barns, windmills, and lighthouses all preserved in a mist of antiquity. But more than anything it was the light, the wild, sea-brewed light, that made them want to return.

Eight months later, an account of the Tile Club's odyssey appeared in the pages of *Scribner's Monthly*. Written by Laffan and Edward Strahan, "The Tile Cub at Play" was illustrated with twenty-seven drawings that had been made during the trip. The article put East Hampton on the artistic map. The next summer, local boarding houses were jammed with young painters in search of natural scenery. During this period, Laffan also wrote a publicity pamphlet for the Long Island Rail Road that was intended to promote tourism and encourage settlement in the outer reaches of Long Island. "No lovelier stretch of country, none more pleasing to the eye of artist or poet, none more peaceful and poetically happy in its outward expression, or more varied and interesting in its contour and color, is to be found anywhere along our Eastern Coast," he wrote.[10] Laffan's conflict of interest—between appreciation and exploitation—would become something of a tradition as the area grew in popularity.

Another writer who visited East Hampton soon after it had been "discovered" by the painters, wrote: "The beach, with its broad reaches of sand and foaming surges, its wrecks, sand-storms, mirages, soft

ABOVE:
Thomas Moran in his garden, East Hampton, c. 1913.

TOP LEFT:
Thomas Moran standing in front of his house in East Hampton, c. 1913.

TOP RIGHT:
A picnic on Hook Pond, East Hampton, c. 1905. George Fowler (with pole), Ruth Moran, and Mary Moran Tass in Thomas Moran's Venetian gondola.

colors, and long line of sand-dunes cut into every variety of fantastic shape by the winds, was equally prolific of wild fancies."[11] Here was the beginning of a modern and romantic interpretation of the Hamptons. What a few years earlier had been perceived as wasteland was now a wonderland of visual delights, miraculously transformed from a "desolate tract" into a paradise of unexploited pastoral bliss.

WHILE MOST OF the early visitors stayed in boarding houses or rented cottages, there were a few who liked the area so much that they decided to settle down and build their own summer houses. As one writer noted, "The advantage of living in such a place is that all an artist has to do is take out his easel and set it up anywhere, and there in front of him is a lovely picture."[12] Thomas Moran, known for his dramatic paintings of the Western wilds, moved out to East Hampton in 1882 and became the most prominent member of the new art colony. Working with a local builder named Stafford Tillinghast, in 1884 Moran designed himself a rather eccentric house in the heart of the village, just across from Goose Pond (now Town Pond). The house was a quirky caricature of the Queen Anne style then in vogue in England. It was, in effect, the first example of "experimental" architecture in the Hamptons. Projecting gables and quaint chimney pots made an odd-looking silhouette against the summer sky. With dormer windows pointing up like

raised eyebrows, the house appeared to be craning its neck to get a better view of the ocean.

The largest room was Moran's studio, a two-story space with a large window at its north end. The interior was filled with an eclectic mix of furniture, oriental rugs, ornate oil lamps, carved chests, and wall hangings that Moran had accumulated on his travels. A visitor to the studio named Lucy Cleveland was delighted by all the exotic clutter: "Suspended from the 'gallery' swing bulbous bronze delights," she wrote. "[They are] deep hued, lustrous as the eyes of a Sultan's favorite or the jeweled splendours of her sandalled feet."[13] Friends and fellow artists gathered at the Moran studio on summer evenings. Moran's wife, Mary Nimmo, entertained their guests with traditional Scottish ballads. Their daughter, Ruth, read poetry aloud. On one of his trips to Venice, Moran purchased a gondola that, supposedly, once belonged to Robert and Elizabeth Browning. Moran had it shipped all the way to East Hampton, where he used it for outings on Hook Pond.

Moran set out from his house on long walks across the moors and dunes of East Hampton, making quick studies as he went. In one of his paintings, *The Watering Hole Place* (c. 1880), Moran captured a herd of cows standing at the edge of the village pond. Trees in the background were bathed in silky summer light. Moran was especially intrigued by the qualities of the beach itself, and spent many hours making studies of the water's restless motion. In one etching, *The*

Breaking Water (1880), he attempted to capture every concentrated line of force in the roiling water. No less a critic than John Ruskin hailed it as the finest study of waves ever executed by an American artist.

In 1891, a few years after Moran's arrival, American impressionist William Merrit Chase arrived in Southampton to become director of the Shinnecock School of Art. Advertised as "America's First Outdoor School of Art," it emphasized the new European approach to painting. Chase taught his students to look at nature with a fresh perspective and to work spontaneously in the open air. "It usually takes two to paint," he said, "one to paint and the other to stand by with an ax to kill him before he spoils it."[14] The school was based in "The Art Village," a utopian compound built for the love of art. It looked like a toy village. Precious and picturesque, each cottage was a shingled confection, articulated in turn with a gable, hipped, or gambrel roof; multiple dormers and bays; diamond-shaped window panes; rough stone chimneys; bracketed overhangs; protected porches with ivy-covered trellis work; and recessed nooks for sitting and reading. The looping road that connected the cottages and studios was shaped like an artist's palette.

Stanford White converted the old Atterbury House into a studio and living quarters for Chase and his family. It stood high up in the Shinnecock Hills, and for many years was the only thing in sight for miles around. "Heather covered hills of sand stretch from the encroaching bays to the open sea," wrote one nineteenth-century visitor, but today the hills are thick with cedar and scrub oak, and the open vistas are gone.[15]

Several other houses were built in the vicinity for artists. In 1899, Grosvenor Atterbury designed "The Creeks" for the painter Albert Herter. It had an unusual plan in the shape of a splayed U, so devised to capture as many views as possible out over Georgica Pond and, at the same time, to allow as much natural light into the interior as possible. Seven years later, Theophilus A. Brouwer, a potter and all-around visionary, built himself a large house in the area. A Moorish-style castle overlooking the Great South Bay, it was supposedly modeled after a castle Brouwer had once visited outside of Seville, Spain (though Brouwer's son claimed his father had never been to Europe). The interior staircase was carved with oak-leaf patterns and sea horses. The outside of the

building had a precarious set of steps—something out of a Dr. Seuss book—that led up to the top of a high tower where a concrete rabbit and squirrel kept a lookout. It was from this perch that Brouwer could gaze out over his 14-acre kingdom and plan the place he would call "Pine-Wold Park." He spent the next twenty-six years planting, building, and filling his enchanted theme park with allegorical figures that he sculpted out of concrete. There was *Ursus the Gladiator* wrestling *Aurochs the Bull*; a lion attacking an antelope; a unicorn; and, best of all, *Lady of Light*, a naked woman suspended on a curving tongue of red flame.

During the summer of 1892, only a year after Chase had moved to Shinnecock, John Gilmer Speed, a writer for *Harper's Monthly Magazine*, tracked him down and filed a twelve-page report. The journalist watched Chase at work in his studio. He followed him on his walks through the Shinnecock Hills and down along the sandy stretches of beach. "For several miles," wrote Speed, "Mr. Chase had been pointing out pictures to me and painting them in his mind. In a walk of an hour and a half the artist's eyes had seen enough of beauty to keep ten men busy for fifty years." Speed explained how normal eyes, "prosaic eyes," weren't sensitive enough to see the virtues in this landscape.[16]

"The simple country people" wrote Speed, "have never found anything to admire in the Shinnecock Hills themselves, or the creeks and bays made by the rising tides. To them the Shinnecock Hills have always been rather unlovely, as they are not fer-

tile, and the sandy roads of even a few years ago made travel very hard across them."[17] In other words, it had taken the artistically perceptive Chase to bring the aesthetic value of such a place to the world's attention. Speed also noted that the same barren property was growing in value now that it had gained recognition. Land that had been worth $2.50 per acre a few years before was now fetching $250.

> It is necessary in the Country House utopia to fill in by play and sport an otherwise desirable vacuity.
> —Lewis Mumford, 1922[18]

IN 1879, JUST a year after the Tile Club's trip to East Hampton, a New York entrepreneur named Arthur W. Benson paid $151,000 for a large tract of land that began at Napeague in the west and stretched all the way to Montauk Point in the east. Benson (for whom Bensonhurst, Brooklyn is named) envisioned an exclusive community devoted to sport and male camaraderie. He invited a group of his business cronies from New York to join him in establishing the Montauk Association.[19] It was all so idyllic: hundreds of acres of unspoiled forests, rolling hills, and meadows for hunting; freshwater ponds and miles of beaches for sport fishing. And they had it all to themselves. But such idealized visions carried a price. Benson wanted to create a retreat of untamed beauty, but without the distraction of the scruffy-looking native population—there was still a community of Montauk Indians living in the area. With friends in high places, Benson was able to have them removed from their ancestral lands. In May 1885, eight Native American families were relocated to "Freetown," an area in East Hampton that had been set aside for freed slaves. For the convenience of a few wealthy sportsmen, the last remaining Montauks were displaced. Each of the families received a few dollars for the inconvenience. Their homes were then burned to the ground.

The Montauk Association compound comprised seven freestanding cottages situated on the high ground between Lake Wyandach (now Fort Pond) to the northwest and the Atlantic Ocean to the south. Stanford White designed the buildings. Frederick Law Olmsted did the landscaping, positioning the houses in a V formation that made the most of the sea breezes and gave each house its own uninterrupted view of the ocean. This arrangement became a model for future East End enclaves. It also established a relationship between architecture and landscape that continues to this day. Instead of being anchored to their sites, the houses were seemingly disconnected from the ground, like ships floating across the landscape. The houses had no kitchens, so everyone ate together in a clubhouse placed near the center of the property. There was also a laundry building and stables.

Concurrent with the artists and sportsmen came members of the clergy. A group of Methodist ministers from Brooklyn established a summer colony on Shelter Island during the 1870s and 1880s. There was a hotel, a yacht club, and a group of cottages built overlooking Dering Harbor in an area that became known as "Divinity Hill."[20] In East Hampton, a group of Presbyterian ministers colonized the sandy reaches to the west of the village. During the early 1870s there was a white clapboard house built for Reverend Stephen Mershon, a shingle-style house for Reverend T. DeWitt Talmage, and a Victorian Gothic house for Reverend W. R. MacKay. The eclectic mix of architectural styles set these first cottages apart from the smaller and more rustic year-round homes of the local residents. Talmage, who was the pastor of the Brooklyn Tabernacle, built several other cottages that he rented out to fellow clergymen. This area, as on Shelter Island, was soon renamed Divinity Hill.

What started as retreats for clergymen and their congregations soon evolved into secular colonies where sport and socializing took priority over spiritual matters. Mixing in with the ministers were affluent bankers, lawyers, doctors, Wall Street brokers, and their families. These people were not coming out to preach or paint the scenery. They were coming out to relax and socialize with their peers. Their summer enclaves tended to be well removed from the year-round, residential neighborhoods. They were built in waterfront areas that had previously been considered undesirable for the purposes of settlement. New houses were built near the ocean dunes or on high promontories to capture panoramic views. In an odd twist, the new summer visitors built their houses in the same places that artists had chosen to paint a few years earlier, establishing a rather incestuous relationship between art and architecture that would loom large in the future development of the region. Scenes of the empty landscape that had been exhibited in New York galleries a few years before (or printed as etchings in popular magazines) were becoming so many construction sites

In the 1880s, an enclave of shingle-style cottages was built for the Georgica Association, an exclusive compound in Wainscott, situated on the western shore of Georgica Pond. Farther to the east, in Amagansett, summer cottages were built along Bluff Road and (in the 1890s) Indian Wells Highway, all within walking distance of the ocean and the Namaganesett Field Club. Since the summer houses were only used for a short season, there was more latitude in their design and setting. While the city homes of these new colonists tended to be restrained and uniform in character, their country houses could be rambling and picturesque, expressing a longing for more romantic places and historical periods. Several of the early cottages had wraparound porches for framing views and capturing the cool ocean breezes. While none were in the grandiose scale of the cottages of Newport or Bar Harbor, some were relatively large. The 1874 Satterthwaite Villa in East Hampton had seventeen rooms. It was a stick-style confection, with "a mingling of the Gothic, Grecian, and Italian styles of architecture."[21] Elaborately carved brackets ornamented the covered porches that wrapped around both the first and second floors of the house. A belvedere on the roof was specially designed for gazing out to sea.

While marginally dependent on the year-round communities for carpenters, plumbers, domestic

Bathers in the ocean surf,
East Hampton, c. 1890.

servants, and gardeners, these exclusive colonies were otherwise autonomous and self-sufficient. They were examples of what Lewis Mumford referred to disparagingly as "country house utopias.... Everyone does nothing except follow his own free will and pleasure, rising out of his bed whenever he thinks good, and eating, drinking, and laboring when he has a mind to it.... As Rabelais puts it, there is but one clause to be observed—'Do what you please.' "[22] While the country house utopias had none of the political beliefs or eccentric practices of genuine utopian communities, they did represent a certain communal ideal, at least for two months out of the year. Summer life circled around a sequence of sporting and social events—tennis, golf, lawn parties, clambakes, dances. Their symbolic center was not the church or the meeting hall, but the country club.

The perception of the beach was changing from a place of shipwreck and mortality to a place of comfort and leisure. Sea bathing was growing in popularity. Canvas tents were erected for the day. Small, portable bathhouses were wheeled down for the season and then removed at the end of the summer. (Sometimes these contrivances were painted in colors and patterns to match the owner's main house.) A bracing dip into the ocean surf—a "saline salutatory"—became a part of the daily routine for hearty summer residents. Groups of swimmers would plunge into the "surging billows" together, holding onto ropes that were anchored to the shore. Reverend Talmage himself wrote an article for *Ladies Home Journal* extolling the bodily and spiritual benefits of sea bathing in East Hampton.[23] Others were alarmed that young women were taking part in the sport. A few had even taken to swimming on the Sabbath.

While it may have been good for bathing, the ocean was still considered a risky place to build a house. Most of the new summer cottages were set well back from the dangers of the ocean, though a few fearless souls chose to challenge the elements.[24] Again, it was a painter who set the fashion. Howard Russell Butler was a founder and president of the American Fine Arts Society. He specialized in painting marine scenes and wanted to get as close to his subject matter as possible. In 1893, he built himself a gambrel-roofed house right near the ocean in East Hampton. It was designed expressly to take advantage of the site. The ocean lay just to the south, with Georgica Pond to the north. There was a wraparound veranda on the ground level and a porch on the second story to look out in all directions and over the highest dunes. From there, without even leaving his house, Butler could make studies of the elusive sea light and the long white swathe of beach.

Even during this first, and generally benign, wave of development, there were those who anticipated trouble. Having just arrived themselves, they could sense the coming ruination of village life and the destruction of the natural environment. "Already the railroad, rude iconoclast, is approaching to destroy the relics of the past and change the whole aspect of the place," worried one newcomer in 1883.[25] It was almost as if an inherent sense of loss, a future foretold, lay dormant in the sandy landscape. Writing in the *American Architect*, another visitor, Charles DeKay, fretted over the possible introduction of such "modern improvements" as express trains, trolleys, summer hotels, boardwalks, and the like. "How long will Montauk preserve its savage loneliness and grandeur? East Hampton its noble village street? The north woods their shady, sandy solitudes? Sag Harbor its air of an old whaling port?" DeKay was so concerned that he encouraged local residents to form a protective organization, "in order to keep some control of roads and bicycle paths and wayside trees.... An organization which might step in and have a word to say when property owners through greed or mere lack of sense start in to destroy the natural beauty of the county."[26] At this point, no one suspected that it may have been the writers themselves who were the advanced guard of exploitation.

THE EAST END'S transformation into a modern summer resort was well underway. What had started with the artist's brush and the writer's pen was taken up by railroad magnates and real estate developers. Austin Corbin, Jr., president of the Long Island Rail Road, extended the line 21 miles from Bridgehampton all the way out to Montauk. This final link was completed in 1895. The summer colonies expanded throughout the decade in a building boom that was, in part, fuelled by the extended railroad. As one local newspaper reported, "East Hampton is fast becoming more and more of a watering place...and the once quiet resort of the few, is fast becoming the favorite spot of many."[27] While some of the local residents resented the intrusion, others encouraged it and profited by renting out rooms, selling property, and providing the newcomers with essential services.

Reverend Talmage, the popular preacher who had been summering in East Hampton since 1873, made frequent references to the beauties of Eastern Long Island in his sermons at the Brooklyn Tabernacle, which were attended by thousands of New Yorkers. Local newspapers also did their part. In 1891, the editorial pages of the *East Hampton Star* encouraged local residents to welcome the outsiders with open arms. "No one should spare any efforts to attract the city people to our town," wrote the editors.[28]

The Devon Colony was built in a hilly area to the east of Amagansett known as the "Highlands," overlooking Gardiner's Bay. A group of Cincinnati businessmen formed the Gardiner's Bay Company in 1908. They purchased 600 acres of land that lay between Fresh Pond and the ocean and began developing it into a parklike setting with winding roads and large houses placed prominently on adjacent hilltops. The cottages were built from reinforced concrete in a beefy, English-cottage style. A communal club was also built on the bay for sailing and tennis, with rustic bathhouses and a "casino" pavilion. This later became the Devon Yacht Club. (Locals referred to the colony as "Soap Hill," as so many of its residents were heirs to the Procter and Gamble fortune.)

East Hampton's summer colony spread out to the west of the village, along the banks of Hook Pond, and along Ocean Avenue and Lilly Pond Lane toward the ocean.[29] Architects such as Joseph

Greenleaf Thorp, Albro and Lindeberg, Polhemus and Coffin, Roger Bullard, and Grosvernor Atterbury specialized in a kind of eclectic cottage style that evoked the spirit of the English country home. "Coxwould," designed in 1912 by Harrie T. Lindeberg (of Albro and Lindeberg) was exemplary. Built for the New York surgeon John E. Erdman, it had stucco walls and hand-split shingles that conformed to the shape of the roof and curved around the building's eaves and windows in a way that resembled real thatch.

AS THE SUMMER colonies grew, they developed subtle differences that distinguished one from the other. In Southampton there was a more conspicuous display of wealth than in East Hampton, where expressions still tended to be relatively understated. In Southampton, the houses were bigger, the lawns were broader, and the privet hedges thicker. Southampton had a large population of Roman Catholics; East Hampton was more Protestant, and its residents prided themselves on a kind of rarified simplicity in their architecture and gardens. Having nothing to hide, they were more likely to leave their lawns open to the road. Summer denizens of East Hampton liked to say that "Southampton [was] for the sporting rich, Westhampton the nearly rich, and East Hampton the really rich." Southampton's summer elite replied that Southampton was for presidents while East Hampton was for vice presidents.[30]

One of the biggest houses in Southampton was "The Orchard," a sprawling summer mansion built for James Lawrence Breese that was completed in 1906. Breese was a successful Wall Street broker descended from a patrician New York family. He wanted his estate to evoke the feeling of a Southern plantation. The house was designed by Stanford White, a close friend of the family. It was all white, with a broad portico supported by eight Doric columns reminiscent of those at George Washington's home at Mt. Vernon. The most extravagant part of the house was the music room, which was decorated in a robber-baron-style of cluttered elegance. There Breese displayed his most prized possessions—spoils from the Old World brought to the New as validation of his success. (White came out to personally supervise much of the work on this room.) Imported gilt columns stood in

OPPOSITE, TOP:
Summer house in East Hampton, c. 1903.

OPPOSITE, BOTTOM LEFT:
Harrie T. Lindeberg, Erdman House ("Coxwould"), East Hampton, 1912.

OPPOSITE, BOTTOM RIGHT:
Stanford White, Breese House ("The Orchard"), Southampton, 1906.

ABOVE:

A diving competition at the Maidstone Club, c. 1928.

each corner of the great room. Eighteen-foot-high ceilings were coffered and hand painted in the style of a Renaissance palazzo. The floor-to-ceiling windows were decorated with stained glass coats-of-arms representing the signers of the Magna Carta. An Aeolian pipe organ was imported from France and installed in the southern end. Walls were hung with medieval tapestries and old master paintings that Breese's agents had looted from various estates in Europe. White also supervised work on the expansive grounds, transforming 16 acres of orchard into formal gardens with boxwood, pergolas, brick pathways, and classical sculptures. White finished his work on the Breese Estate during the summer of 1906, just a few weeks before he was gunned down by Harry K. Thaw.[31]

THE SYMBOLIC CENTER and principle architectural expression of the summer colony was the clubhouse. It was usually set in the most prominent way, dominating the landscape with the green apron of a golf course spread out around it like a *cordon sanitaire* marking out

an exclusive zone of privilege. One of the earliest was the Quogue Field Club, incorporated in 1881, which offered tennis and lawn bowling. Southampton's social set had the choice of several different clubs, including the Southampton Bath and Tennis, a bastion of old money that was affectionately referred to as the "Bathing Corporation." A Scotsman named Duncan Cryder found that the Shinnecock Hills reminded him of the landscape of his homeland, in particular St. Andrews, the birthplace of golf. In association with William K. Vanderbilt, Jr. (and a few others), he created a twelve-hole, links-style course. Then, in 1891, they founded the Shinnecock Hills Golf Club, one of the first golf clubs in America. A standard pattern was established with the clubhouse for Shinnecock Hills. Designed by Stanford White as something of a fusion between an American barn and a Greek temple, it conveyed a properly balanced message of leisure and propriety. It was positioned high on a hill overlooking the course, an idealized pavilion of pleasure with generously wide verandas. The overhanging roof was supported by a colonnade of white Doric columns. The

Maidstone Club, in East Hampton, was originally incorporated in 1891 for the "mutual benefit, social intercourse and recreation" of its members.[32] Architect Roger Bullard designed its 1924 clubhouse as a variation on a Norman farm house with peaked roofs and stucco walls, and placed it like a baronial country seat high atop the ocean dunes.

As summer cottages became bigger and more formal—with many of the larger estates surrounded by formal lawns and gardens—there was less of a connection to the outdoors and more of a need to return to the simple pleasures of summers at the beach. A kind of substitute cottage became popular during the 1920s: the bathhouse or cabana, a small, shacklike structure built right on the beach. In these convenient structures, hosts and houseguests could change into their bathing suits and take showers when they were done. The most elaborate of these cabanas mimicked the architectural styles of their owner's larger houses. When the dashing Broadway actor John Drew built a house for himself in East Hampton, in 1902, he had his architect, James Brown Lord, design a bathhouse that was a miniature version of it on the ocean dunes.

When a new, beachfront clubhouse opened at Maidstone in 1928, it was praised for its "Lido-Like" arrangement. This part of the club, designed by John H. Jewett, was much less formal than the rather stuffy building designed by Bullard. Terraces, a swimming pool, and an open-air restaurant merged with the sandy beach. There were also seventy-two cabanas built out front along the beach, "each decorated according to the individual ideas of its owners."[33] Here, in less formal surroundings, socialites could relax and act out a kind of Marie Antoinette charade. Hostesses who had never lifted a finger in their own sprawling mansions could play house and serve informal (catered) lunches to their weekend guests. These cabanas were often quite sophisticated—fashionably designed by the same interior decorators who were responsible for their clients' principle summer houses. Ironically, these little playhouses became the favorite retreats for many of the wealthiest club members. In a way, they foreshadowed the small, informal beach houses that would proliferate after World War II.

Psychologists have discovered various kinds of fatigue which are not muscular but are caused by nervous strain....Montauk Beach is the antidote for the nervous fatigue of today's executive.

—The Montauk Beach
Development Corporation, 1927[34]

CARL GRAHAM FISHER was a born dreamer. He was a showman, a salesman, and a prince of real-estate development. Among other commercial schemes, he built the Indianapolis Speedway and promoted the idea of the Lincoln Highway, the first transcontinental highway. In the early 1920s Fisher had a hunch and bought a worthless strip of mangrove swamp on Biscayne Bay in Florida. There he created Miami Beach, which soon became the most successful resort in America. Sometime in the summer of 1925, shortly after his triumph in the Florida swamps, Fisher motored out to the eastern tip of Long Island aboard his streamlined speedboat, the *Shadow-K*.

Standing on her deck, he surveyed the rocky shore and rolling hills of Montauk. It was still an unspoiled landscape, with little more than the old lighthouse and the Montauk Association houses. He wasn't quite sure why, but it reminded him of an ancient, romantic place—the highlands of Scotland, perhaps—but it stirred his emotions and made him want to do what he did best. Build.

Fisher pointed here and there, indicating the areas he wanted to work with while his personal secretary stood by his side and took notes. There would be a giant hotel (something medieval), a tower, a yacht club, and elegant country estates placed among the surrounding hills. Ocean liners would sail in from Europe and moor in the harbor. Passengers would disembark, stay in the hotel, swim, sail, play tennis and polo, and then move on to New York by train. He could see it all before him as he stood there on the rocking deck of the *Shadow-K*, his next creation, the Miami Beach of the North.[35]

A few days later, Fisher purchased 10,000 acres and established the Montauk Beach Development Corporation. Within weeks, an army of engineers, architects, contractors, and construction crews were at work. Over 30 miles of new roads were laid. A thoroughfare was cut straight through the Hither Hills. The rolling terrain was flattened like a pancake. Sand dunes were blasted into oblivion, water pipes laid, and

Golf Club House.   Shinnecock Hills, L. I.

MEADOW CLUB. SOUTHAMPTON, N. Y.

The MAIDSTONE CLUB
EAST HAMPTON, LONG ISLAND, N.Y.

The Namaganesett Club, Amagansett, L. I.

DEVON YACHT CLUB
DEVON, LONG ISLAND, N.Y.

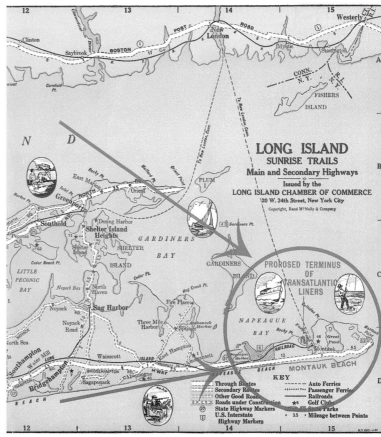

OPPOSITE, TOP LEFT:
Stanford White's 1891 clubhouse for the Shinnecock Hills Golf Club, Southampton.

OPPOSITE, TOP RIGHT:
Clubhouse of the Meadow Club, Southampton.

OPPOSITE, MIDDLE LEFT:
Roger Bullard's 1924 clubhouse for the Maidstone Club, East Hampton.

OPPOSITE, MIDDLE RIGHT:
Clubhouse of the Namaganesett Club, Amagansett.

OPPOSITE, BOTTOM:
Clubhouse of the Devon Yacht Club, Amagansett.

new buildings appeared as if by magic. Local papers tried to keep up with the fast-breaking news. March 19: "Mr. Carl Fisher, father of Miami Beach, announces development plans for Montauk Beach...promises it will be his greatest masterpiece...plans to spend in excess of $10 million." March 26: "45 tractors and other pieces of heavy machinery arrive in Montauk. Wells are drilled. A pier is built in one day...." April 2: "Fisher dazzles locals.... first six-room house is constructed in a day, from foundation to slate roof...."[36]

Fisher also built an eighteen-hole golf course ("as sporty as any in America") with its own clubhouse, a picturesque new railroad station, a yacht club with a mock lighthouse, a polo field, a beach club on the dunes with a boardwalk and bathing cabanas, and the "Fisher Tower," a seven-story office block in the heart of the village. Ideal sites presented themselves for these embellishments "as though Nature had anticipated their necessity," according to a Fisher brochure. "The flat plain on which the polo fields will be completed is surrounded by a wave of hills forming a picturesque amphitheatre."[37]

ABOVE LEFT:
Carl Graham Fisher arriving at Montauk on his boat, the *Shadow-K*, 1925.

ABOVE RIGHT:
A map pointing to Montauk Beach published by the Long Island Chamber of Commerce.

LEFT:
A publicity brochure advertising Fisher's Montauk development, c. 1927.

Schultze and Weaver, architects of the Waldorf-Astoria, designed the Montauk Manor, a Tudor-style hotel high atop Signal Hill. Built in an H plan, the hotel had three dining rooms and more than two hundred guest rooms. It looked like a giant wedding cake with its massive brick walls, half-timbering, and ornate chimneys. In June 1927, a gala dinner was held to celebrate the opening of the hotel. VIPs of all kinds—politicians, actors, sports figures, journalists—were ferried out from Manhattan on special trains. Officers of the Long Island and Pennsylvania railroad companies were also in attendance. Working in partnership with Fisher, the railroads had inaugurated special all-club-car trains that would travel express between New York and Montauk in two-and-one-half hours. During the ceremonial toasts, Fisher was compared to Charles Lindbergh, who had just completed his famous flight—both were giants of the century. The orchestra from Fisher's Flamingo Hotel in Miami had been brought north to provide music. There was a floor show with vaudeville dancers and a special exhibition by a professional wrestler named George Romanoff.

To mark the occasion, a publicity brochure—*Montauk: Miami Beach of the North*—was published that was filled with photographs of what had already been built, along with maps and drawings of what was still to come: "America's finest out-of-doors center, where the real aristocrats of modern America may find new health, new relaxation, new ways to play amid luxurious surroundings.... Millions have been spent to add matchless facilities to this incomparable natural loveliness and create a sportsman's ideal playground. *Montauk Beach is a paradise that eludes the most flattering pen.*" But Si Tanhauser, "Railroad Poet Laureate," attempted some flattery nonetheless in a tribute simply titled "Montauk":

> *I hear thee singing, singing in the dawn,*
> *Where I across the slumb'rous waves would*
> *walk*
> *with eager lips to kiss thy dewy feet,*
> *Thy golden hands, thy fingers,*
> *Oh, Montauk...*[38]

ABOVE:
Schultze and Weaver, The Montauk Manor, Montauk, nearing completion in 1927.

AS OTHERS WOULD discover, the formula wasn't quite right for such an all-out assault. The weather was unpredictable. And there was, after all, something forlorn about Montauk's rolling moorland. The storms were violent and the season was too short to clear a profit. The ocean-liner concept was also a flop. People didn't want to stay at a resort after a long Atlantic crossing. If that wasn't enough, the stock market crash of 1929 put a stop to Fisher's northern campaign. By 1934 the Montauk Beach Development Corporation was bankrupt. Five years later, Fisher himself died from a liver ailment.

Meanwhile, the summer colonies of East Hampton and Southampton continued to grow in relatively discrete ways. An active but restrained social life went on behind thick privet hedges or within the exclusive confines of the country clubs. There were other ill-fated schemes to transform Eastern Long Island into a resort paradise. "Midhamptons" was proposed in 1927 by a group of New York developers for an area in Wainscott along the border between Southampton and East Hampton.[39] A central mall would stretch northward from the Montauk Highway with double carriage avenues, formal gardens, and cross avenues all culminating at a central station building on the Long Island Rail Road. The plan continued north past the tracks, with radiating avenues and wedge-shaped building lots. It was a pure "garden city" concept in the spirit of the British planner Ebenezer Howard, and was inspired, no doubt, by the radial diagrams that Howard published in his book, *Garden Cities of To-morrow* (1902). A later phase would have extended the avenues toward the northeast, where there were to have been a sports club with polo fields, swimming pools, and other incitements. Like Fisher's plan for Montauk, "Midhamptons" deflated with the Crash.[40]

In 1937, long before the advent of zoning, the R. B. Allen Development Corporation created small, quarter-acre lots for a more modest housing scheme that was built just to the east of Amagansett. While not as grandiose as Midhamptons or Fisher's Montauk, "Beach Hampton" was an ambitious scheme in keeping with the realities of the Depression economy. If fully realized, it would have brought hundreds of New Yorkers out from the sweltering city, offering them escape and relaxation at affordable prices. The company published a promotional brochure—*Eastward to the Sea: The Romance of Beach Hampton*—extolling the virtues of the beaches and clean air that promised to make Beach Hampton such a paradise: "Romance? Glamour? Scenic Beauty? Recreation? Historic Memories? Beach Hampton is indeed in the heart of Wonderland.... How this mile of pure, white sands, blue waters and silvery surf does sing to the soul!"[41]

The twenty-five-page brochure included drawings of various styles of houses that could be purchased from the company for as little as $4,000. A map was printed in the back of the brochure that showed how easy it was to get there from the city: "Beach Hampton, less than three hours from New York City, is not just another real estate development, it is an ideal, a vision, a dream that we have made come true. Here, if you will, awaits you, a new world of happiness!"[42]

Three miles of hard-paved roads were laid in a crisscrossing pattern and given beachy names like Treasure Island Drive and Sandpiper Lane. Water mains, electric street lights, and telephone service were installed. Everything was ready. The first houses were finished in 1937–38. The Beach Hampton Surf Club, a handsome white pavilion, was built prominently on top of the dunes. It opened with gala celebrations in August, but only a few weeks later the epic hurricane of 1938 struck the coast, and much of the development, including the club, was destroyed.

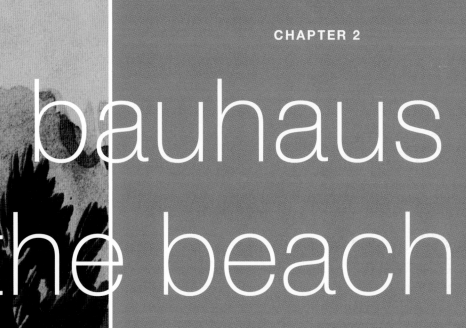

bauhaus on the beach

I object to uselessness. I object to cornices, to pitched roofs, to leaded glass windows, and to shutters. My object in domestic architecture is to provide shelter and protection against heat, cold and wet…that it be so arranged as to be run with maximum saving in drudgery. That it be, in short, a proper house for twentieth-century living.

—Percival Goodman, 1931[1]

WHILE SO MANY visionary plans seemed to fail, there was something about the low, horizontal landscape of Eastern Long Island that provided fertile ground for the cultivation of modernism. The beach made a perfect setting for new ideas washing over from Europe. Several of the American-bred architects who built experimental beach houses in the Hamptons had studied, visited, or worked in Europe, and had returned brimming with a spirit of innovation. William Muschenheim studied architecture in Vienna, Percival Goodman studied in France, Frances Miller made frequent trips to Europe, and Philip Johnson had lived in Germany. Several others were born in Europe and had emigrated to the states: Antonin Raymond came from Prague; Pierre Chareau fled France before the fall of Paris; Paul Lester Wiener and Bernard Rudofsky came from Austria; and Peter Blake escaped Nazi Germany. Together, they brought with them the latest advances in theory and practice.

Modernist ideas were easily transposed and adapted for use in the summer homes of the pre- and postwar periods. The slender *pilotis* of Le Corbusier's Villa Savoye (1929–31) became posts for raising houses to attain better views and for protecting them from hurricane surge. The roof terraces and open porches that Le Corbusier used at his Villa Stein (1927) became sun decks. The glass facades that Mies van der Rohe and Walter Gropius were using in Germany became sliding glass doors and floor-to-ceiling windows for gazing at the sea. The looseness of the open plan was perfectly suited to the informal lifestyle of a new breed of active, sun-worshipping summer residents.

While the first modernist beach houses on Long Island may have looked like virtual transpositions from avant-garde strains in Europe, there was something else going on. In an early manifesto of the mod-

ern movement, the Dutch artist and sometime architect, Theo van Doesburg, wrote: "There is an old and a new consciousness of the age. The old one is directed toward the individual. The new one is directed toward the universal." But the opposite held true in the emerging beach culture of Long Island. The new consciousness was directed toward the *individual*. Modernist ideals that had originated in the socialist culture of Holland, Russia, and Weimar Germany were somehow transformed and pressed into the service of capitalist leisure; updated examples of Thorstein Veblen's "evidence of esteem." The principles of the new beach architecture were closer in spirit to Hollywood than to Weimar.[2]

The very first "modernistic beach house" on the East Coast was built by a Hollywood executive named Glendon Allvine, the publicity director of the Fox Films Corporation. Allvine's stark white house was built in 1928 and made a crisp incision into the dunescape of Long Beach, a community on Long Island's southern shore. Allvine had been exposed to *l'esprit noveau* during a visit he had made to Paris where he saw work by Le Corbusier, Rob Mallet-Stevens, and André Lurçat. During business trips to Los Angeles, Allvine had also seen houses by Frank Lloyd Wright, Richard Neutra, and Rudolph Schindler.[3]

Allvine was excited by the modern movement and encouraged his own architect, Warren Matthews, to try his hand at the new style. In his previous commissions Matthews had specialized in neo-Tudor and Norman-style estates on Long Island's north shore, so the results in Long Beach were predictably clumsy. But he managed to include most of the right ingredients: Bauhaus-style setbacks, flat roofs, horizontal bands of windows, and cantilevered decks with tubular metal railings. The house was oriented toward the sea as if it were a

OPPOSITE:
Elizabeth Bodanzky
Muschenheim (on left) with
her neice, Linda M. Perrone,
on the beach in front of the
Muschenheim Bathhouses,
Hampton Bays, c. 1933.

futuristic ship about to set sail, an image reinforced by four portholes on the beach facade.

In contrast to the white stucco walls, Matthews accentuated the lines of the multilevel roof with black slate coping. Decks were placed in carefully chosen positions to allow sunbathing at different times of the day. Interiors were less austere than the exterior, with more of the sensuality of an Art Deco movie set than a Bauhaus dormitory. Allvine filled each room with specially commissioned work by his favorite modern designers, some of whom he knew from their set design work in Hollywood. There was a tubular steel daybed by Ruth Reeves, a lacquered bed by Paul Poiret, decorative folding screens by Donald Deskey and Paul Frankl, and chairs by Walter von Nessen.

From the beginning, the modern beach houses of Eastern Long Island were showplaces, places of escape. They were not intended as socially responsible housing designed for uniform repetition or mass production, but as expressions of personal freedom. In an article describing the Allvine House, Harriet Sisson Gillespie wrote: "The new art, as the modernist visualizes it, must be an *individual expression* of the forces that surge around us today."[4]

Percival Goodman left New York for Europe in 1925. He was twenty-one years old and had just won the prestigious Paris Prize, which came with a scholarship to study at the Ecole des Beaux Arts in Paris. But, like so many young architects of his generation, Goodman turned against Beaux Arts traditions after being exposed to the radical new directions in European architecture. During his stay, Goodman also visited projects by Le Corbusier, Lurçat, and Mallet-Stevens.[5] He also learned about revolutionary new projects outside of France like the Weissenhofsiedlung in Stuttgart Germany (1927), with its housing schemes by Mies van der Rohe, Walter Gropius, Mart Stam, and others.

Goodman returned to the United States in 1931. It was only two years after the Wall Street crash and while prospects looked grim, the economic crisis also held promise for a socially committed young architect like Goodman. New forms of affordable housing would be essential; the time was right to challenge the bourgeois tendencies of the American building trade. He drew plans for a series of houses to be built in Long Beach, Long Island, not far from the Allvine House. That year, his drawings of a prototypical

housing unit were published in *Architectural Progress*, showing a sharply geometric construction with white stucco walls and a flat, cantilevered roof—not unlike the faculty houses that Walter Gropius had designed for the Bauhaus in Dessau, Germany in 1926. "The end and rationale of all construction is the happiness of the individual," wrote Goodman in an essay that accompanied his drawings, "but the beginning and instrument of all construction is the planning of the community."[6] Then, in 1933, the drawings were included in an exhibition at the Architectural League of New York. This is when a speculative builder named Arthur Colen saw them and proposed a partnership. The idea was to build a series of modestly priced housing units across a 26-acre tract in Hempstead, Long Island. Instead of attached units, Goodman and Colen agreed on a series of freestanding, single-family units—140 of them—built on 40-foot lots. It would be a modernist *siedlung,* just like the one at Stuttgart. Backed by a local bank, Goodman was able to proceed with working drawings for a prototype to be made from reinforced concrete with a flat roof and cantilevered decks at an estimated cost of only $3,500 per unit.

Everything was proceeding smoothly until the actual construction got underway in June 1934. The local builders had never worked on a modern house before. They didn't understand the plans and were reluctant to learn new methods. "The fact that a cantilever could be built was a great shock and surprise to the concrete men," said Goodman. "Apparently, to them there were hieratic methods of construction and any departure from them was an offense against God."[7]

The architect and contractor were in constant dispute and with every squabble the costs of the project escalated. Goodman was quickly learning that suburban Long Island wasn't quite ready for his utopian vision. "There wasn't just a negative feeling about modern architecture in this country at that time," said Goodman, "It was absolutely *anti*. Nobody knew what it was about.... People thought it was just crazy."[8]

The quality of construction turned out to be so inferior and unsafe that Goodman was finally forced to disassociate himself from the project. He stormed into the office of the Hempstead building department and, like some scene out of Ayn Rand's *The Fountainhead*, insisted that his housing prototype

OPPOSITE, TOP:
Warren Matthews, Allvine House, Long Beach, 1929.

OPPOSITE, BOTTOM LEFT:
Percival Goodman, model of aluminum beach house for Montauk, 1932.

OPPOSITE, BOTTOM RIGHT:
Percival Goodman, perspective drawing of modern house for Long Beach, 1931.

be torn down, which it eventually was. Developer Colen, meanwhile, had come to the realization that modern architecture would never make him a profit. "Nobody would ever buy those boxes," he grumbled and decided to go back to building neo-Tudor villas.[9] While it was almost impossible to find work as a young architect during the Depression (especially one suspected of being a communist) Goodman was able to scrape by designing window displays for department stores in New York. But during this same period of struggle, Goodman developed a very different kind of project: a small weekend house for a beach-front site on the eastern tip of Long Island, in Montauk. Perhaps it would not be in public housing but in the privately owned vacation house that modernism would find its American identity. The structural framework of Goodman's beach house was to be made of steel and the outer walls covered with sheets of polished aluminum. Raised off the ground on metal pipes, the house was designed expressly for easy, fast, and inexpensive assembly: "a means by which the city dweller can escape the inevitable claustrophobia brought on by unnatural compactness," wrote Goodman. "It is the proper housing for the health and sport cult, and it is a compromise with economic conditions."[10] Goodman's aluminum house was never built, but it offered a hint of things to come. Here was a different kind of utopian promise, not one that was designed for the masses, but for affluent individuals who could afford a weekend at the beach.

DURING THE SUMMER of 1925, a young American architect named William Muschenheim, went to work in an architecture office in Berlin. After attending Williams College, Muschenheim had studied architecture at MIT, but nothing had prepared him for what he saw in Germany that summer. On his days off, he explored the fruits of Weimar culture: He saw crystalline new structures by Max Taut and visited exhibitions of steel-framed furniture by Mies van der Rohe and Marcel Breuer. He made a visit to Walter Gropius's new campus for the Bauhaus in Dessau while it was still under construction. He attended the theater of Bertolt Brecht, heard the music of Arnold Schoenberg, and saw the paintings of Paul Klee. It was all intoxicating, and Muschenheim wrote letters to his parents with breathless news of his discoveries.[11]

In the fall, Muschenheim began postgraduate studies with Peter Behrens in Vienna. Behrens's atelier was one of the hothouses of avant-garde design in Europe—Gropius, Mies van der Rohe, and Le Corbusier had all worked there early in their careers. Behrens stressed the importance of town-planning and the duty of architects to design good housing for the masses. His methods made a lasting impression on the young architect from New York: "[Behrens] emphasized that the student must learn how to develop his potentialities," wrote Muschenheim, "and be aware of their relationship to a new era, rather than follow any predetermined rules."[12]

Muschenheim's postgraduate thesis was for a "House on the Dunes"—a study in horizontal massing with echoes of the work of Gropius and Adolf Loos. The project was a success and won the prestigious Behrens Prize. In theory the House on the Dunes might have been suitable for any beach, but Muschenheim designed it for a specific site on Long island: a 5-acre plot of land in Hampton Bays with its own private beach and views across Shinnecock Bay. The land was owned by his father, Frederick Augustus Muschenheim, who had plans to develop it into a summer retreat.

While he couldn't afford to build his son's project, the senior Muschenheim did encourage him to convert an old gable-roofed house that was already standing on the property. The house wasn't right on the beach, but it was only a 500-foot walk down to Shinnecock Bay and less than a mile from the ocean beach. Muschenheim would have preferred to tear it down and start from scratch, but his father gave him carte blanche and encouraged him to work with what was there. The remodeling began in 1925 as a kind of work-in-progress where the young architect could experiment with new ideas. He began with lessons he had learned in Vienna and adapted them to the Long Island setting. He left the original gable roof intact as a central form, and worked around it, wrapping it with white walls and flat roofs. Interior spaces were opened up, partitions were knocked out, and new wings were added to the old house in a pin-wheel kind of rotation. Muschenheim used every device possible to open the house to the views, the sun, and the ocean breezes. He added several porches and a metal staircase that spiraled up to a sun terrace. The old parts of the house were delineated from the new

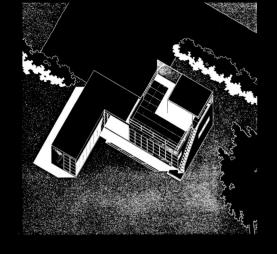

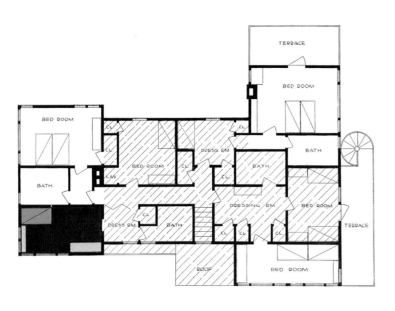

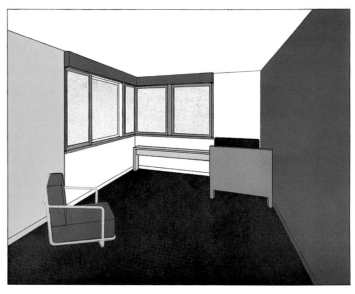

ABOVE:
Muschenheim House, detail of spiral staircase (in ruin).

OPPOSITE, TOP LEFT:
Muschenheim House, floor plan.

OPPOSITE, TOP RIGHT:
Muschenheim House, interior color scheme.

OPPOSITE, BOTTOM:
William Muschenheim, Muschenheim Bathhouses, Hampton Bays, 1930.

parts with primary colors in a way that was similar to what the De Stijl architects were doing in Holland. Window trim on the old parts was painted yellow, while the new parts were clad in white clapboard and given blue trim. Porch railings were also painted yellow, the doors red.[13]

Sometimes it was hard to find the right materials and Muschenheim had to improvise. Where he might have preferred flush metal windows—the kind that Gropius used at the Bauhaus—he had to settle for wood frames fabricated by a local carpenter. It was also difficult to find good modern furniture at that time, so Muschenheim designed his own. As it evolved, the house looked like something caught in the act of becoming, with its frumpy gable poking up. Despite all of his modifications, it still felt like a conventional house masquerading as a modern one. Awkward in its way, it represented a transition from the conventions of his father's generation to a new form of leisure that his own generation was beginning to embrace—with a less structured sense of time and a close connection to nature. Muschenheim and his friends would swim every day in Shinnecock Bay. They would go sailing and lie naked in the sun, or walk to their favorite ocean beach. His father would, on occasion, venture down to the beach, but he never went swimming and was always formally attired in a jacket and tie.

The Muschenheims created their private little enclave well removed from the country-club sets of Southampton and East Hampton. They were socially self-sufficient and imported most of their friends from New York. Muschenheim's father had been trained as an engineer but had turned away from his chosen profession to work with his older brother in the hotel business. He was the co-owner and manager of the Hotel Astor on Times Square and, in this capacity, came to know some of the most influential and powerful people in the city. Among his friends were many prominent musicians and artists, including Arturo Toscanini, Rudolph and Peter Serkin, Arshile Gorky, the dancer Anita Zahn, and Artur Bodanzki, the principle conductor of the Metropolitan Opera House. (Muschenheim married Bodanzki's daughter, Elizabeth, in 1930.) They all came to visit the compound in Hampton Bays.

Muschenheim's father loved to entertain his friends and put on lavish dinner parties. As his granddaughter, Anneli Arms, recalled, "My grandfather gave up engineering for partying." He would drive out from the city in his chauffeur-driven Cadillac, bringing crates of champagne, prime steaks, and other delicacies from the kitchen of the Hotel Astor. (The car was equipped with special little compartments to hold all the weekend supplies.) Tables were set up on the beach and dinner was served by professional waiters brought out from the hotel. As the number of summer guests grew, the compound expanded and the younger Muschenheim designed a guest cottage, a garage, a playhouse for the children, and a cookhouse for the servants.[14]

In 1929, around the time of the Wall Street crash, the elder Muschenheim bought a few acres of oceanfront property not far from the main house, just to the west of the Shinnecock Inlet. At the time there was nothing there except rolling dunes and a single fisherman's shack. At one point, it was suggested that some kind of bathhouse be built on the site. Then, in 1930, Muschenheim designed a grouping of bathhouses for this empty and expansive site. While he had been restricted in the design of his father's house, here Muschenheim was free to try anything. A bathhouse only needed to provide seasonal functions and could take almost any form—it was a perfect medium for experimentation. Muschenheim took the concept of the traditional beach cabana and stripped it of all of its elitist associations. The little buildings, which were attached by wooden walkways, sat perched on the top ridge of a dune, their bold geometric forms rising above the undulating contours of beach grass and sand. The bladelike shapes of four sloping roofs pointed in different directions. Three separate structures provided space for changing rooms, showers, toilets, and sunbathing courts for the Muschenheim family and their summer guests. The slope-roofed pavilions were made from half-inch thick asbestos cement panels. Each panel measured 4 feet by 8 feet and was attached to a structural framework of wood. The joints between the panels were caulked with lead. The roofs of the changing rooms were covered in asbestos shingles.

The ocean beach was the perfect backdrop for the geometric gestures of the modern movement. "It was a fascinating setting for an architect to work in," said Muschenheim, "with that enormous ocean on one side and those soft dunes on the other."[15] The bold outlines of Muschenheim's bathhouses suggested a new kind of relationship between architecture and the beach, one that was both challenging and complimentary, provocative and respectful. During this same period, the modern dancer Anita Zahn was exploring similar kinds of interactions between the human body and the natural landscape. Zahn had been a disciple of Isadora Duncan, and was a close friend of the Muschenheims. (She was said to have been the mistress of the elder Muschenheim.) During the 1930s she came out to the Hamptons and performed her interpretive dances right on the ocean dunes. (Later, she established a school in East Hampton for young dancers.) Her 1935 performance "Three Muses" evoked the same kind of elemental forms as Muschenheim's cabanas.

Muschenheim's bathhouse project was soon noticed by the architectural world. It was chosen by Alfred Barr and Philip Johnson for inclusion in the *Rejected Architects* exhibition that they organized in 1931. The exhibition was something like a dry run for the famous *International Style* exhibition that Johnson and Henry-Russell Hitchcock curated at the Museum of Modern Art the following year. *Rejected Architects* was set up in a storefront on Sixth Avenue as a protest on the part of progressive young architects against the conservative tastes of the Architectural League. In an appraisal of the exhibition, Johnson singled out Muschenheim's project for the diversity of its materials and forms, and for how it represented the best of the modern movement.[16]

During this same period, Muschenheim was also working with Joseph Urban on the New School for Social Research. He made additions to the Hotel Astor for his father; developed the color scheme for the Chicago Century of Progress Exposition of 1933, and, with E. J. Kahn, designed the Marine

Transportation Building at the New York World's Fair in 1939. But the bathhouses in Hampton Bays may have been Muschenheim's most significant contribution to the architectural discourse of the period. With their scale and sculptural presence, the cabanas introduced a modern tribute to the sea and sky and forshadowed the geometric abstractions that would not fully emerge until the 1960s in the work of Charles Gwathmey and his contemporaries.

WHILE THE CRASH of 1929 impeded most new building in the Hamptons, there were a few notable exceptions. Lucien Hamilton Tyng was a New York financier who survived the collapse relatively unscathed, and during the first years of the Depression was solvent enough to build himself an unusually grand summer house in Southampton called "The Shallows." Tyng's original house on Halsey Neck Lane had burned to the ground in 1930, and after the fire Tyng commissioned the architectural firm of Peabody, Wilson, and Brown to design a fireproof structure on the same site. The firm was known for the large country residences that they designed for socially prominent clients. Though they had dabbled in the modern mode, this commission was a serious departure from their normally eclectic menu of Georgian, English, Provençal, and various other styles preferred by their Social Register clients.[17]

Archibald Brown, the youngest of the firm's partners, was able to convince his otherwise wary client that a pared-down, modern exterior was not only stylish but practical. Beside being fireproof, the new style also offered a token concession to the gods of finance—it was a relatively austere and humble expression compared to the lavish displays of architectural one-upmanship that had been built in Southampton during the pre-Crash days. The Depression was no time to flaunt one's success by raising a mock Tudor manor with quaint details and fussy fenestration. It was a time for sober restraint and reflection. In its way, "modern" conveyed a sense of Puritan austerity and, even, repentance. At least this was true on the outside of the house.

The house stood high on its watery site between an inlet of Shinnecock Bay on one side, a pond on the other, and the ocean just to the south. With blank facades, flat roofs, and setbacks, it had the profile of

LEFT:
Anita Zahn and company performing "Three Muses," on an oceanfront lawn in East Hampton, 1935.

Peabody, Wilson, and Brown, Tyng House ("The Shallows"), Southampton, 1931.

a great white battleship steaming out toward Shinnecock Bay. Walls were made from hollow tile covered with white stucco. Trim and flashing were made from lead-covered copper. Copings and balcony floors were made from random rectangles of slate. Overhangs and recessed planes created a cubistlike patterning of shadow and light across the pale stucco surfaces. There was nothing penitential about the interior, however, with more than twenty-four rooms including a grand central hall, a lavishly appointed living room, and a dining room that could comfortably seat thirty guests at a time. On the second floor, which could be reached by an elevator, there were several guest bedrooms, six bathrooms, five "maids rooms," a sewing room, as well as a master bedroom, a boudoir, and a dressing room.

Though it was in the modern idiom, the Tyng House had almost nothing in common with Le Corbusier's idea of a *machine á habiter* (machine for living), and was closer in spirit to the large villas that Rob Mallet-Stevens had designed for wealthy French clients, in particular the houses for Rue Mallet-Stevens in Paris (1926–27), and the Villa Cavrois in Croix, France (1931) which shared a similar sense of scale and massing. There was certainly nothing revolutionary about the interior layout of the Tyng House. It was broken up into a warren of rooms to accommodate all those weekend guests and servants. The owner had insisted that the new house be built on the exact footprint of the original,

burned house, so the architects had been restricted in their desire to create open, flowing spaces. They were, however, able to create a connection to the exterior by carefully placing windows to capture the "finest landscape pictures of the sea and marshes."[18] Six different balconies were oriented toward the bay and pond, while a broad roof terrace commanded views of the ocean.

As a modernist mansion, the Tyng House was a rare exception. When financial markets began to rally again, so would the fondness for eclectic styles of architecture. Modernism wouldn't catch on in the Hamptons until after World War II. Even then it would not be the conspicuously rich who favored the style, but rather a less affluent generation of weekenders who wished to express an image of independence and nonconformity.

FRANCES BREESE MILLER grew up in the lap of luxury. She was the daughter of James Lawrence Breese, a wealthy entrepreneur who had hired Stanford White to design his plantation-style estate in Southampton known as "The Orchard." Miller was educated at home, in Manhattan, by a French governess, but during the summer months she stayed at The Orchard and took part in the summer rituals of Southampton society. Miller performed in amateur musicals, played tennis at the exclusive Meadow Club, and went swimming in the ocean at the Southampton

Bath and Tennis Club. But as she reached maturity, Miller realized that she didn't quite fit in. She was strikingly tall—over 6 feet—and stood out from the other debutantes of the summer colony. She was already developing rather eccentric, tomboyish behavior. Her father treated her more like a favored son than a daughter and allowed her to drive his Pierce Arrow around the village, much to the dismay of the matrons of Southampton society. (Driving an automobile was still considered unacceptable behavior for a young lady of good breeding.)

In 1915 she married stock broker Larry Miller, but she was already beginning to feel alienated from the privileged world in which she had grown up. Through her friends Gertrude Whitney and Julianna Force, she met a group of Greenwich Village artists. "Recognizing how narrow and exclusive a circle I moved in, I felt ashamed. Henceforth I would take every opportunity to widen my horizon." She read books on art and oriental philosophy, attended lectures on modern design, and visited the Peggy Guggenheim Gallery, one of the first in America to exhibit abstract art. Despite her husband's disapproval, she began to study painting.[19]

In 1928 she opened a store on Fifty-seventh Street that was the first in New York to sell furnishings and textiles by the new generation of American designers that included Russel Wright, Gilbert Rhode, and Walter von Nessen. Miller also began to work as a professional interior designer, producing a collection of hand-hooked rugs that she designed with simple geometric patterns. When these rugs became popular with architects, Miller found herself with an unexpected source of income. Meanwhile, her Wall Street husband was increasingly threatened by her growing sense of independence. "I felt suffocated and began to fear that our marriage would destroy me," she wrote. After a period of psychiatric treatment, Frances went to Reno, Nevada and obtained a divorce. "I had to learn to live alone," she wrote, "to conduct an independent private life, to re-examine my beliefs, and try to find out what mattered most to me."[20] The most liberating point in Miller's transformation from debutante to bohemian came when she decided to build a house on the beach. All her life she had wanted to live near the sea. In 1932, two years after her divorce, Miller bought a pie-shaped lot in Brideghampton on Dune Road, a narrow spit of sand

that lies precariously between the Atlantic Ocean and Mecox Bay. Although it was only a few miles to the east, it was a far cry from the manicured lawns and privet hedges of old Southampton.

Miller envisioned a house just for herself. "Tradition would be abandoned," she wrote as if composing a manifesto for her own personal salvation. "No covered porches, no attic, no dining room, no space-consuming staircase, and, since I planned to live without household help, no maid's room." She wanted total immersion in the beachfront setting, so the house would become part of the windswept landscape. Building a house on the dunes was still considered a reckless thing to do, however. Locals warned her that the ocean could break through during storms and cut her off from the mainland, but she went ahead with her plans, undeterred. She made a series of preliminary sketches herself and then hired society architect Lansing "Denny" Holden to prepare working drawings.[21]

"The Sandbox," as Miller dubbed the house, fit perfectly into the wild and windy setting. It had a flat-roofed, geometric profile that was inspired by the modernist architecture Miller had seen on a trip to Europe. There, she had visited many different examples of the new architecture, but had been particularly taken by the experimental buildings that Erik Gunnar Asplund designed for the Stockholm Exhibition (1930). The simple cubic forms of Miller's house had no extraneous trim or detailing. Horizontal redwood siding and open sun porches made a sympathetic counterpoint to the undulating folds of the ocean dunes. There would be no formal gardens, just nature in its rawest form. Miller's only intervention into the surrounding sandscape was to encourage the natural process of wind sculpting. She discovered a way to shape the barrier dune in front of her house so as to provide protection from ocean storms: she placed anything she could find in front of the house—dead trees, bits and pieces of driftwood, old furniture—and over time, windblown sand was trapped by the obstructions, creating a high protective mound.

All openings were positioned to take advantage of favored views. Some of the windows looked out toward the ocean, others pointed to the north. Miller planned the kitchen so she would be able to cook while looking out over the waters of Mecox Bay. The living room had four different exposures. "I wanted

OPPOSITE, TOP:
Frances Miller with Lansing Holden, Miller Beach House ("The Sandbox"), Bridgehampton, 1933.

OPPOSITE, BOTTOM LEFT:
The Sandbox, interior view in 1933.

OPPOSITE, BOTTOM RIGHT:
The Sandbox, floor plan.

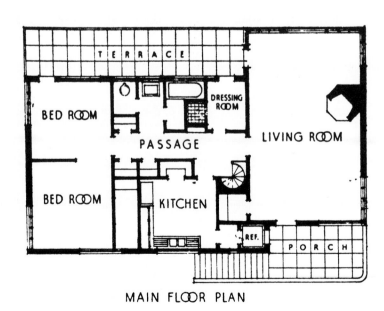

MAIN FLOOR PLAN

TERRACE

BED ROOM

DRESSING ROOM

PASSAGE

LIVING ROOM

BED ROOM

KITCHEN

REF.

PORCH

floor-to-ceiling windows and exposure to sun on all sides," wrote Miller. "Even the bathroom must have sun, and most important, a view from the tub."[22]

The big dune at the side of the house appeared to spill right through the windows and onto the living room floor, an illusion that was further enhanced by the "sand-pattern" rug that Miller had woven herself. She further married the house to its setting by splatter-painting the floors with pre-Pollock drips and swirls of green and yellow paint. Small, artfully selected pieces of driftwood were fashioned into door handles for closets and drawers. The entire project cost only $7,500.

As soon as it was finished, The Sandbox attracted attention. People driving down Dune Road stopped to stare at the "queer little box of rectangular design sticking into the side of the dune." The editors of *House Beautiful* published an article praising it as one the first modern houses on the East Coast, and had Miller write an essay titled "Why I Built That Kind of House." (Miller also self-published a book about the house in 1934 called *Week-End On the Dunes.*)[23]

At first, Miller just spent weekends and summer vacations at the house, but when her two sons left for boarding school, she was able to spend more time at the house, writing, reading, and painting in comparative solitude—learning how to lead a life of quiet introspection. At times her life at the beach seemed almost mystical: "Listening to the surf beyond the barrier dunes," she wrote, "I learned to sense the ocean's moods, to be aware, by the sound, of a change

of tide."[24] The Sandbox became Miller's escape from conformity and the social strictures of her conservative background. She was free to do whatever she felt like doing, unconcerned with what the snobbish crowd in Southampton thought of her eccentric behavior. She took long walks along the empty beach and made a habit of swimming naked every day, no matter how cold it was. The Sandbox was Miller's refuge from the city and the past, a healing and revealing environment that served as a means of her own personal salvation.

FARTHER TO THE east, out on the sandy cliffs of Montauk Point, another kind of summer retreat was being built: the Carera Beach House, designed by architect Antonin Raymond. Born in Prague in 1889, Raymond emigrated to the United States in 1916 and began working for Frank Lloyd Wright at Taliesen in Wisconsin. Three years later he accompanied Wright to Japan to work as project architect on the Imperial Hotel in Tokyo. After completion of the hotel, Raymond stayed in Japan and established a successful career as one of the first architects to bring modernist ideas to Japanese building. In 1937 he decided to leave, however, due to anti-Western sentiment and the looming clouds of war. Back in the United States, Raymond set up a practice in an old stone farmhouse in New Hope, Pennsylvania and proceeded to design a series of houses that used

ABOVE, LEFT:
Carera Beach House, living room.

ABOVE, RIGHT:
Carera Beach House, front door.

the same combination of open plan, natural finishes, sensitivity to site, and other ideas that Raymond brought with him from Japan.

The Carera Beach House, which Raymond began in 1939, was sited in a most sympathetic way, with low, earth-hugging forms that melded into the Montauk landscape. The various levels of the house and its gently sloping roof line echoed the windswept contours of the dunes. The shape was wholly determined by the house's relationship to the ocean views. Divided into three parts, the house had a kind of "scissors" floor plan that combined elements of Japanese architecture and an American "split-level" layout. "A good modern plan is *free*," wrote Raymond, "expressive of the informal American way of living. The relation of the interior to the exterior and the materials used and their finishes are more *natural*, expressive of our re-awakened sense of the physical." Raymond dogmatically declared that "in modern architecture, the only decoration is the construction."[25]

The main living/dining area was sited in the most prominent position and commanded the best views. There were sliding glass windows and a wide wooden deck that reached out over the crest of the dune. A service wing extended away from the beach toward the old Montauk Highway with a kitchen, garage, maid's room, and storage area. Steps from the living area led down to a bedroom wing angled off to the east. As with all of his residential projects of this period, a combination of natural materials was used

to integrate the house even further into its wild setting. Rough Montauk stones were used in retaining walls, fireplaces, and foyer floors. Interior floors were made from oak. Square modular panels of pale gum plywood were used on ceilings and interior walls. Rough-hewn cedar columns framed the views in both the upper- and lower-level decks. Throughout the house, Raymond used a system of sliding *shoji*-type screens. All the windows could be easily boarded up with sliding Weldwood shutters to protect the house against storms. Most of the furniture was spare, Japanese in style, and designed by Raymond's wife, Naomi. Wherever possible, built-in closets and cabinets were used in place of free-standing furniture. Raymond wanted to develop a more intimate connection between house and landscape, to deliver his clients directly to the sensations of the natural beach environment, to create, as he said, an "atmosphere of serenity and calm, life, mobility, and joy."[26]

Although descended from the social ferment of the 1920s, this new architecture of leisure was not designed to improve the social order but, to provide a means of personal freedom. Early experiments in beachfront living by Raymond, Miller, Muschenheim, and others set the stage for what was to come after the hiatus of World War II, when a new generation of artists and architects would discover the Hamptons landscape and interpret it in their own ways.

CHAPTER 3

convergence

The new painting has broken down every
distinction between art and life.
—Harold Rosenberg, 1952[1]

A GROUP OF prominent European artists established a foothold in the Hamptons during World War II. There had been migrations of artists to Eastern Long Island since the Tile Club first came in 1878, but this was different. The refugee artists of the 1940s included some of the most prominent members of the European avant garde. Unlike Manhattan, which many of the exiles found cold and unforgiving, the Hamptons offered a congenial setting in which to wait out the war. The fluid atmosphere of the beach proved more conducive to spontaneous exchange. Many of the exiles first came to East Hampton as guests of Gerald and Sara Murphy, an affluent but artistically inclined couple who had lived as expatriates in Paris during the 1920s and had been friends with many of the pioneers of the modern movement, including Pablo Picasso, Fernand Léger, Gertrude Stein, Ernest Hemingway, and F. Scott Fitzgerald. (Fitzgerald had immortalized the couple as Dick and Nicole Diver in his 1934 novel *Tender is the Night*.)

The Murphys returned to America in the 1930s and spent their summers at "The Dunes," a sprawling oceanfront mansion that Sara's father, Frank Wiborg, had built near the Maidstone Club in 1895. Léger and his companion, Lucia Christofanetti, came out and took up residence at one of the guest cottages on the Wiborg estate. Christofanetti grew to love the area so much that she eventually found her own house and encouraged many of her émigré friends to visit. Salvador Dali and Marcel Duchamp came out during this period. So did Anaïs Nin, Jean Hélion, Arshile Gorky, Isamu Noguchi, and the Chilean surrealist Matta. Max Ernst rented a summer house in Amagansett with Dorothea Tanning. Working with everyday objects, Ernst created a series of chess-related sculptures including *The King Playing with His Queen* (1944).

André Breton, leader of the surrealist pack in Paris, also came to the Hamptons during the war years. He was inspired by the luminous sky and sandy Long Island landscape. Breton had escaped to New York in 1941. During the summer of 1943, he rented a house in Hampton Bays and commuted from the city every weekend on the Long Island Rail Road. Breton wrote his epic poem *Les Etats Genereaux* while summering in Hampton Bays ("There will always be a wind-borne shovel in the sand of dreams," he wrote).[2] On some weekends he was also joined by a young protégé named Charles Duits. Together they sat on the train chugging eastward from the city, composing automatic surrealist verse.

This was a trying period of transition for Breton. Not only was he adjusting to his state of exile, but he found himself sharing the house with his estranged wife, Jacqueline Lamba and her lover, a handsome young sculptor named David Hare. Breton sat on the shady porch while Lamba and Hare swam in the ocean or walked naked along the beach, holding hands and flaunting their passion.[3]

While most of the exiles returned to Europe as soon as the war was over, their presence had a lingering effect and set a high level of discourse for American artists to follow. A new generation soon found their way out to this promised land of open vistas and restless tides. Jackson Pollock and his wife, Lee Krasner, came out to East Hampton in 1945 and purchased a modest two-and-a-half story farm house in the Springs. Robert Motherwell, who had first come out to Amagansett to visit Max Ernst, returned after the war and built himself a house and studio. Mark Rothko came out to visit in 1946, John Little, the painter, in 1947. Willem de Kooning first came out in 1948, as did the Italian sculptor Costantino Nivola and the painter James Brooks. Alfonso Ossorio first

came to East Hampton in 1949 to look up Jackson Pollock and decided to stay. Franz Kline first visited in 1950, then, during the summer of 1954, shared "The Red House" in Bridgehampton with Bill and Elaine de Kooning. Jacques Lipchitz came in 1954 and so did Conrad Marca-Relli, Theodoros Stamos, and Larry Rivers. (Rivers first made his mark not as an artist but playing baritone saxophone at the Elm Tree Inn in Amagansett.) Others who came during this period were William Baziotes, Wilfred Zogbaum, Balcomb Greene, Helen Frankenthaler, Adolph Gottlieb, John Ferren, Hedda Sterne, Iram Lassaw, and Jimmy Ernst, son of Max.

Some of the artists only stayed for a few months, others moved out permanently and, like Pollock, renovated older houses or converted barns for their studios. A few, like Motherwell and Stamos, built experimental houses and studios. The painter Balcomb Greene built himself a studio on the windswept bluffs of Montauk. In 1952 Ossorio, bought "The Creeks," the old Albert Herter estate on Georgica Pond, and proceeded to transform it into a kind of surrealist theme park. He filled the house with exotic caged birds, oriental rugs, and an impressive collection of abstract paintings by Pollock, Jean Dubuffet, and others. He also transformed the grounds of the estate with a collection of rare conifer trees and garish sculptures.

These artists changed the nature of the Hamptons. The South Shore was no longer just a string of pretty villages from Westhampton to Montauk. It was more than a collection of pristine beaches, potato farms, and a few exclusive country clubs. As one resident of the period put it, the place was now crawling with "crazy artists."[4]

Along with the artists came a wave of architects: Pierre Chareau, Peter Blake, Frederick Kiesler, Tony Smith, Paul Lester Wiener, Robert Rosenberg, George Nelson, and others who were struck by the qualities of the sea-reflected light and the all-pervasive sky. The artists and architects were also joined by writers. Harold Rosenberg, art critic for the *New Yorker*, had moved to the Springs as early as 1943 with his wife, the writer May Tabak. His *New Yorker* colleague, Berton Roueché, moved out to Amagansett on a permanent basis in 1948. Truman Capote built a beach house for himself on the dunes in Bridgehampton. John Steinbeck moved to Sag Harbor. Edward Albee moved to Montauk, Dwight Macdonald to East Hampton, Peter Matthiessen to Sagaponack. Even Jack Kerouac, king of the Beat writers, came for a short stay with his mother in North Haven.

The Hamptons proved to be an excellent setting for exploring the depths of the unconscious. Ideas flowed. Boundaries dissolved in the relaxed atmosphere. There was something about the place that freed the imagination. Maybe it was being surrounded by all that water: the ocean, the saltwater inlets and ponds. Maybe it was being located on

ABOVE, LEFT:

Jackson Pollock at work in his studio, the Springs, 1950. Photo by Hans Namuth.

ABOVE, RIGHT:

Pollock's studio floor.

such an extremity, at the very eastern tip of Long Island. "Out here it became more playful and more joyous because nature helped," recalled Ruth Nivola, who moved out to the Springs in 1948 with her husband, Costantino Nivola. "The artists had a real connection with the earth, with the beach, with the poetry of nature."[5]

All of this helped to foster a new energy that, in turn, extended itself well beyond the shores of Long Island. There were heated conversations in artists' studios, drunken discussions at the Elm Tree Inn and Jungle Pete's. Artists lay on the beach talking about each others' work or sharing the latest gossip from the New York gallery scene. Coast Guard Beach, at the western end of East Hampton, became known as Artists' Beach because so many of this first group congregated there.

While this latest invasion was resisted at first by locals and established summer residents, attitudes gradually changed. East Hampton's cultural center, Guild Hall, began to include the new abstractionists in their exhibitions. The first real breakthrough came in 1949 with the exhibition *17 Artists of Eastern Long Island*. The show was organized by Christofanetti and Roseanne Larkin, and included canvases by Pollock, Raphael Soyer (who was then living in Montauk), and seascapes by Ray Prohaska of Amagansett. The next summer Guild Hall mounted *10 East Hampton Abstractionists*, which included work by Pollock, Krasner, Motherwell, and James Brooks. In 1953 there

was *The Sea Around Us*, with works by Pollock, Baziotes, and Stamos.

It was at about this time that a conservative East Hampton type announced that the place was going to the dogs, and warned that reckless events like the exhibitions at Guild Hall would only bring a flood of "Jews, Communists, and other queers."[6] But the flood gates had already opened. In 1957, the abstract artists established their very own East Hampton gallery—the Signa Gallery, operated by Ossorio, Elizabeth Parker, and Little. Signa's first exhibitions included work by Kline, David Hare, Krasner, Costantino Nivola, and Stamos.

Popular magazines and newspapers began to run a disproportionate number of articles about the Hamptons—eccentric artists made good copy. This, in turn, brought out more people. The art scene, as much as the picturesque scenery, was a lure for tourists. The first glossy stories about the Hamptons phenomenon were published soon after World War II. There were several stories about Pollock illustrated with live action photographs of the artist at work in his studio in the Springs, the most famous being a series taken by Hans Namuth. Here was a man absorbed in his work, an artist at the very peak of creative passion, his features blurred, dribbling "ropes" of paint onto a canvas. At the time, these images were better known than the actual paintings.

A spread ran in the 8 August 1949 issue of *Life* magazine called "Jackson Pollock—Is He the

TOP:
Peter Blake and Jackson Pollock viewing their Project for an Ideal Museum at the Betty Parsons Gallery, New York, 1949.

MIDDLE:
Original model of the Project for an Ideal Museum.

BOTTOM:
Mies van der Rohe, Museum for a Small City, 1942.

Greatest Living Painter in the United States?" The March 1951 issue of *Vogue* magazine had colorful shots by Cecil Beaton of slinky fashion models posing in front of Pollock's now famous drip paintings. The June 1948 issue of *Harper's Bazaar* ran a story about Motherwell and his unusual Quonset house in East Hampton with photographs by Ronny Jaques. There was a heightened sense of expectation in these stories. "At night," read one of the captions in *Bazaar*, "the lighted house glows like a beacon."[7] The presence of the artists legitimized the place for weekend visitors and established the foundation blocks for a kind of urban culture that would gradually be transplanted from the city to the rural setting. Eastern Long Island, now popularly referred to as "The Hamptons," was being sold as a cultural melting pot.

Art critic Harold Rosenberg first used the term "action painting" in an article about the new American style in 1952: "What was to go on the canvas was not a picture but an event.... The act-painting is of the same metaphysical substance as the artist's existence. The new painting has broken down every distinction between art and life."[8] And for a golden moment this was what seemed to be happening in outer Long Island. The distinguishing line between art and life was being stretched to the breaking point.

In reaction to the uniformity of postwar life there was a renewed stress on individual choice, on the free expression of the self. Although a man of few words, Pollock himself spoke of how modern painters had chosen to "work from within... expressing an inner world." Explaining his technique, he said, "I usually paint on the floor.... I feel nearer, more a part of a painting. This way I can walk around it, work from all four sides and be *in* the painting.... I want to express my feelings rather than illustrate them."[9] It was a challenge to the rigid, gray-flannel culture of the Eisenhower years. The artist's canvas, laid on the floor like some kind of ritual mat, had become the new template of modernity.

Some of the young architects felt that painters like Pollock were leading the way toward a new sensibility that they were morally obliged to follow. Peter Blake, the German-born architect, critic, and curator, wrote: "What I and others saw in the new painting in New York and in the Hamptons was only the begin-

ning; we were sure that a similar architectural energy would soon manifest itself all around us. And we felt we were ready."[10] But how could an architect interpret the kind of energy and "unframed space" that the painters were talking about? By its very nature architecture is a planar, right-angled art form. Architecture requires walls, roofs, doors, and windows. Or does it? Some of the experimental houses of this period were conceived on the border between sculpture and architecture. Frederick Kiesler made literal attempts to create a free-flowing continuity in his Endless House projects. Architect/sculptor Tony Smith worked with crystalline networks to create a less predictable kind of continuity.

To several architects of this period there was a sense that the open landscape of outer Long Island offered the equivalent of Pollock's empty canvas. Some spoke of the area as being without context, a clean slate upon which to leave one's imprint. There were few if any trees or hedges to block views. Everything was exposed. The sky loomed large, dipping down to meet the low-lying potato fields and dunes. Anything that was built in such a setting would stand out as if magnified. "All the buildings I would do were an interpretation of that landscape," said Blake.[11]

Blake also confessed to a sense of almost mystical awe upon first visiting Pollock's studio in the Springs: "I was absolutely overwhelmed—incredibly impressed," recalled Blake. "I'd heard a little about him but never seen any of his work, and it was—well, the sun was shining when I walked into his studio, *shining in and into the paintings*. It was like walking into the Hall of Mirrors at Versailles—dazzling, incredible!"[12]

The two became friends and this friendship lead to a collaboration between the artist and the architect on an "Ideal Museum" space for Pollock's paintings. Inspired in part by Mies van Der Rohe's 1942 project, Museum for a Small City, the idea was to hang Pollock's paintings as free-standing walls dividing the internal space of an all-glass pavilion. The architecture would be an extension of Pollock's art, with his mural-sized canvases floating within the ephemeral space, disconnected from all other references but that of the natural landscape lying just outside the membrane of glass. "It seemed to me that the ideal exhibit would be one in which these very large canvases of his would hang in the landscape, in relation to the water and the trees," said Blake.[13]

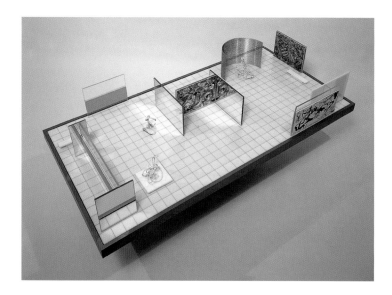

Blake raised enough money to build a half-inch scale model of the project, which he fabricated himself out of wood, glass, and peg board. He used miniature versions of eight of Pollock's largest paintings as free standing elements: *Gothic* (1944), *Alchemy* (1947), *Summertime: Number 9A* (1948). *Number 10* (1949), *The Key* (1946), *Number 1A* (1948), *Number 24* (1949), and *Number 17A* (1948). The paintings were either supported by poles or suspended by wire from the ceiling. They stood at right angles to one another to create a free-flowing, Miesian articulation of space, or as Blake himself described it, "a dream of endless, infinite space in motion." Blake also used mirrored walls in relation to some of the paintings as "an attempt to put paintings into the landscape and have them be reflected into infinity."[14] Pollock participated to the extent of making three miniature sculptures, something like three-dimensional versions of his drip paintings. He twisted wire, dipped it into wet plaster and then spattered it with paint. One of the sculptures was placed on a low plinth while another was set apart by a semicircular wall of perforated metal.

The scale model was included in *Murals in Modern Architecture*, an exhibition of Pollock's newest work that opened at the Betty Parsons Gallery in the Fall of 1949. Photographs and plans of the project were published a few months later in *Interiors* magazine and were accompanied by a glowing essay by Arthur Drexler: "The project suggests a reintegration of painting and architecture wherein painting *is*

the architecture," wrote Drexler, "but this time without message or content."[15]

In a perfect world, the horizontal slab of transparency would have been built in back of Pollock's own house overlooking Accabonac Harbor in the Springs. Though the project was never realized, it did anticipate a daring new attitude in domestic architecture in which inside and outside, foreground and background would be seamlessly merged.

JUST A FEW miles away from Pollock's studio, another painter, Robert Motherwell, was struggling with his own demons. The thirty-year-old Motherwell had moved to outer Long Island around the same time that Pollock had, searching for peace and concentration away from the city. Unlike many of the other artists of his generation, however, Motherwell had money that he had inherited from his father, who was a president of the Wells-Fargo Bank in San Francisco. Land values in East Hampton were incredibly low in 1945, and Motherwell was able to buy a 4-acre lot on the corner of Georgica and Jericho roads for about $1,200. He then turned to his friend, the French émigré architect Pierre Chareau, to design a house and studio on the site. Motherwell had first met Chareau during the war at Jane Bowles's house in East Hampton. Chareau was best known for his modern furniture and the revolutionary house in Paris known as the Maison de Verre (1932). But now

ABOVE, LEFT:
Model of the Project for an Ideal Museum.

ABOVE, RIGHT:
Model of the Project for an Ideal Museum photographed outdoors at the Pollock property, the Springs, 1949.

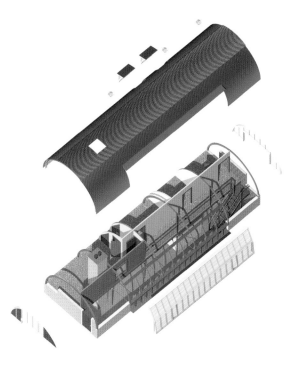

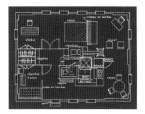

ABOVE:

Pierre Chareau, Chareau
Cottage, East Hampton, 1945,
exterior and floor plan.

TOP:

Pierre Chareau and Robert
Motherwell, Motherwell
House, East Hampton, 1946
(demolished 1985), exploded
view and exterior. Renderings
by Paul Domzal, Edge Media.

Chareau was destitute. He and his Jewish wife had been forced to flee Paris with no possessions and hardly any money. He had been able to get a small job designing the Free French canteen at the French Consulate in New York, but it wasn't enough. So when Motherwell asked him if he would be interested in designing a house in East Hampton, Chareau eagerly accepted. As part of the deal, Chareau would be able to build himself a small, concrete cottage on the property.

The Motherwell House had few similarities with Chareau's earlier projects. He worked with industrial elements, as he had in the Maison de Verre, but there the comparison ended. The house for Motherwell was raw and rudimentary, designed out of immediate necessity. There was no extra money for the kinds of elegantly crafted details that Chareau had used in his glass house. To be sure, it was an improvisation conjured up from the most readily available materials of the period. The Quonset hut was a prefabricated building system developed early in the war by Navy architects at the Quonset Point Naval Air Station in Rhode Island. Throughout the war years, engineers and architects had adapted the squat, barrel-vaulted structure to every imaginable purpose, from barracks and field hospitals to machine shops, garages, air bases, and storage depots. The semicylindrical shelter was easily demounted and could be shipped as a kit of parts with an outer membrane of corrugated steel, a structural frame of curving steel ribs, a pressed-wood

lining, and a layer of insulation.[16] Chareau was fascinated by the possibilities of the Quonset hut system and encouraged Motherwell to incorporate it into the design of his house. (The idea of living in one of these metal huts wasn't as radical as it might have seemed. During the postwar housing crisis, as many as 50,000 people in the U.S. used Quonset huts as temporary shelter.)[17]

Motherwell was able to purchase two surplus Quonset kits from the government for a total cost of $3,000. One kit was to be used for the house, and the other for a separate studio building. All the metal parts arrived one day heaped in the back of a truck. The basic framework went up very easily but construction turned out to be much more complicated than either Motherwell or Chareau had anticipated. "Building any house is an ordeal," said Motherwell, "but this was a nightmare because everything had to be custom made and no one wanted to do it."[18] All the foundation work, windows, doors, and interior walls had to be crafted by hand. Motherwell had originally allocated $10,000, but the construction budget soon escalated to $27,000 and he had to ask his mother for help in covering the extra costs. At one point he even threatened to scrap the whole project and only reconsidered after pleas from Chareau.

When finished, it was an eccentric looking structure—the last thing you'd expect to find in the refined estate section of East Hampton. It was a complete subversion of the standard American house.

None of the neighbors approved. Among the conservative old guard of East Hampton's summer colony, the house seemed scandalous, another product of the "crazy artists" who appeared to be taking over and yet more evidence of how badly the community was starting to slip.[19]

While Chareau may have been the architect of record, there was an unfinished roughness that was all Motherwell. "I wasn't trying to make a manifesto," said the artist, "I was just trying to make something that suited me."[20] Inside, the house had a free-flowing, open plan. The few partition walls that did exist were made from combed plywood. The ground level was excavated several feet below grade, the concrete floors were painted red, and the retaining walls were made of concrete block. There was a small open kitchen at one end of the living space, and a free-standing fireplace at the other that rose toward the ceiling in stepped-back levels of brickwork. The living area was flooded with natural light from a 36-foot-long window that Motherwell and Chareau had salvaged from an old commercial greenhouse. During storms, rain poured down the overlapping panes of glass "in a delicious waterfall."[21]

"We sited the house on January 21," said Motherwell, "in the dead of winter, when it would be exactly south. I remember that the heating bills were incredibly small, like fourteen dollars a month. We had hit on a solar system without really knowing it."[22] Structural elements were left exposed. The curving steel crossbeams that supported the roof were revealed, and to give them further emphasis Motherwell painted them a bright circus red. "It looked very much like a Calder inside the house," said Motherwell. "Alexander Calder was a friend of mine and I asked him what kind of paint he used on his mobiles and he said he used a kind of lacquer that was made for coach striping on expensive automobiles."[23]

The open staircase at the far end of the space rose to a long narrow balcony that led to the bedrooms. The floor on the second level was made from oak discs pressed into concrete, "set like stepping-stones into cement" that made for an uneven, cobblestone-like surface. "We wanted to use tiles," recalled Motherwell, "but I couldn't afford them. During construction someone cut a disc of oak—I can't remember why—and suddenly I thought that it could be used for the floors."[24]

In fact, the house can be seen as an extension of Motherwell's best work during this period—canvases such as *Montauk* (1945), *Viva* (1946), and *The Poet* (1947), were all painted in East Hampton and combined collage elements, graffiti-style writing, and traces of pigment that were rubbed, splashed, or worked roughly in the action mode of the moment.

BELOW LEFT:

Pierre Chareau at the Motherwell House, 1948.

BELOW RIGHT:

The Motherwell House in *Harper's Bazaar*, June 1948.

ROBERT MOTHERWELL'S
QUONSET HOUSE

ABOVE:

**Motherwell House,
floor detail.**

BELOW:

**Pierre Chareau and Robert Motherwell, Motherwell Studio,
East Hampton, 1946. Addition by Robert Rosenberg c. 1954.
Elevation redrawn by Bret Sanders, Barnes Coy Architects.**

ABOVE:

Motherwell House, interior.

ABOVE:
Motherwell House, exterior.

BELOW:
Robert Motherwell in his house, East Hampton, c. 1948. Photo by Hans Namuth.

ABOVE:
Robert Motherwell, *Untitled (Elegy)*, 1950. 30 x 38 inches. © Dedalus Foundation, Inc./Licensed by VAGA, New York.

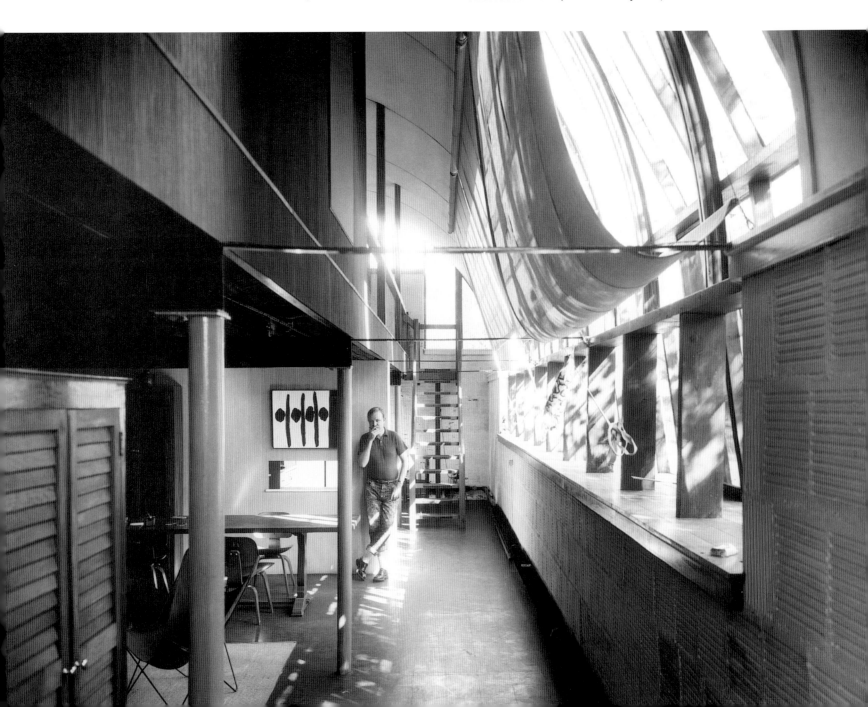

The ad hoc spirit of the architecture had similar qualities of layering. The use of surplus materials suggested the ready-made objects of Dada. There were echoes of cubist collage in the textures of the oak floor and corrugated roof, and constructivist tendencies in the exposed structural elements.

As with most experimental architecture, the house proved to be a challenge to live in and demanded a state of constant vigilance. Something was always leaking or breaking, and it could be sweltering during the summer months with so much glass along its southern side. But despite the difficulties (not to mention the deterioration of relations with his wife, Maria) Motherwell found inspiration in the East Hampton setting. "I did the best pictures of my life there," he confessed.[25]

Just as his own work had influenced the design of the house, the architecture of the house exerted an influence on the painter's work. As Motherwell observed during this period: "Structures are found in the interaction of the body-mind and the external world; and the body-mind is active and aggressive in finding them."[26] A photograph by Hans Namuth taken during the period confirms this connection. The photograph shows the artist standing in the house with one of his first "Spanish Elegy" studies hanging on the wall behind him. It's hard not to see a connection between the painting and the house that envelopes the space around him, with its steel ribs and sectional walls bisecting the curve of the roof. As with any new habitation, there must have been a period of adjustment, of trying to get used to the surprising arrangement of spaces, and someone as sensitive as Motherwell would have surely digested the geometry of those unusual rooms. "It is natural to rearrange or invent an order to bring about states of feeling that we like, just as a new tenant refurnishes a house," he wrote the same year as he built the house.[27]

Despite their abstraction, some would insist on making literal interpretations of Motherwell's "Elegy" paintings—bulls' tails and testicles hung side by side on a wall, suggested one critic—but there was also something unmistakably architectonic about those black shapes pressing against one another.[28] They evoked an oddly familiar sense of place, as if extruded from the curving walls of Motherwell's own house.

COSTANTINO AND RUTH Nivola moved out to East Hampton from New York City as part of the wave of artists that had followed Pollock and Motherwell. During the late 1930s, the Nivolas had been forced to leave their native Italy in a hurry: Ruth was Jewish and "Tino," as his friends and family called him, had connections to the anti-fascist movement. When it became clear that it was no longer safe to stay in Milan, they emigrated to New York. Nine years later they bought a 35-acre property in the Springs and began to fix it up.

The property consisted of an old farmhouse with a barn and a chicken coop out back. Tino and Ruth restored the house and stripped out its interior partitions, while painting the walls white and the floors a bright taxi-cab yellow. Meanwhile, Tino began to tinker in the garden. It started with a simple enough plan—to create a pleasure garden, a place to gather with family and friends in the summer—but then it grew into something quite special. While Nivola was an accomplished artist in his own right, his most singular contribution may have been this garden and the way it combined elements of painting, landscape design, sculpture, and architecture. "For Tino art was part of life," said Ruth Nivola. "It was not a separate activity. It *was* life, an expression of how he would see life." Out in the garden, new ideas kept multiplying and, in a sense, flowering.[29]

The grounds were completely overgrown when the Nivolas bought the property. There were cedar trees and some venerable old white pines (now grown to over 50-feet high) as well as a giant willow and maples. Tino selectively edited what was already there and began to add new elements. One year he brought a cactus back from his native Sardinia and planted it in the middle of the garden, but it died from the cold.

The general layout of the garden was developed in collaboration with the Nivolas' friend, Bernard Rudofsky, an Austrian architect who is best remembered today for *Architecture without Architects*, a seminal 1964 book and exhibition at the Museum of Modern Art that heralded the genius of vernacular design. "When Tino and Rudofsky worked together it was a little like children playing in the garden," said Ruth Nivola. Their idea was to organize the property into a sequence of open-air "rooms" using a combination of paths, free-standing walls, fences, and natural plantings to define each area. All of these elements would be

combined to create what Rudofsky once described as an "interplay of wall surfaces, sunlight, and vegetation."[30]

Rudofsky's concept was in keeping with the modernist goal of merging landscape and architecture into a seamless whole, but where Mies van der Rohe or Philip Johnson would dematerialize the walls of the conventional house with floor-to-ceiling glass, Rudofsky offered his version of the "outdoor house" or "habitable garden." It was an idea, he explained, that was understood well before the revolutions of the twentieth century, one that predated the Roman Empire. "These ancient gardens were an integral part of the house; they were contained within the house," he wrote. "All were true *Wohngarten*, outdoor living rooms, rooms without roofs, but still invariably regarded as rooms." Rudofsky had already experimented with this device at the Arnstein House in Sao Paulo, Brazil, where every interior space had a corresponding outdoor area attached by a veranda.[31]

Nivola, who had grown up working as a mason in Italy, did most of the work himself. He laid out rough stone paving for pathways and terraces. He built pergolas for creeping wisteria and slatted fences. A variety of free-standing masonry walls were stuccoed over and painted with abstract murals. Near the center of the garden, the largest of the outdoor rooms was defined by a high fence of horizontal slats painted white. Standing perpendicular to this was a freestanding wall of stucco onto which Nivola incised a *graffito* drawing of a group of allegorical

figures directly into the freshly trowelled concrete. A third wall was suggested by a line of evenly spaced trees. At the center of this area, rising from a bed of lillies-of-the-valley, was a fountain made from spade-shaped pieces of copper that "teased water down an aerial stairway."[32]

The adjacent "room" was an outdoor cooking terrace with a free-standing fireplace, a barbecue grill, and a tall chimney painted white. Originally, the boundaries of this area were defined by a skeletal framework of wood painted red, as if it were the diagrammatic outline for some kind of architectural illusion. To further emphasize the concept of the outdoor room, another free-standing wall was punctured by a square window through which the branch of an old apple tree was allowed to grow. This wall was left white, but shadows moved across its surface as a kind of kinetic mural. "Such a wall becomes a piece of sculpture," Rudofsky once wrote, "a foil and projection screen."[33]

The Nivola house and garden soon became a center for socializing. "At that time we were young and strong and there were so many people who would drop in," said Ruth Nivola. "It was very informal, people would sleep all over the place—in the studio, on the porch, wherever there was room. It just happened.... We would have lunch parties in the garden every weekend for twenty or more of our friends."[34] Jackson Pollock and Lee Krasner were just down the road. Other regulars included Willem

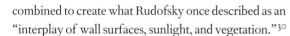

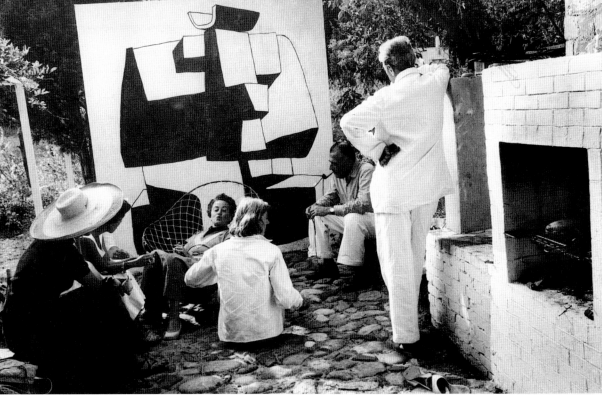

de Kooning, Mark Rothko, Franz Kline, James Brooks, Hans Namuth, Dorothy Norman, and Saul Steinberg and his wife Heda Sterne, who lived just across the street. Many architects came too, including Rudofsky, Peter Blake, Frederick Kiesler (who rented a house a few doors down), Paul Lester Wiener, and Paul Tishman, the developer.

Nivola also built a solarium, another kind of outdoor room, one without a roof or any opening in its four walls. Those walls reflected the rays of the sun to such a degree that nude sunbathing was possible even in the winter. "We could take sun baths there in the middle of January," said Ruth Nivola. "It was completely protected and warm." The walls of the solarium, both inside and outside, were also painted with murals.[35]

Over the years, the garden continued to expand in different directions, evolving as an experimental laboratory for Nivola's own work and a place of continual inspiration. Nivola placed many of his own sculptures in unexpected places around the property. An arrangement of giant peach-shaped spheres, carved out of concrete, still sits on the front lawn. These petrified fruits, which had originally been made for a children's playground, have an erotic undertone that characterizes much of Nivola's best work.

Nivola built himself a studio at the back of the property, and it was there that he developed his own patented system of casting. While playing with his children on the beach, Nivola had made a discovery. "My father was very good at making sand castles," recalled his son, Pietro. "He loved to sculpt with wet sand on the beach. Then one day he wondered what would happen if he poured fluid plaster over the forms he had made."[36] Nivola learned to carve directly into the sand at low tide using his hands or a trowel and then pour plaster into the negative forms he had made. When it was set, he would then paint the castings with water-based pigments. This technique made for a fairly primitive and rough-edged work, as one critic has suggested, a kind of "action sculpture," created in rhythm with the tidal ebb and flow.[37] Nivola gradually refined the technique and laid out an entire field of sand beside his studio where he was able to create larger castings under more controlled conditions, such as the bas relief panels for the Mutual of Hartford Insurance headquarters in Connecticut (1958). What had started as a game for his children turned into a promising new direction in his career.

THE MOST ENIGMATIC of all the Nivolas' visitors was probably Charles-Edouard Jeanneret, better known as Le Corbusier, the Swiss-born master of the modern movement. On his first visit, in September 1950, he arrived and told his hosts: *"Votre maison est tres jolie, mais elle est besoin d'un mural."*[38] So the Nivolas generously offered him two blank walls in their living room.

Le Corbusier sized up the space and began to do rough sketches in pencil and watercolor, which he then glued together on a piece of cardboard. He proceeded to develop a composition of bright colors and abstract forms with the intent of creating a more animated sense of space in the otherwise cramped interior.

Using cans of leftover paint that were found in the barn, Le Corbusier worked quickly, painting directly onto the plaster walls of the old farmhouse. This sort of impromptu performance was a fairly common occurrence at the Nivola House—the couple encouraged such spontaneous acts of creativity. The mural on the shorter of the two walls produces an illusion of shallow depth. A door-like shape with the concentric graining of wood echoes the real doorway at the other end of the same wall. In between these two doors stands a humanoid form painted in deep red that seems to be undergoing some kind of metamorphosis.

The wider of the two walls was given little if any sense of depth, but a thick serpentine line of black paint helps to dematerialize the obtrusive corner where the walls meet. The actual door, to the left of this wall, is outlined in black. A sweeping, arm-length stroke of paint ends with a stylized hand that appears to be encircling an emblematic eye, a red bird with female genitalia, and a restless composition of Picassoid faces. It took Le Corbusier about a week to execute the two-part mural. He finished painting the shorter wall first. (It is signed and dated 30 September

1950; the longer wall 1 October 1950.) During a later visit, Le Corbusier appropriated Nivola's method of casting and carved out his own ideas in the sands of Barnes Hole Beach. He hollowed out the forms of a bird, a fish, a bowl, and left the imprints of his hands in the sand. He then filled the negative impressions with freshly mixed plaster.

When he wasn't working on one of his murals or sand castings, Le Corbusier took walks along the beach and played with the Nivola children. He also got the chance to meet some of the younger artists who were beginning to make their mark in the art world. He went up the road to see Jackson Pollock and some of his all-over drip paintings, but wasn't very impressed. He casually dismissed Pollock as being a "hunter who shoots without aiming." A few days later, Le Corbusier got a ride into New York with Pollock. It was one of those odd moments that could have only happened in the Hamptons—the aging modern master riding down the Montauk Highway with the *enfant terrible* of the new avant-garde. Apparently they barely spoke to one another on the way into the city, but Le Corbusier was impressed by Pollock's driving and commented afterwards that he made a much better driver than painter.[39]

ABOVE LEFT:
Costantino Nivola,
Study for Mural, **1950.**

ABOVE MIDDLE:
Mural by Costantino Nivola
in the Nivola Garden, 1950.

ABOVE RIGHT:
Costantino Nivola
standing in his garden.

OPPOSITE, TOP ROW:
Le Corbusier sculpting
in sand on Barnes Hole
Beach, 1950.

OPPOSITE, MIDDLE LEFT:
Le Corbusier working on
sand casting with the Nivola
children on Barnes Hole
Beach, 1950.

OPPOSITE, MIDDLE CENTER:
Le Corbusier with
sand casting in the
Nivola Garden, 1950.

OPPOSITE, MIDDLE RIGHT:
Le Corbusier at work at
the Nivola House, 1950.

OPPOSITE, RIGHT:
Murals by Le Corbusier at
the Nivola House, 1950.

TOP:

**Frederick Kiesler with model
of the Endless House. Photo
by Hans Namuth, 1959.**

JUST AS POLLOCK and the other abstract expressionists were reinventing the meaning of painting with mural-sized canvases, architects like Tony Smith, Peter Blake, and Frederick Kiesler were struggling to invent a new approach to architectural space. If the canvas of the action painter became Harold Rosenberg's "arena in which to act," then the new architecture would be an arena in which to experience the pure sensations of space and landscape—a kind of "action architecture." In both paintings and buildings of this period, the individual "self" became the primary subject matter and, equally, the primary "view." The summer house and its inhabitant would be placed right in the middle of the picture—by the water's edge, on the crest of a dune, in the heart of a potato field—instead of off to one side. This upset conventional figure-ground relationships that applied to architecture as much as they did to traditional easel painting. Instead of merely interpreting nature, both painting and architecture became forces of nature.

The architect/artist Frederick Kiesler started visiting the Hamptons in the 1940s along with the surrealist artists. During the 1950s he came out on a regular basis, renting the Ayerst House in the Springs, not far from the Nivolas' home. There, in a barn-studio, Kiesler developed a series of unrealized plans for the "Endless House," a biomorphic shell structure that he hoped would become a new template for the modern house, breaking away from the tyranny of the right angle and the grid that had dominated domestic architecture for so long. (He referred to conventional houses as "voluntary prisons.")

Over the years, Kiesler conceived several different versions of the Endless House, including one for a wealthy client named Mary Sisler on a site near the beach in East Hampton. "While the concept of the house does not advocate a 'return to nature,'" wrote Kiesler, "it certainly does encourage a more natural way of living, and a greater independence from our constantly increasing automotive way of life."[40] To achieve such an open, organic living space, Kiesler

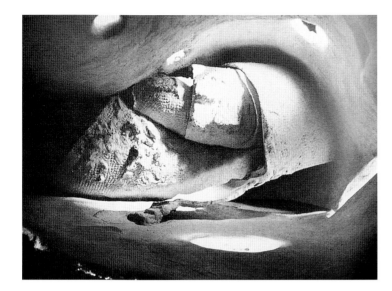 

proposed a construction method he called "continuous tension" in which exterior walls would be cast in a double-shell of reinforced concrete over wire mesh. "The 'Endless House' is called 'Endless' because all ends meet, and meet continuously," he wrote.[41] Columns and beams were eliminated in favor of this continuous shell. Windows were irregularly shaped openings covered with molded plastic, not the "window holes" of conventional cubic architecture. There would be separate cells or "space-nuclei" for different functions: an area for communal living around an open fire; a separate space for seclusion and quiet meditation; another for eating and cooking.

Then there was the Project for a Beach House that the architect Sanford Hohauser designed in 1956 as "an attempt to combine architecture and sculpture into a single unity." The house was a smooth white ovoid that appeared to have been washed up on the beach. Its framework was to have been made from wire netting sprayed with concrete. "House and furniture form a unit," wrote Hohauser, "the flow of lines of one merges imperceptibly into that of the other."[42]

These kinds of literal interpretations were impossible to realize as actual buildings and would, for the most part, remain as unbuilt visions. There were too many planning permits, building codes, and labor unions to allow for this kind of spontaneity in the building process. Conventional practice still called for planar walls, right angles, and standard wood framing.

There had to be another way to translate the energy and movement of painting into built form. While you couldn't exactly pour architecture out of a can or dribble it from a paint brush, you could make it more open and fluid. Architects would attempt to explode the conventional house frame just as Pollock and others were exploding the picture plane. They would try to integrate it directly with the landscape so that the houses flowed into their settings through floor-to-ceiling windows, open decks, multilevel porches, breezeways, and walkways reaching out onto surrounding dunes. They would break down the boundaries between inside and outside by pulling back walls, tilting axes, opening, fracturing, splaying, dematerializing building envelopes, or otherwise uprooting the house from its conventional base, thus creating a new kind of domestic space that pushed the very boundaries of livability.

TONY SMITH, LIKE Peter Blake, was another young architect who had close personal contact with Pollock during the 1950s. Smith, who would later become famous for his own geometric sculptures, was a drinking buddy of Pollock's and shared many of the same interests; they even collaborated on a few projects. It has been said that Smith helped Pollock paint *Blue Poles* (1952), one of his most famous canvases, during a long drinking bout. Smith began to develop plans for a Roman Catholic church in 1950 with a scheme to

ABOVE;

Tony Smith, Untitled (c. 1949–50). Courtesy of the Tony Smith
Estate ©2000 Tony Smith Estate/Artists Rights Society, NY.

BELOW, CLOCKWISE FROM TOP LEFT;

Tony Smith, sketch of Stamos House, Greenport, 1951; Stamos
House under construction; Stamos House; Tony Smith, drawing
for Parsons House, Southold, 1960; Theodoros Stamos
with painting. Photo by Hans Namuth.

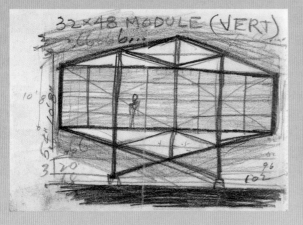

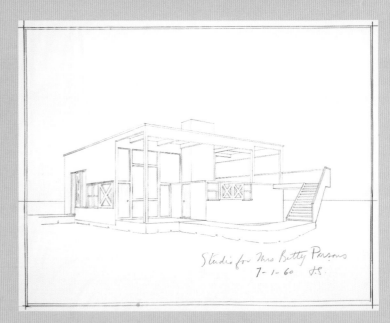

have Pollock execute a series of murals for it. "The church was to be a hexagon," recalled Alfonso Ossorio, "like a honey-comb, interlocking and cantilevered, and Jackson was to do the undulating ceiling with a band of stained glass going around."[43]

Working in partnership with Theodore van Fossen, Smith designed a series of experimental residential projects between 1944 and 1962. While most of these projects were never realized, three were actually built on Eastern Long Island. "Tony has done some exciting houses," wrote Pollock in a letter to Ossorio in June 1951, and was working on "a studio for [Theodoros] Stamos in Greenport."[44] Stamos, a

fellow painter of the New York school, had bought a piece of property on the north fork and Smith had drawn up plans for a hexagon-shaped house that was raised on posts to gain views over Long Island Sound, which lay to the north.

With the Stamos House, Smith subverted the idea of the traditional house. He detached it from its context as a geometric volume and placed it on a cradle of criss-crossing trusses, as if it were the Ark awaiting the Flood. Like so much of his work, the extruded hexagonal form derived from Smith's interest in complex geometries. He was fascinated by crystalline structures, the domes of

ABOVE LEFT:

Peter Blake, early study for the Pin Wheel House, Water Mill, 1953.

ABOVE RIGHT:

Pin Wheel House, plan.

R. Buckminster Fuller, and the tetrahedral kites of Alexander Graham Bell.

It was hard to come to grips with the Stamos House—a bit like entering a self-contained thought, suspended for a moment in the mind of its creator. With its two "roofs" pulling from the center, it exerted a strange tension between up and down and in and out. In their correspondence, both owner and architect referred to it as the "Box-Kite." A Japanese painter who came to visit told Stamos that the house combined the singular and plural, while a Greek visitor thought the house was "all health."[45]

Apart from its crystalline logic, the Stamos House could be seen as a pun on suburban iconography, challenging the norms of those postwar Monopoly-board houses that were appearing everywhere at the time, especially farther west on the plains of Levitt. Smith recognized the tyranny of the single-family house as a "symbol and pretense of order."[46] It was almost as if he had taken the standardized "builder's special," flipped it on its low-pitched head, then mirrored it with another roof. This odd impersonation was made all the more unsettling by Smith's use of diagonal bracing that suggested the kind of neo-Tudor facades that were so popular at the time.

Smith went on to design a house (in 1960) for Pollock's dealer, Betty Parsons, atop a wind-blown point in Southold only a few miles away from the Stamos House, but he was growing more and more

frustrated with the tedious realities of architectural practice. An architect isn't as free as an artist to create forms. There are too many restrictions and conflicting personalities involved in the process. Smith gradually moved away from the profession to make pure sculpture. And while the Stamos House was one of the more successful of Smith's commissions, it was less a completion than a point of departure. Not fully resolved as an architectural entity, it foreshadowed the geometric poetry of his sculptural work.

SOON AFTER PETER BLAKE had finished the museum project with Pollock, he decided to build a house for himself in the middle of a potato field in Water Mill. He called it the Pin Wheel House because of its shape and the way its walls could be slid open on steel tracks. "When I did the Pin Wheel House," said Blake, "I was looking for a piece of land to be very open to the landscape from which you could look out in every direction. It would be a very open space."[47] The house was raised four feet off the ground to provide a distant view of the ocean. In an early study, Blake used the photo of a barren, wind-swept landscape as a background. In the foreground he superimposed his little spaceship of a house. It was almost as if he had taken the Cartesian cube of a city apartment, removed it from the urban grid, and plunked it down in the middle of a desolate wilderness.

ABOVE;

Peter Blake with model of the Pin Wheel House.

RIGHT;

Pin Wheel House, 1954, with walls in different positions.

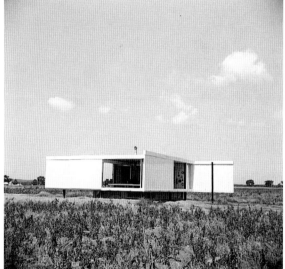

In plan it was only 24-feet square. There were two very small bedrooms and a bathroom downstairs. (Blake and his wife only had one child at that time.) The four exterior walls could each be moved in or out on overhead tracks like barn doors, so that the house could be opened up in any number of ways. When open, the house was a fully exposed platform for viewing and experiencing the landscape in the most direct way possible. During the off-season or for protection against hurricanes the house could be shut up like a box. "It always had to do with architecture and the landscape or painting and the landscape," said Blake. "It never had to do with the kind of architecture you see in the Hamptons today, most of which I despise."[48]

While it's easy enough to see how the Pin Wheel House was a variation on the glass pavilions of Mies van der Rohe, Blake's "all-view" strategy was equally influenced by his friend Jackson Pollock in the way that it engendered a sense of free-flowing space. The perimeter line between inside and outside, between architecture and landscape, was effectively dissolved. A sense of unbroken continuity was further emphasized by the spare, low-lying benches and tables that Blake used to furnish the interior.

At one point Blake asked Pollock to paint murals on the sliding walls. "I asked Jackson if he could do paintings that would be on the outside, it would be four very large paintings, suspended in mid-air that would be the walls. He thought that was fine but the amount of money it was going to cost was prohibitive, so we never got it done."[49]

In Blake's connection with Pollock we glimpse a possible new synergy between art and architecture—an overlapping of interest in light, continuity, transparency, and integration. For a brief period there was a sense that a new hybrid was in the offing, one that never reached fruition but was hinted at in the letters, sketches, and the ephemera of unrealized projects.

Hans Namuth, the photographer who took the iconic shots of Pollock at work, came over to shoot the Pin Wheel House and captured Blake in the act of pulling one of the sliding walls into place. The intention was clear. Here was Action Architecture realized: a house that could respond to the weather, the views, and the personal moods of its inhabitant.

BELOW:
Action architecture: Pin Wheel House with Peter Blake pulling wall.

OPPOSITE:
Pin Wheel House, interior.

Petty Nelson Blake and
children at the Pin Wheel
House, c. 1957.

BY THE MID-1950s, many of the postwar pioneers were already concerned that Eastern Long Island was getting spoiled. Hard on the heels of the artists had come an influx of journalists, photographers, editors, psychiatrists, and advertising executives—what one journalist referred to as "prosperous Bohemians."[50] There were so many theater people one summer that old Coast Guard Beach in Amagansett was dubbed "Off-Broadway Beach" and East Hampton Main became "Sardi's Beach." The 1950s was also a thriving period for live television, and many of the "television boys" who worked in this new medium found their way out to the Hamptons. "Directors and actors followed producers and writers," recalled one writer of the period, "and very soon the action was not just limited to television, the beach becoming completely dominated by people who operated in TV, the theater, and New York films."[51]

With Fire Island already overcrowded, the homosexual community started to summer in the Hamptons. Two-Mile Hollow Beach in East Hampton became the designated "gay" beach, where much nude sunbathing took place. As East Hampton's chief of police put it crudely: "On any given weekend afternoon you can go down to Two-Mile and see three-four hundred head of queer."[52] Favored gay nightspots were Out of this World in Wainscott, and the Elm Tree Inn in Amagansett (which later became Martel's during the singles "grouper" era of the seventies.) Gays learned that the town was a good deal less tolerant than they had hoped as the police carried out a series of group arrests of nude sun bathers, making headlines in the local papers.

It was obvious to everyone that the place had changed. In 1956, the journalist James Tanner wrote:

> East Hampton, once a citadel of Society, has become a new kind of melting pot, a solid gold one, to be sure. . . . Rents and real estate have climbed to dizzying heights; and year by year, taxes rise as if by levitation. The journey to New York, over a hundred miles away, has become something of an ordeal, what with the catastrophic decline of the Long Island Rail Road and the nerve-wracking congestion of the motor roads. In the flux and upheaval of the past ten years, the shape of the houses, the look of the people, and the very landscape have changed. Out of the solid gold melting pot has emerged a different kind of beach resort.[53]

Quite a few of the pioneer artists chose to leave before it was too late, heading up to Cape Cod or to other unspoiled retreats further north. As early as 1953, Robert Motherwell decided that East Hampton was getting too glitzy. He sold his experimental Quonset house to Barney Rosset, the publisher of Grove Press, and moved to Provincetown. (Pierre Chareau had died of a heart attack on 21 August 1950, and was buried in East Hampton's Roman Catholic cemetery.) On 11 August 1956, Jackson Pollock died in a car accident in the Springs that raised his mythical status to an even higher level. To some, Pollock's sudden death signaled the end of a golden period and the beginning of the Hamptons' ultimate demise.[54]

"East Hampton has reached the stage of diffusion when artists no longer give it its character," warned the art critic Harold Rosenberg. "Now it's like New York," he grumbled, referring with derision to the new group of professionals who were infiltrating in successive waves. According to Rosenberg, the worst of the new arrivals were the architects. They were the ones who did the most lasting damage and knew how to ruin the paradise. "The most ominous influx in the past few years has been the architects," he said ruefully, "I've always maintained that they were the tomb builders."[55]

laboratories of leisure

New expressways have abridged the miles, long weekends have created more leisure, and easy credit has enabled the city dweller to buy or rent a "second home." — William K. Zinsser, 1963[1]

NEVIL SHUTE'S POPULAR novel, *On The Beach*, suggested a double meaning for the beach getaway. The book was published in 1957, the same year that the Soviets launched the Sputnik satellite into orbit, and was made into a Hollywood movie starring Gregory Peck and Ava Gardner two years later. Shute's doomsday romance was set during the final days of the planet following a nuclear exchange between the United States and the Soviet Union. For Cold War urbanites, a weekend at the beach held the promise of literally getting away from it all—not just escaping the city but, somehow, the horrors of nuclear annihilation.

If the down side of Cold War domesticity was the private bomb shelter built in so many American basements during the fifties, the upside was the beach house. It may be hard to imagine that the Korean War, the Berlin Wall, or the Cuban Missile Crisis were intrinsically linked to postwar weekend culture, but they were all part of the same mind-set. What better carrot could American-style capitalism offer the world to offset the threat of collectivism and a Soviet Big Brother? The weekend house was the object of desire, the *target*, the ultimate destination of the happy consumer. It was even patriotic. As one editor of the Cold War period put it: "A vacation house should create an atmosphere of complete relaxation, where the cares and tensions of everyday living can be forgotten. During the past few years, its growth has been phenomenal, proof perhaps that *this urge to escape is basic and necessary to the national welfare*."[2]

But what exactly was this "urge to escape" that was so necessary? How did this idea of doing nothing evolve from the Calvinist work ethic that helped make America such a global power? Was leisure just a reward for good behavior, for fulfilling one's work quota, or was it something that ran even deeper in the

human spirit—the unalienable right of every individual who lived in the free world? In its 3 August 1959 issue, *Life* magazine announced rather boastfully that two-million American families owned second homes. (This item ran beside reports of Chinese Communists overthrowing Tibet.) The editors of the magazine also estimated that 75,000 more weekend homes would be built in the coming year. "Rising incomes, longer vacations, more holiday weekends, and constantly improving highways all tempt the wage earner to seek out a change of scene for his leisure time," wrote *Life*'s editors. They continued:

> The second house usually has certain distinguishing features. The setting is one that gives particular pleasure to the owner and his family, whether it be the mountains or the seashore, and the house itself is designed to take maximum advantage of the site. It is easy to maintain on weekends that are devoted principally to leisure and pleasure. Most owners do not want to invest heavily in their seconds homes, but they have found that simplicity and ingenuity of design, as shown on these pages, can provide comfortable quarters for little money.[3]

And there, filling most of one page, was evidence of the phenomenon: a photograph of a modernist weekend house in Water Mill, Long Island.[4] It was a stark looking tableau—far removed from any conventional image of home and hearth, but compelling in its own way. There was no sense that the house was grounded to its site; it seemed as if it had flown there on its own power, Jetsons-style. There were no trees or shrubs around the house, just a barren lawn sloping to the water's edge where the owners sat reading in the sun while their children repaired the family rowboat. It was a perfectly modern and peculiarly American version of Arcadian bliss.

"A House Away From Home," read a large-type caption. "This marvel of ingenuity," explained the editors, was built for only $13,750, a sound financial investment, not a frivolous excess: "Many families have found that a second home, properly financed, costs less than annual summer vacations, with a tangible asset left after the loan has been paid."[5] In other words, it paid to take long weekends. It paid to lie in the sun. It paid to have fun. What better proof could there be of the success of free-enterprise capitalism? American citizens worked hard and had something to show for their labors at the end of the week. Millions of Americans could now afford not one but two houses for themselves, and most of these individuals weren't even millionaires. Meanwhile, Soviet citizens waited for years to get their foot in the door of a cramped little socialist apartment.

During the same summer that *Life* was celebrating the vacation-house boom, the American National Exhibition opened in Moscow. It was part of the first cultural exchange between the two countries since the Bolshevik Revolution and was organized by Jack Masey, head of cultural exhibitions for the United States Information Agency (USIA). The idea was to present the best of American culture to show the Soviet people all the benefits of free-market capitalism. In turn, the USSR would mount an exhibition about Soviet life in New York.

The exhibition, which was set in Moscow's Sokolniki Park, presented a surprisingly progressive, even avant-garde selection of themes. Several of the same architects who were then building innovative houses on Eastern Long Island were involved: George Nelson was in charge of designing the entire exhibition. Peter Blake and Julian Neski designed an exhibition on recent American architecture. The entrance pavilion was a 200-foot diameter geodesic dome by R. Buckminster Fuller made from Kaiser aluminum panels that were anodized a gold color. Visitors entered the dome and were welcomed by *Glimpses of the U.S.A.*, a visually stimulating display of daily American life created by Charles and Ray Eames. Films were projected onto seven different screens that were suspended from the ceiling of Bucky's dome. There were scenes of American highways and airports, scenes of Americans at work and at

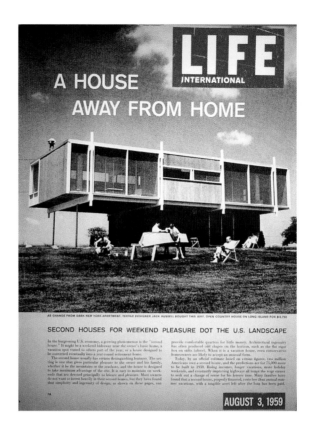

play, including an entire sequence about the American weekend that showed people at the beach, washing their cars, playing golf, sailing, and pursuing other leisurely activities. It made for a dramatic introduction to the exhibition.

The most controversial display of all, however, was not the Eames's multimedia event or Fuller's dome but a model home that had been flown in and reassembled on a patch of grass in Sokolniki Park. It was called the "Leisurama" and was supposed to represent a typical kind of American house, one affordable for middle income citizens. In fact, Leisurama was not just an average suburban home. It was designed, as its name implied, for vacation living and was one of the first mass-produced vacation houses in America. The version built in Moscow became the setting for one of the seminal moments of the cultural Cold War: the so-called Kitchen Debate between Vice President Richard Nixon and Soviet Premier Nikita Khruschev.

Nixon was leading Khruschev on a tour through the exhibition and they stopped for an inordinate amount of time inside the model house. The two world leaders stood there, side by side, gazing at the

all-electric GE custom kitchen as they discussed the merits of capitalism versus socialism.[6] The argument wasn't about disarmament or world hunger, but rather the apparent excesses of capitalism. (In a speech earlier that day, Nixon had tactfully reminded the Soviets that three-quarters of all Americans owned their own homes. They also owned 50 million TV sets, he announced, and 56 million cars.) Nixon was explaining the advantages of a free enterprise system and how such a house was within the grasp of an average American worker, but Khrushchev refused to believe that workers could afford such luxury. He thought that the house was a "Taj Mahal beyond the means of all but the rich," and that its many appliances seemed frivolous and represented the worst of American consumerism. Khrushchev was most offended by an automatic device for squeezing juice out of a lemon. "What a silly thing for your people to exhibit in the Soviet Union, Mr. Nixon," he said. "All you need for tea is a couple of drops of lemon juice.... I don't think this appliance of yours is an improvement in any way. In fact, you can squeeze a lemon faster by hand."[7]

Despite the premier's disbelief, the Leisurama was indeed available to the masses: hundreds of pre-fabricated versions of it were built as second homes by lower-middle class Americans. The basic Leisurama concept was the brainchild of a developer named Herbert Sadkin, president of All-State Properties on Long Island. The overall design was by the Raymond Loewy-William Snaith Corporation, and the prototype was created by Andrew Geller, chief designer for Loewy's housing and home components division. (Geller was already designing some of the most flamboyant beach houses on Long Island.) Marketing for the houses was handled by Macy's: a complete, full-scale Leisurama model was constructed on the ninth floor of Macy's flagship Manhattan store and another was built out in the parking lot of a Macy's at Roosevelt Field on Long Island.

Merchandising specialists at Macy's worried that their target clientele might not be inclined to buy a vacation home if they had to spend extra money on furnishings, so they decided to supply a complete kit of necessities. All you had to do was pick a building site, order the house, and move in a few months later. The houses were "ready for your leisure pleasure" and came complete with beds, tables, chairs, sofas, rugs, a forty five-piece Melmac dinner service for eight, napkins, bath mats, curtains, towels, pillows, sheets, and blankets. There were even brightly colored toothbrushes supplied for each member of the family. Two hundred of the houses were built for vacation use in Montauk and hundreds more were built in a leisure community in Florida.

No man who owns his own house and lot can be a communist. He has too much to do.

—William Levitt, 1948[8]

THE IMPORTANCE OF the freestanding, single-family house as a symbol of postwar American culture can not be overestimated. In 1944, there had been only 114,000 new single-family houses started in America. By 1950 that number had climbed to 1.7 million.[9] Along with the car, it stood for everything most cherished in the American Dream. Unlike Europe, where housing was still perceived as a societal responsibility, the house in America was still idealized as a separate, free-standing element with a deeply imbued aura of individuality that seemed to have survived, somehow, as a vestige of frontier mythology.

At trade shows and building expositions after the war, the house was featured as a kind of cultural icon; in the parking lots of countless shopping centers Americans lined up outside full-scale model homes to witness the thrilling possibilities of modern living. The attraction wasn't just the architecture, but also the appliances and accessories with which the demonstration homes were equipped: Formica kitchens, freezers, garbage disposal units, built-in dishwashers, automatic garage doors, and so many other "labor-saving" devices.

In 1949 Marcel Breuer was commissioned by the Museum of Modern Art to design a full-scale suburban house for a "typical" young American family of four. Breuer designed a thoroughly modern house with a butterfly roof, sliding glass walls, and multi-level interiors. It was constructed in the museum's garden and attracted thousands of visitors.[10] While many of those visitors may have been inspired by Breuer's model house, the reality of postwar building was quite different. The greatest success story in postwar housing was Long Island's own Levittown, conceived by William and Alfred Levitt and built in the town of Hempstead to meet the rising demand for postwar housing. The Levitt's massive development was the mother of all postwar housing developments. Between 1947 and 1951, over seventeen thousand new homes were built on former potato fields. With the help of federal loan guarantees, war veterans were able to purchase their first homes at a cost of $7,990 (with a $90 down payment and $58-a-month payments). Unlike Breuer's model home, however, these houses were conventional—there were no butterfly

roofs or walls of glass. The Levitt brothers opted for more traditional Cape Cod and ranch style houses with quaintly pitched roofs and conventional fenestration. The fields of Hempstead were quickly filled with identical little Monopoly Board houses. While the Levitt houses may have been cut from traditional cloth, the site plan for Levittown was thoroughly modern. Endlessly repeated configurations of 60-foot-by-100-foot plots were set astride looping roadways, looking more like printed circuitry than a residential landscape. Aerial photographs of the subdivisions became prime symbols in the iconography of modern suburbia.[11]

Countless magazine articles and books were published in the postwar period extolling the virtues of the house as a symbolic foundation for the American way of life and proof positive of democracy's success. *Tomorrow's House*, by George Nelson and Henry Wright, was published in 1945. *If You Want to Build a House*, by Elizabeth Mock, was published by the Museum of Modern Art in 1946. *The Book of Houses*, by John P. Dean and Simon Breines, also came out in 1946, as did *The Book of Small Houses*, by Harold E. Group. *Homes* was published by the editors of *Progressive Architecture* in 1947. These books were all filled with the same brand of optimism and reverential prose. An aura of almost mystical value was attributed to the single family house. It was not seen as mere shelter, not just a house for raising the family, but something much more personal. "Don't think of your house as an impersonal shelter of so-and-so many rooms," wrote one author, "but as an outgrowth and expression of the best conceivable pattern of your life." Another wrote that "individuality is possible only in a modern house because no other approach to building expresses life as it is today. And without expression there can be no individuality." Such sentiments had nothing to do with the social order, the city, the community, or even the neighborhood, but were rather focused on the individual self. The house would not only provide a roof over one's head but act as a kind of mirror image for one's own personal development. "Your home should be more than shelter for the body," read the sales brochure for one postwar builder. "It should be *a haven for your soul*."[12]

Patterns of American work and leisure were changing dramatically. This was due to new levels of

Long Island

The Sunrise Homeland

Long Island Sound

SUFFOLK

NASSAU

QUEENS

NYC

KINGS

Atlantic

Ocean

1947 ISLAND-WIDE SURVEY OF COMMUNITIES
BOROUGH, COUNTY TOWN and VILLAGE INFORMATION

THE LONG ISLAND ASSOCIATION

postwar prosperity, easier terms of credit, and a general urge to make a fresh start or otherwise seek movement in both the social and physical dimensions. The demographics of Thorsten Veblen's leisure class were expanding to embrace an entirely new population of aspiring consumers, including many Americans who had come back from the war and were educated and mortgaged on the G.I. Bill. In a previous generation, this same group might have continued to work and live in the old industrial centers, as their immigrant parents or grandparents had done. Now they were able to fulfill much higher expectations.

To many of those veterans returning to the New York area, Long Island seemed like the place to make a fresh start. By 1947, Long Island had a population of almost five million, one third the total population of New York State. Over the next twenty years it continued to expand at a precipitous rate and, in many ways, mirror the growth of Southern California during the same period. Business groups like the Long Island Association helped to promote the image of a dreamland of postwar expectation. Their 1947 brochure, *Long Island: The Sunrise Homeland,* listed its many virtues and described how it was a safe, clean place to raise a family, to build a house, to find new career opportunities: "Suffice it to say that Long Island has everything except mountains, cataracts and the Grand Canyon and all within the space of 120 miles."[13]

Flat farmland stretched eastwards and provided fertile ground for new development. Nassau County became one of the great spawning grounds for suburban sprawl. It gave birth to Levittown and countless other developments, fanning out in weblike patterns, with looping roadways and endlessly repeated houses, each built on its own postage stamp lot, each with its own front lawn and princely little driveway. Along with the new communities, there were new parks, schools, hospitals, and shopping centers, and a booming economy to support them. Long Island-based companies like Grumman Aircraft, Republic Aviation, and Sperry Gyroscope prospered during the war with government contracts. These same companies were now expanding and offering employment.

Most importantly, there was easy access to all of these new communities and work centers. The Long Island Rail Road had the most extensive commuter train system in the country with 420 miles of track and 760 commuter trains running daily. (By 1947, the LIRR was transporting a total of 80 million passengers a year.) Long Island had five major airports, including Idlewild (now JFK International), then the world's largest, and dozens of smaller ones. Long Island also had one of the most sophisticated road systems in the country. As conceived by New York's Commissioner of Parks, Robert Moses, there were 1,500 miles of interweaving highways, parkways, and two-lane roads. Some parts of the parkway system, however, dated back to the 1920s and were already showing signs of obsolescence.

In 1956, the U.S. Congress passed the Highway Act, which provided a gush of federal funds ($26 billion) for new building. Pre-existing roads like the Southern and Northern State Parkways were repaved and widened. The Sunrise Highway (Route 27) was also widened and improved with high-speed sections. But this wasn't enough to keep up with the rapidly expanding populations of Nassau and Suffolk counties. A convincing argument was made for the construction of an east-west artery that would allow for the speedy movement of commercial traffic, since trucks weren't allowed on the parkways.

Construction of just such a route had begun a year earlier, in 1955, when the New York State Transportation Department commenced work on a six-lane, 90-mile "Expressway" (Route 495) that started in Queens at the mouth of the Midtown Tunnel and went straight as a ruler down the center of the Island. By 1958, the Long Island Expressway (L.I.E.) reached as far as Shelter Rock Road in Nassau County (Exit 35). By 1962 it reached all the way to the Suffolk County line (Exit 48).[14] (This upgraded highway system was part of the same national program that General Lucius D. Clay had originally recommended as a defensive measure against Soviet attack. At least that was how the multibillion dollar program had been pushed through Congress.)

Highway opponents, like Lewis Mumford, warned of the consequences of the new program. "The current American way of life is founded not just on motor transportation but on the religion of the motorcar," wrote Mumford, "and the sacrifices that people are prepared to make for this religion stand outside the realm of rational criticism. . . . In using the car to flee from the metropolis the motorist finds that he has merely transferred congestion to the highway and thereby doubled it. When he reaches his destination, in a distant suburb, he finds that the countryside he sought has disappeared: beyond him, thanks to the motorway, lies only another suburb, just as dull as his own."[15]

Despite Mumford's dire predictions, it seemed true, for a short period anyway, that the gleaming new highways would leap over the hinterlands and deliver urbanites to a better place. While the western and central sections of the Island were filling in with subdivisions and shopping complexes, the eastern end was still a pristine wonderland of sandy beaches and unspoiled farmland: "Where Vacation Begins…" wrote the editors of *Long Island: The Sunrise Homeland*. "Here is a panorama of natural beauty, thriving communities and health-giving recreational facilities." These health-giving areas were now becoming all the more accessible.[16]

Even though it soon became hopelessly congested and was dubbed "the longest parking lot in the world," the L.I.E. eased the trip from the city to the beach. There were fewer lights and traffic jams. The weekend-man could feel a rush of freedom as he drove east, past the crumbling Gatsby estates of the North Shore, past Garden City, past Levittown, past Babylon, as if the overhead traffic signs were encouraging him: *Yes! You can have it all; good career, apartment in the city, kids, second car, and now…a second home at the beach.* As one magazine reported: "Every Friday night, in a car distended with portable cribs, portable babies, and other familial gear, he leaves New York and hurtles to outer Long Island, drawn to his goal as obsessively as any pilgrim."[17]

Improved roads helped to create the illusion of a direct link between city and beach that hadn't existed before. In a sense, the hard-surfaced umbilical chord of the L.I.E. annexed to New York City an area that had traditionally been linked to New England. The beach became an *extension* of the city rather than a *destination* unto itself. And a cosmopolitan set of values would reach out and nurture a modern sensibility in the most distant peripheral zone. As the critic Harold Rosenberg had warned, the Hamptons were getting to be more and more like New York.

THE BEACH HOUSES of the postwar period were not only designed as ways to escape the city, but as ways to escape the past. Free-spirited beach houses expressed all the best impulses of the modern age: health, sport, sun, sex, freedom. Like the social milieu that created them, these houses were about "seeing" and "being seen." From the inside they were designed to work like a camera: "a box, glazed on one side, with the glass wall pointed at the view."[18] From the outside they were sculptural and photogenic objects, frequently published in the pages of popular magazines. In fact, Eastern Long Island began to change in direct proportion to the exposure it received in the press; media coverage had as much an influence on growth as highway extensions and the population explosion.

One magazine satirized the Hamptons' weekend ritual and predicted that things were only going to get worse:

On Sunday night, broiled by the sun, washed externally by the ocean and internally by gin, [the weekender] bundles his cranky children into the car, hopeful that by starting early he will 'beat the traffic,' and turns his headlights westward for the long voyage home, one which doesn't beat the traffic and which never seems to end.[19]

More and more "escape houses" were published. *The New York Times Magazine* ran regular stories about unusual Long Island beach houses, and several other publications, including *Life*, *Esquire*, and *Vogue* followed suit. If new highways enabled weekenders to get to their beach houses a bit faster, these articles lured more people to come out. Every seductive photograph brought an indeterminate number of carloads east.

The editors of *Holiday* magazine showed a particularly strong interest in the vacation house phenomenon, and in 1950 started to run a series called the "Holiday Handbook of the Second Home," with photographs and thoughtful essays that chronicled the rising class of second-home owners. Then, in May 1951, *Holiday* published an issue devoted to something called the Holiday House, ("Today's Design for Leisure Living,") with a cover illustration painted by Ludwig Bemelmans, of Madeline fame.

The house was built in Quogue, near a private tennis club, and was designed by George Nelson, *Holiday*'s architectural consultant. The idea was to

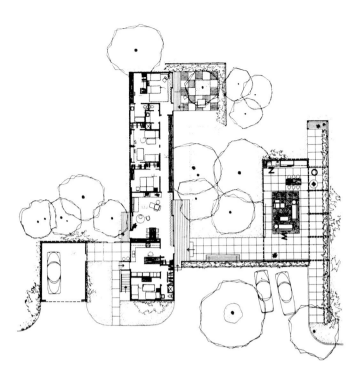

create a new kind of vacation house that could be managed without servants, a house that addressed the needs of the active, upwardly mobile postwar family. As the editors explained, it was "initiated to explore the full possibilities of modern vacation living," and was presented in such a way that made it seem as if the reading public needed to be educated on these possibilities:

> *Holiday* believes heartily in what has come to be termed the "modern house," but recognizes that to many lovers of period and conventional homes some interpretations of contemporary architecture connote only *flat-roofed blisters* on the landscape. The "Holiday House" may lack appeal for some people simply because it is a modern dwelling, yet its innovations and design cannot fail to suggest improvements which can be applied to any type of home.[20]

Nelson pulled apart the components of the conventional American house and put them back together in a way that was better suited for modern living. Here was a chance for Nelson to test many of the ideas that he had written about in *Tomorrow's House*. His plan was fast and loose, without a conventional hierarchy of spaces. Traditional rituals of entry were displaced by a splayed sequence of flat-roofed pavilions linked to one another by walkways, terraces, and a shady lawn. Natural materials were used in juxtaposition to

new synthetic fibers and plastic laminates. In an early study, Nelson drew out the site plan as a nonobjectivist composition of interlocking colored rectangles—blue, yellow, and brown, progressing from the south to the north and beginning, of course, with the garage, in honor of the vehicle that transported the weekender out from the city. (Nelson, who lived in the Holiday House himself for a while, drove out from the city in a sporty Jaguar convertible.) A small side path lead to the long rectangle where the dining, kitchen, and bedroom functions were all crammed into a narrow, barrackslike arrangement, "a kind of deluxe boxcar." Most of the furniture was designed either by Nelson or his friend Charles Eames.

The distinction between inside and outside was purposefully confounded at the Holiday House by shifting planes and screens of various materials that could be opened or closed to create a variety of spatial effects. A split sapling fence provided a barrier against the busy road. A Celotex-sheathed wall blocked the garden from the parking lot. Accordionlike partitions in the bedrooms slid into place to create extra rooms for weekend guests. The adjustable slats of a nylon "Thru-Vu" blind veiled the dining room from a garden terrace.

Then, across a 40-foot-wide lawn, there was the "Garden Room," another low rectangular structure that was open to the elements along its two longest sides. Spidery outrigger beams stretched out from the roof of this structure and created an arcade that could be entered directly from the parking area. A bamboo

TOP LEFT:
**Summer evening at
the Holiday House.**

TOP RIGHT:
**Holiday House,
Garden Room.**

BOTTOM:
**Holiday House, view
from parking lot.**

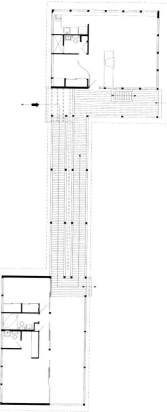

curtain was used to block the rays of the sun, while a curtain made from a new synthetic material could be unfurled on the other side. This was the heart of Nelson's plan—a place where Mr. and Mrs. Weekend could unwind and entertain. They could enjoy intimate contact with nature—beneath the shade of several towering ailanthus trees—while still tethered to a modern dwelling and all of its conveniences.

For all of its sporty intentions, however, the Holiday House was more an exercise in PR than gracious living. Wherever the architecture lacked resolution, Nelson made up for it with technology: "Holiday House does not encourage quiet contemplation… instead it asks you to step right up and try out its science, its mechanical accomplishments, in short—its gadgetry."[21] Holiday House was a test pad for domestic technologies, with automated curtains, electrically operated windows, and intercom systems. All of this, explained the editors of *Holiday*, put the operation of the house into the hands of the "button-pushing

squire," just as he had been in control of the car that brought him there on Friday evening. One wall of the Garden Room contained a kitchen and entertainment center with stereo, storage compartments, and "intercommunicator." Lighting fixtures were equipped with dimmers and could be slid along a track in the ceiling. All of the electrical appliances in the Garden Room were neatly concealed behind sliding panels of yellow and blue checkerboard Naugahyde.

Seen as a reinterpretation of the American pastoral, the Holiday House combined a heady new sense of weekend leisure with a love of gadgetry to transform and, in a sense, urbanize the country: "When evening falls, you may dim Gotham's lighting fixtures, paint a silvery glow on the under surface of the ailanthus leaves by spotlight, and have your dinner. From then on, it's up to you whether you will settle back in contemplation, create the sociable atmosphere of an outdoor cafe, or drown out crickets with music or television."[22]

Holiday House, Garden Room
with custom-designed fur-
nishings by George Nelson.

> Here was his land and his piece of ocean, and he
> would build a house for his family. It would not be a
> scared man's house hiding behind a high dune, or
> a careful man's house facing the back of someone
> else's house. It would be a defiant house, bravely
> facing the sea.   –*Life*, 1962[23]

THE WEEKEND HOUSE became an important point of orientation in the looping Mobius strip of modern life that stretched from city to suburb to country in the great new vector of postwar mobility. These new weekend machines were removed from the restraints and rituals of the conventional home, and they demanded new perceptions of place, space, and time. They were about escape, leisure, sport, and the experience of nature in the most direct way possible. The most successful beach houses of this period were active and transitional. Any sentimental notions of "arrival" or "settling down" were negated: there were no cozy nooks, no hearths, no ceremonial points of entry. The view through the windshield of a car speeding eastward from Manhattan was further extended by the floor-to-ceiling windows that gave the modern beach house its panoramic views of sea and sky.[24] Both the windshield and the picture window represented a similar sense of yearning for the natural "moment." The mind, weary from the work week, could now expand out toward the endless void of sky and sea with nothing to interrupt its flow.

Weekends were brief and compressed. The shorter the turn-around time, the more intense the experience needed to be. A little beach house with wrap-around views and flaring decks could jump start the most jaded sensibilities. Plate glass windows offered a panorama of the sublime: wild seascapes, frothy whitecaps, line squalls, scudding clouds. But these houses represented a distinctly urban perception of the natural environment. Not so much *nature-in-the-raw*, as *nature-seen-from-a-transparent-bubble*. One critic of the 1960s wrote that "[these vacation houses] form the architectural frame for a way of living different from the routine life of a town dweller. The essential features of this sort of existence are close contact with nature and informality." He was careful to point out, however, that this existence was decidedly modern and should not be mistaken for a "sentimental back-to-nature philosophy."[25] The sea and sky appeared to be an all-encompassing spectacle, like one

of those wide-screen Cinerama productions Hollywood was pushing during the same period. Just as in a movie theater, the home owner remained a thoroughly passive and detached spectator, an illusion that was only occasionally disrupted by hurricanes. This wasn't his "real" home. There was a suspension of reality. There were no lasting attachments. He could depart at any moment. The telephone and automobile kept him connected to the city.

Three years after *Holiday* magazine had presented its answer to the perfect weekend house, the magazine *American Home* carried a feature story about another kind of experiment in living. On the cover of its July 1954 issue was the image of a house perched precariously on stilts. The Lewis House was built right at the water's edge in the Springs, on a narrow whisker of sand called Louse Point that runs between Accabonac Harbor on one side and Gardiner's Bay on the other. The photograph, taken by Paul Weller, was shot during an exceptionally high tide, and it made the house look like a boat moored to its site. Here was a kind of weekend sublime realized—a true "adventure in living," with the waters of the bay lapping right at the front door. Here there was no longer a question of the house being positioned to take advantage of the view. In this case, the house *became* the view.

As the editors explained, it was a "crow's nest of a house, perched on piers." Its architect, Robert Rosenberg, had been a naval architect during the war, and he made the structure "seaworthy" by resting it on concrete piers that had been cast directly in the water. The main living area was only 20-by-20 feet square and could be divided in half by a sliding wall on tracks. There was a small master bedroom and a kitchen with an open counter. An "eight passenger" bunkhouse was attached to the back of the house with sleeping quarters for the Lewis children and weekend guests. Each of the four tiny bunkrooms was equipped with surplus Navy bunks—"simple, and easy to keep shipshape as any seagoing cabin."[26]

The cover photo of the house showed outdoor steps that led right into the water and a sporty red car parked beneath an overhanging deck. This was an important gesture. The arrival of the car from the city defined a new kind of architectural procession—one that lead from the point of arrival up to the sun deck and beyond. Le Corbusier anticipated this kind of pit-stop

arrangement in his Villa Savoye, about which he wrote: "The auto enters under the *pilotis*, turns around the common services, arrives at the center, at the door of entry, enters the garage or continues on its way for the return journey: this is the fundamental idea." And this was the fundamental idea of so many beach houses of the postwar period. In a sense, the Lewis House was the realization of a drawing for a beach house that Le Corbusier drew in 1928, Villa by the Sea, with its front *pilotis* standing right in the water like straws sipping from a drink.[27]

The car and the new highway system created what social historian Russel Lynes called a "breeze-way" between city and country. "The automobile," wrote Lynes, "is a part of domesticity, an extension of it…a means of joining town house or apartment with country house, just as a breezeway used to join two log cabins."[28] Both car and weekend house were about speed and forward momentum, portable symbols of postwar aspiration and mobility. Many, like the Lewis House and Peter Blake's Pin Wheel House, were as sleek and "convertible" as the cars themselves—some were hardly bigger. They could be opened or closed for the season with sliding doors hung from metal tracks or big wooden shutters. Ramps, ladders, and spiral staircases were used in place of conventional stairways to evoke a sense of flowing, uninterrupted space. In some cases the houses were assembled from prefabricated kits, and like cars could be easily replicated at a moderate cost. Blueprints of the Lewis House were offered for sale in the back of *American Home* ("the plan is ideal for a Shangri-La anywhere," wrote the editors), and several versions were built in different parts of the country.

NEW HOUSES STOOD out prominently against the sky, but how should an architect interpret the loaded exchange between sea and land? The sandy shoreline wavered back and forth from season to season, fluctuating, eroding, building back up, and then being swept away again. Before the war, modernist houses were still a relatively rare sight on Long Island. There had been those odd exceptions, like Miller's Sandbox or the Muschenheim compound in Hampton Bays, but by the early 1950s more and more modern houses were appearing along the beaches of outer Long Island. Modern design was tolerable, even preferable, when it came to the weekend. While flat-roofed modernism

still stood out from the crowd, it wasn't nearly as provocative a statement as it had been in the 1930s. "When it is a vacation house, even conservative home-owners are likely to accept an unusual form," reported *Life* in 1959, while another magazine made the point that "people have fewer preconceived ideas about the way a summer house should look and so they are willing to accept shapes, forms, structures, colors that they might resist in their year-round homes."[29]

Who were these new clients who were willing to accept such unusual forms? They were a new class of weekend pilgrims. While attracted by the artistic milieu of the Hamptons, they were not themselves artists nor were they the offspring of old patrician families. For the most part these "prosperous bohemians" were visually cultured individuals who had progressive ideas about home, family, and education.[30] They had grown up during the Depression without much money, seen service during the war, and now wanted to create new identities for themselves. They were ambitious and tended to work in fast-paced professions like advertising, television, film, fashion, and magazine publishing. (William Lewis, who had hired Robert Rosenberg to design his beach house in the Springs, was in advertising and radio.)

They were part of a glossy new group that was typified by the restless characters in *Dune House*, a 1960 novel by Geraldine Trotta. The story takes place in Bridgehampton during the summer of 1954, and traces the lives of six New Yorkers who share a summer rental on the beach: "The house on the dunes [was] an ugly wooden square," wrote Trotta, "set high and lonely on the crest of the Bridgehampton sands at the edge of the water…. The living room, one flight up, was planned for parties and sprawled over the entire second floor. A

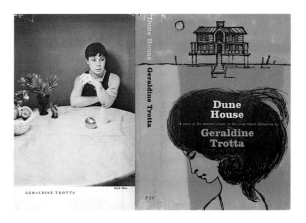

ramshackle verandah ran all around it, like the rim of a battered hat, from which, on the ocean side, a ribbon of worn steps fluttered down to the beach."[31]

The novel follows the protagonists from weekend to weekend as they survive a sequence of beach parties, broken affairs, and midnight skinny dips. They are all in their early thirties and work in Manhattan. (One is a fashion photographer, another a filmmaker, another a travel magazine writer.) They are sexually promiscuous, prone to divorce, and hard drinking with a preference for "double-dry Martinis." They travel extensively, are open-minded about psychiatry, are interested in modern design, and like to drive sporty cars. "Unlike the idle rich of the twenties who lounge-lizarded on inherited income, they were the ambitious offshoots of the fifties, who earned what they had and spent it with style. For lack of a better name, they made up the self-starter set…and were now prepared to enjoy the rest of their days with no conscious sense of obligation or guilt." Learning how to summer in the Hamptons was just another part of their postwar re-education. For them, the dune house hovering above the surf was a glowing metaphor for their own aspirations: "The house was ringed in mist when they got back, rising romantic and unreal from the vapors. A light shone from somewhere inside it, a hesitant yellow in the hollow hull of an enormous lantern."[32]

The new weekend houses, like the one in *Dune House*, sat ever so lightly on the landscape. They were only grazing on the surface or hovering in place like the spacecraft to which they were so often compared. They tended to be well removed from traditional village centers and were quite often built in unexpected areas. They were not found within the established summer colonies of East Hampton or Southampton, but away from the country club enclaves, out on their own—in the middle of potato fields in Water Mill, straddling dunes in Bridgehampton, overlooking the inlets of the Springs, perched high on bluffs in Montauk.

The natural environment was left alone. Native dune grass, bayberry, and beach plum were allowed to grow wild. If a tree had to be planted for aesthetic or screening purposes, it was often a Japanese black pine. These could grow in sandy soil and possessed the kind of sculptural branches that modernists preferred. There were no elaborate gardens, no lawns to mow or hedges to clip—no upkeep. Decks and terraces might sport an occasional pot of geraniums, but there was almost no

intervention into the surrounding landscape other than a dirt driveway and a narrow pathway leading down to the beach. A formal garden implied a certain level of continuity and that wasn't the desired message.

The modern approach allowed a house to be in direct concert with the natural landscape and to express a greater sense of individual choice. Instead of having to follow a predictable hierarchy of domestic spaces, the modern architect, like a jazz musician, was free to improvise on the spot as he interpreted the mood of the site. A 1952 article in the *New York Times Magazine* called Robert Rosenberg's all-glass beach house in East Hampton "A Window on the Sea," and that's just about all it was—a window with a kitchen and a bathroom.[33] The low, Miesian pavilion sat atop the secondary dune, overlooking Two Mile Hollow Beach. The house practically vanished into the scenery of rolling dunes and was surrounded by thick clumps of beach plum and bayberry. From the north you could see right through to the dunes and ocean that lay beyond. Except for a tiny bathroom enclosure, everything was revealed. It couldn't have been simpler.

Transparency was an inevitable part of the modern experience. After all the death and devastation of war, the glass house represented a new beginning, a fresh start. In the age of x rays and radar it also implied honesty, even a kind of moral courage in the face of an uncertain future. If everything were revealed through a transparent membrane, there could be no dark corners or hidden agendas. As the architect Antonin Raymond noted: "It is an interesting detail that an increase in the size of windows is indicative of an increase in civilization."[34] Glass was easily cleaned. It had no history or sense of the past. It rewrote itself every morning in the flickering light and shifting reflections of the sea, sand, and sky.

The idea of total transparency had been much discussed during the early days of the modern movement. But the concept of architectural display took on a different meaning in the New World, where nature, or the idea of nature, tended to be *wild* rather than domesticated. The Austrian-born architect Rudolph Schindler, who designed what may have been the first modern beach house in America—the Lovell Beach House in Newport Beach, California, in 1926—predicted that one day the "distinction between indoors and outdoors will disappear [altogether]." And he was right. New kinds of safety glass developed during the war helped to break

OPPOSITE, TOP LEFT:
Robert Rosenberg, Rosenberg House, East Hampton, 1952.

OPPOSITE, TOP RIGHT:
Rosenberg House, terrace.

OPPOSITE, BOTTOM:
Rosenberg House, living room.

the barrier even further between inside and outside, allowing for wider spans of transparency. "Why block off scenery behind blind walls?" read an advertisement for one glass company. "Open up your vacation home to light and views with large expanses of clear glass."[35]

Of course there were many problems with the concept of a glass house. There was such a thing as overexposure. During stormy weather, the all-glass treatment was sorely tested. "Much as we like to sit in a flowering meadow in June," wrote T. H. Robsjohn-Gibbings in *Homes of the Brave*, "a transparent cover between us and the slush and drizzle of a winter evening may be over-subtraction." A cartoon published in that book showed three ladies having a tea party inside a modernist, all-glass living room holding parasols over their heads to block out the sun.[36] All-over transparency also implied a kind of invisible social barrier. To many, the idea of a glass house seemed an elitist abstraction removed from the problems of the real world. In the *New Yorker*, a cartoon by Alan Dunn showed a couple lying under the covers in their all-glass bedroom while a homeless man stood outside staring in at them. But while the problems of glass architecture may have been prohibitive for a year-round house, they weren't as problematic in a vacation house, where issues of real time and real space were temporarily put on hold, at least until the end of the weekend.

Two of the most influential houses of the postwar period were studies in extreme transparency. Mies van der Rohe designed the Farnsworth House (1950) in

Plano, Illinois as a summer retreat for Dr. Edith Farnsworth. It was a glassed-in space supported by the most minimal of structural elements. A slab roof and travertine floor were suspended from eight steel columns. A low entry porch was used as another floating element in the composition. As one editor wrote at the time, the Farnsworth house was "a kind of architecture that declared itself almost by its absence." Philip Johnson went even further in his own Glass House in New Canaan, Connecticut (1949). The only nontransparent elements there were a cylindrical bathroom unit that penetrated the slab roof and a set of kitchen cabinets. Everything else was nakedly exposed.[37]

When Johnson came to visit the Rosenberg House, he called it a "poor man's version of the Glass House," referring to his own house in New Canaan. And it truly was the most rudimentary form of shelter. The house sat low to the ground on a platform of basket-weave brick that served both as interior paving and exterior terrace. The north and south facing walls were floor-to-ceiling glass, but since sliding glass doors were too expensive for Rosenberg's meager budget, none of the windows could be opened—all the glass was fixed in place. (The 5-acre ocean-front site had only cost $5,000 and the house itself less than $10,000.) The interior was basically one open room. A sleeping area could be closed off from the rest of the space with a sliding curtain. A separate bunkhouse for children and weekend guests was added later. In the early years the house didn't have any electricity; because

ABOVE:
Philip Johnson, Farney House, Sagaponack, 1946, living room.

TOP LEFT:
Farney House, exterior.

TOP RIGHT:
Peter Blake and Julian Neski, Russell House, Water Mill, 1956.

ABOVE RIGHT:

Peter Blake, Blake House, Bridgehampton, 1960.

Rosenberg's neighbor wouldn't permit electric lines to cross his property, Rosenberg and his family learned to make do with kerosene lamps. There were more important things than electric light. The views were spectacular and the Rosenbergs were completely immersed in the surrounding beachscape.[38]

Philip Johnson himself had designed one of the first flat-roofed blisters on Eastern Long Island—a house for Eugene Farney. It was Johnson's first architectural commission and was completed in 1946, the same year that he became director of the Department of Architecture and Design at the Museum of Modern Art.[39] While it is easy enough to see the influence of Mies, Johnson's mentor, in the project, the Farney House also shows the mark of Marcel Breuer, with whom Johnson had studied at Harvard. The horizontal profile of the house was just high enough to peek over the ocean dunes of Sagaponack. The central living/dining area was laid out like a glass-enclosed breezeway that separated two more discrete pavilions. Considering the exposed, weather-beaten nature of the site, Johnson chose to shield both ends of the house in a protective layer of vertical cedar siding. One side concealed three small bedrooms and the other contained a kitchen and a maid's room. It was a sensible plan for the beach and became something of a template for many future beach houses. (A few years later, Johnson proposed a similar breezeway plan on a much grander scale as a summer house for Henry Ford II to be built in Southampton.)

PETER BLAKE BUILT a dozen houses in the Hamptons between 1954 and 1962. All of them were extreme studies in the art of weekending. There were no softly padded comfort zones, overstuffed couches, or quiet corners for self-indulgent thoughts. Blake's houses were pure mechanisms of antibourgeois behavior that challenged existing norms of lifestyle and forced their inhabitants to go one-on-one with Nature herself. Working with his partner, Julian Neski, Blake completed a beach house in Mecox for Jack Russell, a textile merchant, in 1956. *Life* magazine called it a "flat cigar box on stilts"—it hovered above the site supported by pencil-thin *pilotis* and outrigger-type bracing. "It was a perfectly nice piece of land," recalled Blake, "but you couldn't really see anything and so I got some scaffolding and we climbed up and looked around. Once you climbed about ten feet up in the air you got these fantastic views of the ocean and the dunes and Mecox Bay so I decided to have a house that was up in the air." This variation on the glass house theme would become a standard solution as water views became more scarce.[40]

After a few years of experimental living, Blake found his own Pin Wheel House to be inadequate. "It was very tiny," said Blake. "We had a second child and needed more space." So in 1959 he sold it and bought a waterfront lot in Bridgehampton. Again, as with the Pin Wheel and the Russell houses, the design strategy was generated by the views—this time a

ABOVE:
Blake House, view
through breezeway.

BOTTOM LEFT:
Peter Blake, Hagen House
and Studio, Sagaponack,
1960, during lunch party.

BOTTOM RIGHT:
Hagen House, catwalk
and stairs.

more focused view to the west into the sunset and out over the waters of Mecox Bay and beyond to the ocean. "My second house was designed totally for the landscape," said Blake. [41]

The central breezeway was angled like the lens of a camera toward the prettiest part of the bay, and the rest of the house took shape around this "lens." The plan was broken up into two square sections, both 24 feet by 24 feet (as if Blake were attaching two Pin Wheel houses.) One side had four bedrooms and two bathrooms. The other had a living/dining area and a kitchen. These two parts were separated by the breezeway, 12 feet wide, that framed the view. All of the rooms opened to a narrow porch that skirted the perimeter of the house. "A lot of people would come in straight from the beach," said Blake, "and the idea was to get them into the house without tracking in all that sand." [42]

During the same period, Blake designed a house in Montauk as another kind of framing device. Because of the risk of erosion, the Armstrong House (1961) had to be set well back from the cliffs along the shoreline. In an attempt to capture the elusive ocean view, Blake created what he called an "upside down" house with bedrooms on the ground level and a living/dining area and terrace on the second floor, high enough to see over the edge of the cliff.

The house in East Hampton that Gordon Bunshaft designed in 1960 for himself and his wife, Nina, was also a platform for looking, but in this case there was a double purpose of viewing art on the inside and the natural landscape on the outside. The house was planted right into its setting overlooking Georgica Pond like a little white temple. Famous for designing glass-sheathed skyscrapers like Lever House (1952) on Park Avenue, Bunshaft brought a truly cosmopolitan sense of space to his weekend

pavilion. In fact, it was almost a direct transposition of his New York apartment, where he had used the same pale palette and marble surfaces.

The house opened to the south with a terrace and floor-to-ceiling glass looking out over a broad lawn that sloped down to the pond. The all-white interiors made a museum-like setting for the Bunshafts' extensive collection of modern art, which included works by Léger, Miro, and Giacometti. Natural light flooded through the glass walls and clerestory windows and reflected off the concrete ceiling and travertine floors. There was a living/dining area in the center, a master bedroom to the east, and a small guest room and studio to the west. There were no interior doors, just dividing partitions. The most noteworthy feature of the design was the system of precast concrete T-beams that gave the roof a floating, slightly disembodied effect. It was the same clerestory system that Bunshaft would use on a much larger scale for the headquarters of the American Republic Life Insurance Company in Des Moines (1965).

"IT HAS BEEN forever my fate to want to bring order into chaos," wrote the architect Paul Lester Wiener, who summered in Amagansett from 1953 until the time of his death in 1967.[43] Wiener was among the group of European émigrés who had found their way out to the Hamptons after the war. He was born in Leipzig, Germany, in 1895 and immigrated to the

United States in 1913 but later returned to Europe to study architecture. In 1942 he partnered with José Luis Sert in Town Planning Associates, an architectural and urban planning firm that designed major projects in Latin America, including master plans for the cities of Bogotá, Colombia and Havana, Cuba. During the war, Wiener helped to develop prefabricated, demountable housing systems. Then, in the late fifties and early sixties, he designed a series of summer houses on Eastern Long Island that reflected his philosophy of bringing order into chaos by creating serene, reflective spaces that would help to counteract the discordant effects of urban life.

For Beatrice Simpson, a fashion editor at *Vogue*, Wiener placed a glass pavilion in the middle of a wild flower meadow in Amagansett. Using simple effects, he was able to create the illusion of more space than the 1,875 square feet the 1963 house actually possessed. The interior was divided into the most elementary areas. At one end, a living room spilled out into the surrounding meadow through floor-to-ceiling glass. There were two bedrooms at the other end with a small kitchen and dining area in between. Wiener contrasted the structural elements of the house against its thin, transparent envelope. To enhance the sense of a glowing inner landscape, he devised a lighting system that used reflector panels suspended from the ceiling. Walls and ceilings were painted white, while vertical and horizontal members were stained in a dark brown color that was suggestive of traditional Japanese

ABOVE LEFT:
Gordon and Nina Bunshaft in front of their house during its construction, East Hampton, 1962.

ABOVE MIDDLE:
Night view of Bunshaft House, 1963.

ABOVE RIGHT:
Bunshaft House, front lawn.

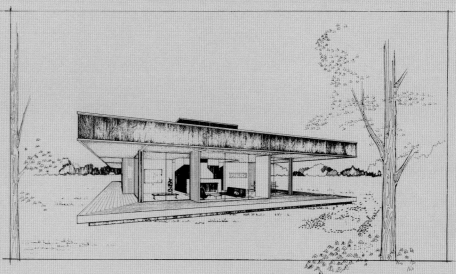

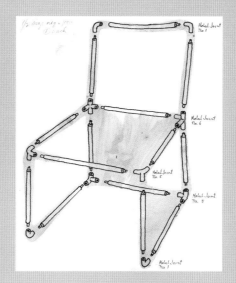

CLOCKWISE FROM TOP LEFT:

Paul Lester Wiener at his studio in Amagansett, c. 1963; Wiener and Richard Bender, Saypol House, perspective rendering; Wiener and Bender, Simpson House, Amagansett, 1963; Wiener and Bender, De Cuevas House & Studio, Amagansett, 1962; Wiener and Bender, Scull House, East Hampton, 1962; Wiener, drawing for kit-of-parts chair, c. 1958.

architecture. The roof of the house was given sloping fascia "fins" that ran along each side to create the feeling of a dark cloud hovering above a series of slender columns. A wide overhang helped to break the intensity of the summer sun. "The roof extends the possibilities of the glass-wall house," wrote Wiener, "and breaks architectural clichés."[44]

Another European émigré who found his way out to Long Island during this period was the architect Guy G. Rothenstein, who, in 1959, built himself a cube that floated above the dunes of Fire Island. Rothenstein was born in Germany and studied architecture in Frankfurt, but chose to leave when the Nazi Party assumed power. He moved to Paris in 1934 and was able to find work in Le Corbusier's atelier. After emigrating to the U.S. in 1941, he worked for Skidmore, Owings & Merrill and became a specialist in factory-produced housing systems. He also began to experiment with the possibilities of sprayed plastics in construction. For his own small beach house he tested out several of the ideas he had been developing for mass housing. The house slept six and took advantage of every inch of available space. Exterior walls were sheathed with modular asbestos panels that measured 4 by 8 feet.

Rothenstein used "easy-to-clean" plastics throughout the house. Floors were covered with sand-colored vinyl. All surfaces in the kitchen and bathroom were covered in plastic laminate. The front wall of the living room was made from multicolored screens of

honeycomb fiberglass that could be swung up to become roof screens on the deck. These screens helped to eliminate glare from the sun and extended the living area outward. The house's flat roof had a spiral-shaped solarium made from translucent fiberglass that the Rothensteins used for private sun bathing. All the furniture in the house was designed by the architect to save space. There were chairs made of molded plastic that could be easily stacked, a folding chaise for lying in the sun, and an ingenious couch with a hinged backrest. In the daytime it could be directed out toward the beach while at night it could be flipped to the opposite side so that it faced the fireplace.[45]

MODERNIST BEACH HOUSES were the most visible manifestation of the changing Hamptons scene. In the press they took on an almost cultlike status. *Harper's Bazaar* described the new houses as "rectangles with plate-glass ocean facades in the Bauhaus style." The French magazine *Aujourd'hui* ran an eight-page color spread about experimental houses in the Hamptons called "*Habitations d'Artistes a Long Island.*" In its May 1963 issue, *Horizon* magazine ran a twenty-four-page spread written in a breezy style by William K. Zinsser that was accompanied by photographs of the colorful people and their houses: "Onto this natural playground," wrote Zinsser, "the new settlers have grafted their playhouses in every conceivable and inconceivable shape.... These

houses, quite close together, appear to sit in mid-air. They are on stilts, theoretically safe from high seas that might crash over the dune, and each is a novel projection of ramps and decks which enable their owner to bask in the sun all day, clad in a bathing suit, playing Scrabble and listening to LPs of Broadway shows, without going near the water."[46]

In reaction to the coldness and predictability of the doctrinaire modernist box, several architects began to break from the fold and experiment with much more expressive and "inconceivable" forms. "Many avant-garde architects are creating roofs in bold and captivating shapes to crown modern houses," reported the *New York Times Magazine* during the summer of 1959. "What the boxy modern house needs is a little charm and playfulness," said the architect Alexander Knox, who designed a "transparent tent" for himself in Bridgehampton during the same year.[47]

Knox's plan for his 1,800-square-foot house began with a twelve-sided glass pavilion that would capture all 360 degrees of the surrounding waterfront view. The most distinctive element, however, was a pleated parasol roof that looked like a beach umbrella folded into twelve pie-shaped sections. The roof was made from Duraply, a kind of plywood used for building boats, and was held in place by a system of steel cables and columns. The peak of the roof had a plastic bubble skylight, like the ones that had been used for gunner's turrets in World War II bombers. This domed skylight flooded the living area with natural light, while the roof's deep and zig-zagging overhang provided shade around the circumference of the living space. The tent-like pavilion was connected to a glass breezeway with a dining and kitchen area. This wedge-shaped space had 8-foot-wide sliding glass doors on both sides to provide cross ventilation and open it up to adjoining terraces. "On a sunny summer weekend the house *unfolds*," wrote the editors of *House & Garden* magazine, describing the open-air charms of Knox's weekend retreat.[48]

OPPOSITE TOP:
Alexander Knox, Knox House, Bridgehampton, 1959.

OPPOSITE, BOTTOM LEFT:
Knox House, living room.

OPPOSITE, BOTTOM RIGHT:
Knox House, deck.

BUILDING A HOUSE near the beach was an obvious gamble, but that was part of the attraction. Hurricanes challenged the precarious placement of the new houses and tested the soundness of their experimental designs. So much glass and open-sidedness had their drawbacks. Nineteen fifty-four was a particularly bad year. During the last week of August, the eye of Hurricane Carol crossed the eastern portion of Long Island, bringing gale-force winds and surging tidal waters. Many waterfront houses were destroyed. The experimental bathhouses that William Muschenheim designed in Hampton Bays (which had somehow survived the devastating hurricane of 1938) were swept into Shinnecock Bay. The brick and glass studio that the painter James Brooks built in Montauk was also swept off of its foundations and taken out to sea.

Others fared better. The Sandbox, Frances Miller's little beach house in Bridgehampton, had been built high enough on the dune to survive the worst. The waters of Gardiner's Bay flooded all the way across Louse Point Road in the Springs and reached as high as the railing of William Lewis's deck, but Robert Rosenberg's design proved to be seaworthy after all, and the house was left relatively undamaged. Over in Water Mill, Peter Blake reluctantly took refuge inside his Pin Wheel House: "I was locked up inside those sliding walls and the house vibrated like crazy," recalled Blake. "It was really a mad experience. I was there by myself while my family stayed in New York. They were smarter than I was, but the house and I survived the storm, to everyone's surprise."[49] Here was another test for the modern architect: trial by wind and water.

The painter Theodoros Stamos and his companion Bob Smith endured the worst of the storm squirreled inside the hexagonal space pod that Tony Smith had designed for them three years earlier. "Carol has come and gone," they reported in a letter to Smith:

> It was quite a rip—the house is sound and stalwart. We were in the center of the storm. It blew at over gale winds from the NE and then we had an hour's lull and it blew back from the SW. We nailed the door shut and prayed. Except for every window leaking and a torrent blowing in through the skylight, no damage.... The only weak spot in the house seems to be the side

ABOVE:
Ruined house after storm, Westhampton beach.
Photo: Jay Hoops.

BELOW:
Beach houses after winter storm.

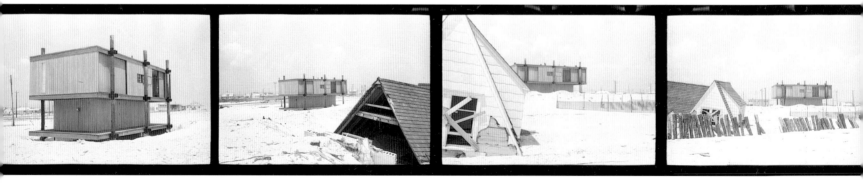

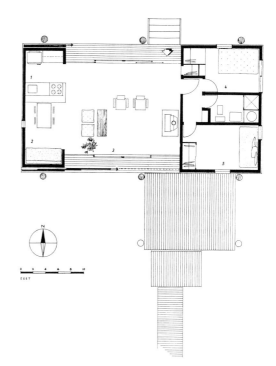

ABOVE LEFT:

Peter Blake, Kent House, Water Mill, 1956.

ABOVE RIGHT:

Kent House, floor plan.

walls. They buckle before the blasts.... At the height of everything Stamos wept, "Why did I build this waterfall?" Since the storm, which beached yachts, sent cabins half a mile inland etc. we have been on the wreckage tour. The rubberneckers come to see if we are still standing. A third of the beautiful cedar trees in front, blew past the windows.[50]

Carol was soon followed by Hurricane Edna. Then, in 1955, the very next summer, Hurricane Diana came pounding on shore. Architects took note. It wasn't just about suntans and cocktail parties anymore. There were lessons to be learned from the violence and unpredictability of East End weather. And the life and death component to beach house design only added to its appeal. "A man whose house overlooks the beach may ostensibly have his eye on the steak that he is barbecuing, or on the bikini wiggling by. Actually his eye is on those dark clouds forming in the west," wrote Zinsser.[51]

In 1955, less than a year after Carol, Peter Blake was contacted by a physician who wanted to build a house right on the narrow barrier beach that ran between the ocean and Mecox Bay in Water Mill. It was common knowledge that this stretch would become completely inundated from time to time, but this didn't phase the client, who was in love with the

site and wasn't particularly concerned about the consequences of building there. Blake agreed to carry out the work but insisted on certain safety measures. "I raised it off the ground on massive wooden piles so it wouldn't be washed away by hurricanes," said Blake.[52] Six telephone poles were driven deep into the shifting sands to anchor the Kent House against floods. It was a fairly predictable modernist box. Interior spaces were divided into a breezeway plan and views were open on both sides of the house through wide panels of glass toward the ocean on one side and Mecox Bay on the other. Blake designed sliding walls made of wood that could be pulled closed to protect the glass during storms.

Following the hurricanes of the 50s, there may not have been quite the same reckless abandon when it came to siting new beach houses. Architects may have warned their clients a little more forcibly to consider the dangers of the beach, to pull back 20 feet or more from the crest of the dune. Foundation pilings may have been driven a few feet deeper, roofs reinforced with extra braces, and storm shutters added. But when gentle breezes were blowing and the sun shone gold across tranquil waters, memories tended to be short. People continued to venture out to the Hamptons to build crazy beach houses that challenged both aesthetic sensibilities and the natural elements.

the anticube

Onto this natural playground the new settlers have grafted their playhouses in every conceivable and inconceivable shape.   —William K. Zinsser, 1963[1]

ELIZABETH REESE WAS the quintessential New York career woman of the 1950s. She was strikingly good looking, tall, single, ambitious, smart, and, like her prewar counterpart Frances Miller, fiercely independent. She grew up in Detroit, where her father was a well-known newspaper man. She followed in his footsteps by entering the world of PR. In the 1950s, she started to work for industrial designer Raymond Loewy, soon becoming his director of public relations. To get away from her hectic life in Manhattan, she bought an oceanfront lot on Daniels Lane in Sagaponack that ran 150 feet along the ocean dunes. This was when beachfront in that area was virtually untouched. There was nothing but ocean and empty potato fields.

Reese visited the site every chance she got, walking back and forth along the ridge of the dune, trying to imagine the house she would build there. One weekend she brought a friend who took a sequence of overlapping photographs of the site with Reese standing in the middle of the scene. Reese then cut and matched the photos and stapled them together to create a panoramic view. This was what she showed to the different architects she contacted.

From the start she knew that she wanted something different: a house that would bring intimate contact with the sea and release her from the rat race of weekday obligations. And it would have to be built for practically nothing. She had spent most of her savings buying the land and hardly had anything left for the house. After meeting with several prospective architects, she decided on Andrew Geller, who she knew from the Loewy office. He had designed the Leisurama model for Macy's and she liked his ideas. In early studies, Geller drew a fairly conventional modernist pavilion with a flat roof and glass walls, but Reese wasn't convinced. She confessed that she

only had $5,000 to spend and that so much glass would be prohibitively expensive. Then, on a scrap of paper, Geller drew a rough little sketch of an A-frame structure that could be built for much less money. Reese approved and they went ahead with the project.

Reese's slim budget became a joke among her friends to the extent that one architect sent her a cartoon of a house that could be built for $3,024. "Dear Client: Please forgive—your ravishing beach house is $24 over budget! Otherwise all details worked out—no heat, no electric, no plumbing, no walls."[2] The cartoon wasn't far from the truth. Geller employed the cheapest techniques available to bring the house in for roughly $7,000, only $2,000 over her original budget.

Geller was also concerned about the risks of building a house right on the dune. Over the years this stretch of beach had been particularly vulnerable to flooding: local residents recalled a time when the ocean had broken all the way through to Sagg Pond. Geller perched the house on the top of the dune and made a storm-proof foundation with locust posts that were sunk 10 feet into the sand. Geller also believed that a triangular shape would be better suited to hurricane force winds. (It also happened to be the cheapest way to build a roof.) He addressed early complaints from Southampton's building department by explaining that the design was inspired by local potato barns. This seemed to satisfy their concerns and they approved his plans.

The Reese House was the most rudimentary sort of shelter, more a campsite than a formal house. To get there you had to drive in a Jeep down a sandy road that ran between the potato fields. There wasn't a phone and there wasn't electricity—just Kerosene lamps. "My house is for fun," said Reese, "for pretending to be a camper, for improvising without any

services or corner stores, for telling ghost stories to children, and for taking off one's high-heel shoes."[3]

The house was built using wood-frame construction with cedar shingles on the roof and board-and-batten siding on the walls. When finished, in 1957, it looked like an artifact that had washed ashore in a storm. The shingles turned the color of driftwood and gradually curled back like fish scales. Sun decks ran the length of the house, both on the front and back. A 5-foot-wide "widow's walk" was cantilevered precariously along the ocean side, and this provided a place for naked sunbathing and quiet meditation. It also doubled as a *brise soliel* to shade the living room from the direct rays of the summer sun.

Inside, the house was spartan and conspicuously low tech. Timber framing was left exposed and raw plank floors were covered with rattan mats. There was no central heating and no insulation. In winter, the house was closed, the water pipes drained, and the windows boarded over with plywood. The living room measured only 13 by 22 feet but it felt much bigger, as it spilled through a large window onto the ocean dunes. A long, low couch was built into the other side of the room and could be turned into extra bedding.

One feature that Reese insisted on, despite her tiny budget, was a freestanding fireplace with windows on either side. "The glass around the fireplace is pure indulgence: we can see the sun setting through one window and the sea is visible through the other."[4] In a pointy space above the fireplace was Reese's own

bachelorette's lair, where she could escape from weekend guests. It was accessible only by a ladder that could be retracted with a system of pulleys and counterweights. A conventional staircase would have taken up too much room. Sail-shaped panels of canvas were used to screen the bedroom from the rest of the house.

Reese loved her new life at the beach. She quickly settled into the house and established her own kind of rhythm. She took long walks on the beach and learned to go surf casting for striped bass. As one magazine described it: "An urbanite beats a fast retreat to the beach, builds a unique summer haven and discovers she can get along nicely without city frills in her *Playhouse on a Budget*."[5] Reese also liked to have her friends stay for weekends; one of her guests that first summer was John Callahan, a reporter for the *New York Times*. He was impressed and took some photographs of the house that were then published in the *Times*'s real estate section. They ran on the front page beneath the heading: "Summertime Living Becomes even Easier at New Long Island Beach Cottage."[6]

The images struck a chord. Here was the beach house dream made real. Even more importantly, as one of the captions noted, the Reese House was surprisingly inexpensive. A week after the article appeared, a stream of cars came crawling down Daniels Lane, hoping to get a closer look. A Wall Street broker named Leonard Frisbie saw the story

Runabout sweaters:
three-quarter pants

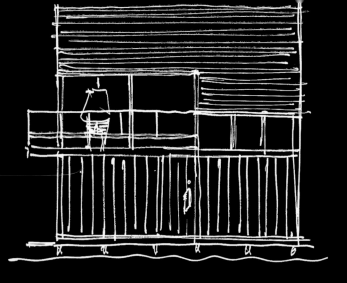

Photographs by Farrell Grehan

Betty Reese (in striped shirt) says of her Geller house, set in a grove of oak and dogwood in Bridgehampton, "I don't care if I never see another box of a room. My windows frame the treetops and the sky." Her fireplace is built of local fieldstone, and the catwalk above the living room connects extra sleeping platform and outside sun deck at one end with upstairs bath and bedroom. Kitchen, ground-floor bedroom and another bath are behind fireplace.

Cedar shingles, a favorite Geller building material, have been used on Long Island houses for 250 years. But triangular windows, punched out as if by a beer-can opener, are a Geller innovation. They cast an even light into Betty Reese's house from all directions. The top of fanlight looks out from an upstairs bedroom, the bottom from a bedroom downstairs.

HOUSES THAT UNSQUARE THE CUBE

Out of cedar shingles, glass, sunlight and very little money, Andrew Geller creates his antic summer houses for people escaping the compartmented world of Manhattan

Of all the forms of dwelling place," says Designer Andrew Geller, "none allows so much room for fun as a summer house. Furnaces and carports and laundry rooms are left behind in the city, and the elements one works with are sunlight and space."

Andy Geller spends his weekdays as an industrial designer for Raymond Loewy/William Snaith, Inc. On weekends he creates houses for fun, averaging 10 a year, each tailored to an individual client. His three latest summer houses, shown on these pages, all have the air of fantasy that is a Geller signature. There are catwalks and circular staircases and hardly a vertical wall to be found. There are fanlight windows, stained glass windows and windows punched out of walls. Most Geller houses are on eastern Long Island, a resort area where 18th century shingled saltboxes, 19th century Victorian mansions and 20th century glass cubes provide a capsule history of U.S. architecture. Geller houses borrow from all their neighbors. Slanting shingled walls recall an Easthampton

windmill; stained glass and fanlights, a Victorian attic. "Attics are friendly places" is a Geller maxim. His critics, who get vertigo at the thought of canted walls, call Geller houses "Andy's antic attics."

Antic or not, there is method in these apparent caprices. Most of his clients live in the cube of a Manhattan apartment, work in the cube of a Manhattan office and feel liberated in the new definitions of space around them. All of them want a maximum square footage for a minimum investment. So Geller builds spaciousness into the living areas, with ceilings that soar and windows that bring in the outdoors from unexpected quarters, ventilating the spirit as well as the house. His catwalks and open stairwells have railings of plumber's pipe painted black. Using his World War II experience as a designer of Liberty ships, he engineers storage, cooking, bath and sleeping space into shiplike minimums. And by thus keeping the cost per square foot under $12, he builds his airy summer havens for less than $12,000.—FRED R. SMITH

CONTINUED

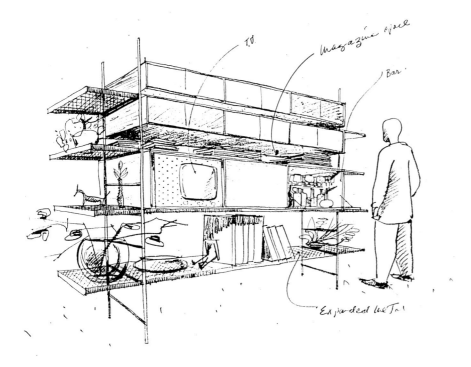

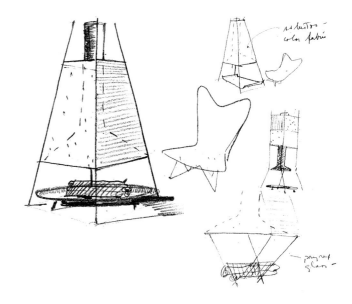

and commissioned Geller to design a similar house in Amagansett. (Frisbie paid Geller's design fee with mutual fund shares.) Soon there were many similar requests, and Geller found himself with a new career. His mission, as he saw it, was to liberate the vacation house and become the most vigilant crusader in the battle against geometric conformity. "I think human beings, once they put their imprint on anything on earth, create some sort of havoc," he said, "and it might be the solution to be contrary and not try to compliment direction or landscape."[7]

To be sure, the beach was not a place to come and hide one's light behind a bushel. Rather, it was a place to stand out, to make a statement, to announce one's arrival as prominently as possible. In 1963 *Sports Illustrated* published an article about Geller that was entitled, appropriately enough, "Houses that Unsquare the Cube," which was exactly what he tried to do. Whenever he got the opportunity, Geller would subvert the standard architectural cube by tilting it on edge, skewing it, or crushing it altogether.[8]

Geller grew up in Brooklyn during the Depression. His father was a socialist sign painter and artist who emigrated from Hungary in 1905 and became a follower of Norman Thomas. "The day I was born," said Geller, "my father was in jail doing time for his political activism. In those days, everyone who wasn't Anglican was considered a bed-wetting commie red." Eventually, he enrolled in Cooper Union, where he studied architecture with Esmond Shaw and Samuel

Paul. He also learned life drawing from Robert Gwathmey (father of architect Charles Gwathmey). Geller's studies were interrupted by World War II, when he joined the Army Corps of Engineers and helped design Liberty Ships. After the war he worked as an architect/designer in Raymond Loewy's office, designing department stores around the country, including buildings for Filene's, Macy's, and Lord & Taylor. It was during this period that he first met Betty Reese.[9]

Following his success with her house, Geller designed a series of free-form beach houses that were structurally daring and challenged the status quo in irreverent ways. These "summer-use play-houses," as he liked to call them, were purely sculptural objects in the landscape, and each was christened with a pet name: "Butterfly," "Box Kite," "Milk Carton," "Monopoly House." "Designing homes like this offers a release for me from my everyday work," he said. On first impression, Geller's little beach houses seem like caricatures, but they represented a kind of everyman modernism that was both playful and accessible to people with moderate incomes.[10]

"Most of [Geller's] clients live in the cube of a Manhattan apartment, work in the cube of a Manhattan office and feel liberated in the new definitions of space around them," wrote Fred Smith in *Sports Illustrated*. "All of them want a maximum square footage for a minimum investment."[11] They were built as simply

ABOVE:

Andrew Geller, Irwin Hunt
House, Fire Island, 1959.

LEFT:

Hunt House, living room.

and economically as possible with exposed structures, single-layer skins, and no insulation. Most cost less than $10,000, or under $12 per square foot. A master of organizational detail, Geller knew how to take advantage of every square inch of space.

Irwin Hunt and his wife, Joyce, wanted an inexpensive Fire Island beach house that would be, above all, unconventional.[12] For this manufacturer of cardboard boxes, Geller designed a long box that sat on edge. The tilted form contained an open ground floor with living/dining areas and a second floor that was reached by a collapsible staircase. The master bedroom opened onto two different balconies, one overlooking the ocean, the other the bay. Two tiny bunkrooms were ingeniously squeezed into the diamond-shaped spaces at either end of the upper level. Triangular portholes provided ventilation.

As with the Reese House, Geller raised the Hunt House off the sand on cedar stilts so that flood waters could flow beneath without causing damage. Broad shutters could be lowered into place to seal off the interiors during storms. Once these flaps were in place the house became an aerodynamic object with its leading edge pointed toward the ocean; hurricane winds would blow under and over its sloping walls without ever hitting a vertical surface or window.

The Hunts thought of their new house as a biscuit box tipped on its side. Geller called it the "Box Kite." Others gave it more derogatory

names. But however odd it might have appeared, the design was based on fairly sensible principles. Its floor plan was generated by the narrow shape of the building lot—a strict set of setback regulations had limited the area with which Geller could work. But to get a building permit he was only required to submit a first floor plan, without elevations. Geller presented what looked like a conventional plan, and the zoning board approved it. They had no idea that it would end up as such a controversial looking structure.

Not far down the beach from the Hunts' was another concoction designed by Geller for Rudie and Trudy Frank. It stood on top of one of the highest sand hills along the beach, floating like a magic lantern amid the stunted pines. Rudolph Frank was a German émigré who manufactured Good Humor ice cream. His wife, Trudy, was a fashion illustrator. Like most of Geller's clients, they lived in New York and came out for weekends craving immediate release from their hectic schedules. Geller gave them 360-degree views and shaped the house so that its walls sloped inward like a mastaba, accentuating the upward flowing lines of the site. To further enhance this ascending sense of movement, he designed a catwalk that floated across the open living area. It then penetrated the all-glass facade and cantilevered 12 feet out like some weird pulpit. Trudy Frank liked to lie up on the catwalk and watch the clouds go by. In the daytime, the Frank House was like a camera pointed at the view, but at

night, glowing brightly from within, it resembled another kind of device: an oversized television set. There, on the inside, sat Rudie and Trudy Frank, stars of their own private sit-com.

Throughout the fifties and sixties, Geller managed to produce dozens of one-of-a-kind houses while still working full-time in the Loewy office. "In those days," he said, "I only required five hours of sleep. Three A.M. was the best time to be at the drafting table and the music was always good on WQXR. I remember starting out east in Montauk at 5 A.M., working on one house, then driving all the way into the city to work at Loewy's studio. Then, after five, I would drive down to the Jersey shore where I was designing another beach house. I didn't know if I was coming or going."[13]

Geller's most ingenious fabrication of the period was for Arthur Pearlroth, an entrepreneur who was also involved in New York City politics. Here, Geller designed two diamond-shaped pods that hovered on point above the dunes of Westhampton Beach. An antenna-style chimney and lunar-landing staircase added further to the impression that alien spaceships were on the attack. "When first seen by local people it caused a stir," recalled Geller. "They weren't used to seeing any dwelling on the dunes and they were shocked because of the shape." A local newspaper announced that the "extremely ultra modern" house had already become a topic of debate between tourists and locals who thought it looked "out of this world."[14]

The house only cost $6,500 to build and had just 600 square feet of interior space. "The double box-kite or the square brassiere, as we called it, was connected by two diamond-shaped forms," said Geller. "The floor plan was predicated by these two shapes that telescoped toward the ocean. On the left-hand side there was the master bedroom and on the right-hand side there was a guest room facing the ocean."[15] A central living area was suspended between the two pods, and a free-standing fireplace rose up through the middle of this space. Geller was able to squeeze three bunkrooms and a bathroom on the upper level and to provide an additional 75 square feet of storage space within the angular recesses of the house.

Geller further refined his escape-pod aesthetic in 1958 when *Esquire* magazine commissioned him to design a beach house for swinging bachelors. The "Esquire Weekend House" was a small, portable unit that could be raised on stilts and erected along any beach for $3,000. "It does not have room for more than one guest," read the accompanying text. "Its refrigerator will not hold more than a weekend supply of tonic and soda.... However, the Esquire Weekend House has no lawns to mow, no sash to paint, and can be opened for the season in four minutes flat. A ship's ladder can be drawn up through the house's trap door in case of prowling wolves or unwanted guests."[16] Here was the *reducto ad absurdum* of the weekend aesthetic.

ABOVE:
Andrew Geller's Esquire Weekend House in the May 1958 *Esquire*.

TOP LEFT:
Andrew Geller, Pearlroth House, Westhampton Beach, 1959.

TOP RIGHT:
Pearlroth House, view onto deck.

OPPOSITE, CLOCKWISE FROM TOP:
Andrew Geller, Jossel House, Fire Island, 1959; Andrew Geller's George House, Bridgehampton, 1963; Jossel House.

ABOVE:

Andrew Geller, Lynn House,
Westhampton, 1961.

BOTTOM LEFT:

Lynn House, living room,
with swinging chair.

BOTTOM RIGHT:

Lynn House, corner window.

With the 1961 Lynn House, also in Westhampton Beach, Geller took the standard modernist box and quite literally squashed it, breaking it open at the four corners. The client was an advertising executive at J. Walter Thompson. The house was divided into two pavilions connected by a deck. Geller referred to the pavilions as the "raspberry baskets." Each structure had sloping walls and diamond-shaped windows at the corners. Interiors were lined with cork for sound insulation, which proved to be so effective that the Lynns couldn't hear their newborn baby and had to install an intercom system.

A free spirit and loose canon, Geller never fit in with the architectural mainstream. His weekend houses had more to do with personal lifestyle than architectural theory. While his projects rarely made it into the cliquish pages of the architectural journals, they appeared quite frequently in popular magazines like *Life*, *Sports Illustrated*, and *Esquire*. Even if some criticized them for being gimmicky, they captured the underlying exuberance of the period, and his clients loved them. Said one satisfied customer: "Geller's houses are real, honest-to-God beach houses."[17]

Wreckage of the Reese House after storm, March 1962.

AFTER HURRICANE DIANA passed in 1955, there was a five-year respite from mother nature. Then, in 1960, Hurricane Donna hit. While the storm caused erosion and blew down power lines, it wasn't catastrophic. Far worse than Donna was the nor'easter that arrived without warning on Wednesday, 6 March 1962. Unlike a hurricane, which often passes in a few hours, this nameless storm wreaked havoc for four days. Heaviest damage was reported on Fire Island, where more than forty-one houses were destroyed during the first day alone. Dozens more were lost along the Dune Road area of Westhampton Beach, where surging waters created a new, 300-foot-wide inlet.

Further east, in Sagaponack, the entire line of barrier dunes was undermined. The stretch where Betty Reese had built her A-frame was particularly vulnerable. Reese's caretaker, Shammy, immediately phoned her in the city and explained that things were looking bad. The locust post footings were starting to give way after twenty-four hours of pounding surf. Reese's housekeeper, Alice Rogers, mailed this note to Reese late on Wednesday:

Things at the beach house are in a "sad state" as Shammy has told you. Everything in living room (except rugs) were gone when the house collapsed. Mr. Mitchel and his sons were down there, so I took the liberty of telling him to save what they could (not too much). I have typewriter, flag and a few rugs. (This was done after the tide went down.) I told them to take no risks whatever. Langmans [Reese's neighbor] is expected to go, and Deans [another neighbor] is undermined. Trust I've done the right thing. I still have drapes here from fall also.

In a haste,
Alice Rogers[18]

During the next high tide the house was lifted off its cinder-block foundation and dumped onto the beach like a wrecked ship. When Thursday dawned, the winds were still blowing and the surf was still rising. The house was washed away completely with the next tidal surge. "My plucky little house went out to sea," wrote Reese in a letter to *Life* magazine, "broken but standing on Wednesday, totally gone on Thursday at dawn."[19]

On Friday the papers carried front page stories about the devastation. More than forty lives were claimed by the freak storm, and hundreds of houses were destroyed. President John F. Kennedy declared Long Island a disaster zone and ordered emergency relief. The *Times* carried photographs of flooded streets and abandoned cars. And beside a photo of a wave crashing against a boardwalk was a sickening image of Reese's house—right there in the same newspaper that had first published it—leaning at a weirdly disjointed angle, its beams cracked, windows smashed, and chimney askew. The accompanying caption read: "East Hampton, L.I.: Summer home wrecked in storm."[20]

The vacation-house boom is national in scope. Clusters of holiday homes are springing up everywhere…to satisfy the American desire to "get away from it all."

—*House Beautiful's Vacation Homes*, 1968 [21]

DESPITE NOR'EASTERS AND hurricanes, the boom in beach-house construction continued unabated. In 1965, Abercrombie & Fitch, the famous sporting goods outlet, built a model beach house on the roof of its flagship store on Madison Avenue. The six-room "House-in-the-Sky" was co-sponsored by *Sports Illustrated*, a magazine that had been promoting the beach-house craze for several years. It was a prefabricated kit produced by a company called Stanmar, "specialists in leisure," and could be built anywhere for $14,340 (unfurnished) and erected in less than three weeks. "It is not just another vacation house," said Bud Holman, the interior designer, "but one that uniquely answers the needs and reflects the tempo of the active outdoor family." All furnishings were available from Abercrombie & Fitch, including fabrics by DuPont and kitchen appliances by Kelvinator. Thousands of New Yorkers trooped up to Abercrombie's roof and walked through the nautically themed rooms or sat on the "generous deck" and imagined themselves transported to their favorite beach. [22]

This house, standing twelve stories over Manhattan, was an odd apparition, but there was something fitting about it being up there, vying for air space among the towers of midtown. The modern beach house had become a thoroughly urban artifact. A new level of prosperity allowed many more urban professionals to consider building a vacation home. The beach-house fad was now a populist uprising, not just an option for those "prosperous bohemians" who thought of themselves as nonconformists. Now it was for all the upwardly mobile masses to enjoy.

Construction of second homes in the United States increased from an average annual rate of twenty thousand units during the 1940s to fifty-five thousand units during the 1960s. Many of the same individuals who had been able to get their first mortgage through the GI housing bill could now afford to build a second home far away from the noisy city. Builders recognized a lucrative new market. [23]

The U.S. Census taken in 1960 reported that 1.7 million Americans owned second homes, but this figure was considered conservative. Marketing surveys of the same period put the second home inventory at over three million, with starts exceeding 150,000 in 1968 alone. Publishing companies launched special editions on vacation living such as *House Beautiful's Vacation Homes & Leisure Living* and *House & Garden Guide For Young Living*, and these were packed with colorful stories about off-beat beach houses. Several books were also published during the period that documented the phenomenon. There was William Hennessey's *Vacation Houses* (1962); Karl Kaspar's *Vacation Houses* (1967); and *The Architectural Record Book of Vacation Houses* (1970). A good proportion of the examples illustrated in these books were built on Eastern Long Island.

In a housing study published in 1967, 23 percent of the Americans surveyed either owned, rented, or shared a vacation house. Another study concluded that one out of every ten households was in the process of saving toward the purchase of a second home, and since there were close to sixty million households in the U.S. at that time, that meant that six million families had plans to build a second home. "Families have more *real* income," explained one building journal, "consequently more discretionary income; financing is easier. There's more leisure time and better highways to desirable locations." By far the strongest incentive seemed to be the desire to get away from the routines and restraints of modern life. In that 1967 survey, the primary reason given for owning a vacation house was personal freedom. Of those surveyed, 91 percent answered that their second home was a "place where you can do just what you want." [24]

Much of the leisure propaganda of this period was directed at women. With their emphasis on outdoor living and their small, efficient kitchens, vacation houses would deliver housewives from domestic drudgery. There tended to be less formality and more equality in domestic chores. If nothing else, the man of the house was expected to ignite and maintain the outdoor barbecue. Liberation was a theme that went back at least as far as Frances Miller's Sandbox of 1934, but it was now a growing trend that could be used in the marketing of mass-produced vacation homes. The beach house might even be seen as a small step along the path of feminism. The brochure for a housing exhibit at the New York World's Fair of 1964 included the model kitchen for a modern beach house.

ABOVE:
The cover of William Hennessey's 1962 book *Vacation Houses*.

ABOVE, LEFT:

Beach House in the Sky on the roof of Abercrombie & Fitch, New York, 1965.

ABOVE, RIGHT:

Rendering of Claiborne House on the cover of *Interior Design*, August 1965.

LEFT:

"Mother can enjoy the shore, too, when she has a casual summer kitchen," claimed a brochure for the All-Formica Model Kitchen, 1964.

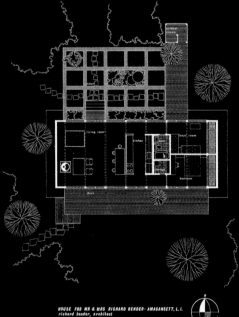

HOUSE FOR MR & MRS RICHARD BENDER · AMAGANSETT, L.I.
richard bender, architect

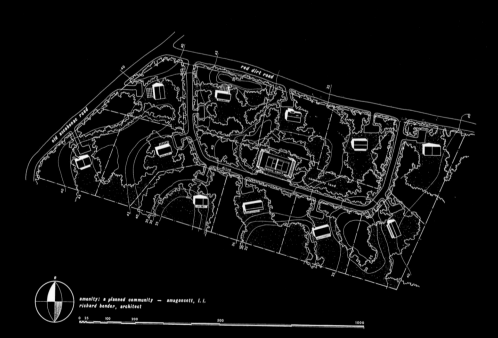

amenity: a planned community — amagansett, l.i.
richard bender, architect

0 25   100   200   500   1000

The kitchen had a central island with counters and cabinets made from that "wipe-clean wonder," Formica. "Mother can enjoy the shore, too, when she has a casual summer kitchen," said the brochure.[25]

There was also a strong "buy-now-retire-later" angle to the leisure boom, and this would be used as another incentive: "A vacation home built in your younger years can become an excellent place in which to retire," explained the editors of *House Beautiful* magazine. Of those polled in the 1967 housing survey, 28.3 percent had plans to retire to their vacation homes. More than 50 percent of all those surveyed had plans to eventually buy a vacation house with retirement in mind.[26]

Andrew Geller had merely scratched the surface of the affordable beach-house market. Hundreds of new construction companies went into business to keep up with the "Second Home Urge," as one magazine called it. Many of these companies specialized in packaged housing kits with prefabricated units, modules, and shells—companies such as Serendipity Homes ("Serendipity swings with exciting fun homes for leisure living"), Stanmar Homes Inc. ("We Build Leisure Homes…Anywhere!"), and Deck Houses ("For a Real Home Away from Home"). They all offered low-budgets, speed of assembly, and ease of maintenance.

One of the most minimal vacation houses to come on the market was the flat-roofed "Nutshell" by Acorn Structures of Concord, Massachusetts. It was an instant house for five that came in several parts and could be ready for occupation for only $4,000: "Put a Nutshell into your favorite mountain, or beach, or backyard, or…anywhere!" Dozens of vacation home plan books were published and were filled with easy-to-build floor plans that usually called for simple and open arrangements. Prefab metal fireplaces and spiral staircase kits were commonly used since they were easy to install. There was also a flood of inexpensive new materials on the market that made construction cheaper and allowed for "carefree" maintenance: new kinds of textured plywood and composite paneling such as Masonite, Marlite, and Homasote. There was vinyl and aluminum siding, translucent Acrylite paneling, and a variety of space age laminates like Formica.

The East End saw a number of local attempts at building affordable vacation housing. In 1950, William Muschenheim developed plans for a low-cost housing project with small, prefabricated units to be built along the beach in Hampton Bays. Plans were filed but never realized. Edward Durell Stone designed a vacation subdivision in 1953 called Northaven Shores. Low-cost modernist houses were built overlooking the channel between Shelter Island and North Haven. The architect Richard Bender, Paul Lester Wiener's younger partner, came up with a plan for "Amenity," a mini-utopia of modestly-priced summer homes that was built in the woods of the Springs (1960–63). Bender had wanted to build a house in the Hamptons but couldn't afford a good piece of property on his own. Together with a number of acquaintances, he purchased a 20-acre lot on Red Dirt Road that was then subdivided into eleven smaller lots. Bender designed his own flat-roofed pavilion as the prototype unit, and variations of this were built around a looping drive "like a cluster of cabanas."[27] The center of the property was preserved as "common land" with a communal tennis court and wooded area. The Amenity houses were designed using a modular system, standard building parts, and prefabricated framing to save costs. The 850-square foot houses had small sun decks, Japanese-style landscaping, and cost less than $15,000 to build (including furniture and landscaping but without central heating).[28]

Farther east, real estate that Carl Fisher had marked out for development was finally filled in with reasonably priced summer homes. The houses at Soundview Estates, Montauk, were white and modern with breezeways attached to a garage. They had sloping shed roofs and large picture windows overlooking Gardiner's Bay. Two hundred of Macy's Leisurama houses, of Kitchen Debate fame, were also built in Montauk in the early 1960s, most on third-of-an-acre plots near Culloden Point. These units cost between $11,000 and $17,000.[29]

In the early 1960s, an advertisement for the Techbuilt Company appeared, showing a small house hanging dramatically over a sandy beach. This was the same advertisement that convinced my own family to build their beach house in Amagansett. The photograph evoked all that was best in the pastoral tradition. The smooth white beach curved into the distance with rolling dunes. The house had a low-pitched roof made from asphalt shingles, large sliding glass doors with aluminum frames, and a deck that

POST AND BEAM CONSTRUCTION POST AND BEAM CONSTRUCTION POST AND BEAM CONSTRUCTION POST AND BEAM CONSTRUCTION POST AND BEAM

In conventional construction a house is supported by both the exterior and interior walls. In terms of the architectural end result this means that the outside walls must be made of materials that can carry a load. Inside walls must be located at regular intervals and must extend to the ceiling or to the roof in order to offer support.

Bold geometry. Strong shapes. A richness and diversity of spatial arrangements.

Combining modern technology with the classic structural technique of post and beam construction, the Techbuilt system is uninhibited by the confining requirements of ordinary building methods.

In the Techbuilt system the house is supported by a frame of vertical posts and horizontal beams. Neither the outside skin nor the inside walls are called upon to carry the weight of the house. Exempt from this restriction, a Techbuilt home can assume virtually any interior proportions. Walls can slant, curve, be made of glass or be eliminated entirely. Space can be divided for functional or aesthetic purposes without limits imposed by structural necessity.

Given this freedom, the possibilities for architectural variety both inside and outside the house become greatly expanded.

Since the Techbuilt system imposes very few limitations on what is possible, we invite you to contact your Techbuilt Representative and bring along your wildest dreams.

AT HOME WITH TOMORROW

by **CARL KOCH, designer of the TECHBUILT House,** with **ANDY LEWIS**

A new concept in contemporary living…

TECHBUILT

ABOVE:
Cover of a Techbuilt brochure.

OPPOSITE, TOP:
Diagrams from *A Total Environment for Living*, a Techbuilt publication.

OPPOSITE, BOTTOM:
The book jacket of Carl Koch's *At Home with Tomorrow*, designed by Gyorgy Kepes, 1958.

hung over the beach with ample room for sunbathing. According to the ad, it was "the perfect answer to anyone wanting a vacation house in a hurry."[30]

The idea for Techbuilt was developed by architect Carl Koch, who had traveled to Germany to study at the Bauhaus under Walter Gropius and Marcel Breuer after finishing his architectural studies at Harvard in the 1930s. Inspired by what he had seen of European modernism, Koch returned to the U.S. and helped to develop prototypes for mass housing at MIT. Like so many architects of his generation, he hoped to solve the great design dilemma of the postwar period: how to create an affordable, mass-produced house with architectural distinction. Koch conceived a plan that would combine assembly-line technology with a less severe look than the Bauhaus formula. The modestly pitched roof and broad overhangs of his Techbuilt prototype vaguely suggested traditions of Japanese architecture.[31]

Techbuilt may have been the first housing prototype launched by television. A program called "Excursion," sponsored by the Ford Foundation, featured the building of a Techbuilt house and followed the progress of its construction from foundation work to finishing details. The two-part program, narrated by Burgess Meredith, was aired in February 1954 and was watched by millions. The company was immediately swamped with orders. The Techbuilt houses were especially popular with younger families looking to build their first vacation homes. With the

help of television, Koch had struck on something very shrewd: an affordable answer to beach house mania—Levittown with sand.[32]

The success of Techbuilt surprised even Koch. In 1958 he wrote a strangely rambling book about his prefab housing system called *At Home With Tomorrow*: "We may come to select our houses with the same splendid innocence with which we choose our automobiles: according to the shape of tail fins, or the number of blondes the advertisement shows wedged in the back seat."[33]

Techbuilt expanded its business through a network of franchises that opened in different parts of the country. One of these was established by a builder named Edward Pospisil, who assembled more than fifty Techbuilt units on Eastern Long Island during the early 1960s. Since he was also in the real estate business, Pospisil was able to sell both house and land as part of a package deal. Once a year he took a suite at the Plaza Hotel in New York and met with prospective clients, explaining the various design options and helping to customize their plans.

The houses cost less than $20,000, depending on how many extras you wanted. They came in several different sizes and styles, ranging from 576 to 768 square feet. They could be ordered directly from the factory, shipped in sections to the site, and erected in a matter of days. All the parts arrived in a single truck. The preassembled wall panels had fiberglass insulation. Precut beams, windows, and sliding

ABOVE:

A Techbuilt beach house under construction.

RIGHT:

The Techbuilt logo.

A
TECHBUILT®
CLASSIC

BELOW, LEFT:

Techbuilt beach house (Otis House), Amagansett, 1964.

BELOW, RIGHT:

Techbuilt beach house, East Hampton, c. 1961, living room with single-layer walls.

glass doors were also provided. By using a simple post-and-beam system of framing, interiors could be partitioned and arranged in a variety of configurations to suit the client's needs. Craig Claiborne, the *New York Times* food editor, for instance, created an unusually expansive kitchen area in his Amagansett unit. "That's what Techbuilt houses are all about—flexibility. Techbuilt gives you your pick of as many or as few rooms as you want—where you want them—the size you want. Unlimited combinations with post-and-beam construction—modular

panels—sky-high windows—crisp, clean, contemporary lines—and handsomely carefree materials."[34]

With the success of companies like Techbuilt, previously unspoiled areas of beachfront real estate began to fill in with new houses. What had begun as a democratization of the second home urge was now threatening to turn the Hamptons into a sprawling *resurbia* (resort-suburbia). To stand out from the pack and make an impression would demand greater risks and new levels of architectural audacity. Just having a deck and big windows wasn't going to be enough.

twist and shout

Sun, sand, and blue skies are the sea-embracing
elements one thinks of and plans for in a beach
house. An early morning dash for a swim; break-
fast with a view; a cool drink or a game of handball
on the beach—a house by the sea should provide
for all the leisurely, enjoyable activities one might
wish. It should also make activities convenient,
easy to do, and require a minimum of setting-up,
picking-up afterwards, or other upkeep. Daily
chores should be made as fun as possible to do.
—*The Architectural Record
Book of Vacation Houses*, 1970[1]

THE SIXTIES WEEKEND had little to do with traditional notions of rural repose. Instead, it represented a frenetic set of recreational options and social opportunities. The dividing line between rural and urban became less and less clear. Everyone wanted to get away, but while so many more were heading east to escape the pressures of New York, city and country began to merge in unforeseen ways. "Long Island is Becoming Long City: 118-Mile-Long Metropolis," ran a 1964 story in the *New York Times Magazine*.[2] The city was transforming the rural ambiance just as the rural ambiance was helping to diffuse the pressures of the city. The means of exodus—the Long Island Expressway and the Sunrise Highway—were reaching a bit further every season, making the trip more tempting to those who hadn't been there before. By 1972 the final section of the L.I.E. was completed and stretched all the way out to Riverhead, the very doorstep to the Hamptons.[3]

At the same time, the East End could no longer be perceived as a string of small villages with lovely beaches, rustic windmills, and eccentric artists. With more houses, more media coverage, and extended highways, it was something different. The area had become the modern phenomenon known as "The Hamptons."

The 1960s were a time of discovery. Old boundaries were crossed and new extremes were explored in music, art, sexuality, fashion, and cinema. The Beatles invaded in 1964 and brought with them an entirely new sense of style. Women wore miniskirts and hotpants. Men wore their hair longer, lapels became wider, and pants flared. In keeping with the times, younger professionals were inventing new roles for themselves, new attitudes about work, family, and leisure.

The East End itself was becoming more and more like a multimedia event, or in the parlance of the day, a "happening." It started on Memorial Day weekend and continued all the way through Labor Day weekend. There were reports of wild parties on the beach, police crackdowns on pot smokers, and free love in the dunes. Mitty's, the first discotheque on the East End, opened in Water Mill. L'Oursin, a club that featured psychedelic light shows, opened in Southampton. On 31 August 1963, the debutante party for socialite Fernanda Wanamaker Wetherill turned into an all-night bacchanal. Affluent young guests rioted and practically destroyed an oceanfront mansion in Southampton. All the windows were smashed and people were actually seen swinging from the crystal chandeliers. The party made front-page headlines and marked something of an end to old Social Register ways. Meanwhile, Allan Kaprow and other New York artists organized a series of happenings. Rock bands played on the beach, a garbage dump was filled with foam, girls in bikinis had flowers painted on their stomachs—all of it documented by a television crew for the CBS program "What I Did On My Vacation."

As the decade progressed there was a noticeable shift in perspective, a shift away from the relatively restrained and pristine functionalism of the fifties beach house—those "flat-roofed blisters" of Peter Blake, George Nelson, and Robert Rosenberg. A younger generation of architects brought a new intensity to the East End scene. Blake didn't like what he saw and decided to move away in the 1960s. So did Nelson, who found the beaches too crowded and felt the area was being ruined by the kind of media exposure that he himself had helped instigate.

The houses of the new generation were more gestural and vertical, more agitated and urban in temperament, representing the hyperactive and youth-oriented culture that epitomized the decade. Like sixties pants and collars, the houses went flaring in all

OPPOSITE:
**Gwathmey House
during house tour.**

directions. Most were relatively small, single-family residences designed for upwardly mobile New Yorkers. Rituals of domestic behavior were challenged, norms of middle-class comfort subverted. The architecture was characterized by thin planar surfaces and transparent volumes combined in ways that derived from the collage aesthetic of synthetic cubism, the fascist architecture of Giuseppe Terragni, and the early villas of Le Corbusier. Younger architects were rediscovering the vitality of early modernist design while reacting against the repetitive blandness of modern corporate architecture.

Traditional house forms were reduced to the most elementary geometries. Floor plans were turned about to create dynamic spaces. Walls were pulled back and fragmented. Planes were shifted and made to intersect other planes. Facades were infiltrated, removed in part, and otherwise displaced. The architectural passwords of the day were "penetration," "rotation," and "erosion." Axes were skewed, points of entry shifted, underlying structures revealed. The thin membrane between inside and outside was pushed to the breaking point with ever-larger panels of glass and interpenetrating elements. Transparent voids were "incised" into cubic forms. Bridges and ramps were used in place of conventional stairways.

While they may have been sculpturally intriguing, these architectural explosions could also make for painfully tortured interiors with acutely angled corners, unusable recesses, windowless bathrooms, and pinched little guest rooms. The rewards of living in such environments, however, were thought to outweigh the problems. The modern beach house provided another means of personal transformation, an architectural equivalent to the encounter groups, gestalt therapy, and "consciousness raising" that were all the rage in the sixties. (It is no coincidence that several of the most conspicuous houses of the period were designed for psychotherapists.) One of the new beach houses was hailed in print as "First Person Bliss." Another was called "a house that feeds the imagination," while a third was described by its owners as a "house that sets us free." "Sometimes the house has such purity it seems almost spiritual," confessed the lucky new homeowners.[4]

The new structures were even more detached from the natural landscape than the previous generation of houses, riding above the ground like so many abstract sculptures. "I didn't care about the context," said architect Charles Gwathmey. "As far as I was concerned, it was like a clean palette." The new houses were very much *drawn* objects, products of the drafting table, what architect Peter Eisenman called "cardboard architecture."[5] The favored mode of presentation became the axonometric projection, a type of perspective in which vertical and horizontal dimensions are drawn to scale and depth is distorted. These projections, often drawn from the perspective of a mole, could make the most banal potting shed look elegantly complex.

The house in all of its geometric glory displaced the ocean or the bay as the primary object of view. "The house, in effect, defines the site by its presence," wrote architect Richard Meier. Critic Paul Goldberger described the daring new beach houses as being "…objects that [are] pure and perfect things in themselves."[6] This apparent detachment from the land also symbolized a degree of social detachment. Clients and architects were, for the most part, blissfully ignorant of everyday issues that effected the year-round communities, except for those that had a direct impact on property values, such as beach erosion, taxes, and restrictive forms of zoning.

Designing a house in the Hamptons became one of the fastest routes to architectural stardom. Indeed, it was something of a professional rite of passage for a young architect. A signature residence in the Hamptons guaranteed instant exposure. With its distinctively flat terrain and media saturation, the area was an ideal launching pad. Each new creation was an event, much discussed within the community and analyzed in the press. Everyone had an opinion. Magazines rushed to publish the latest architectural extravaganzas in all of their photogenic glory. Unusual designs by Julian and Barbara Neski, Gwathmey, Meier, and others were published internationally and made an impact well beyond the immediate area. As Gwathmey said: "The opportunity [to design a house in the Hamptons] comes with a good deal of pressure—the pressure of expectations, visibility, and scrutiny—placing the designer and his building in a continually competitive cycle."[7]

The new wave included a group of ambitious young architects who were known as the "New York Five," or merely "The Five." Eisenman, Gwathmey, Meier, Michael Graves, and John Hejduk were close

ABOVE:
Richard Meier, Hoffman House, East Hampton, axonometric view, 1966.

OPPOSITE, TOP:
Charles Gwathmey, Gwathmey House, Amagansett, 1965.

OPPOSITE, BOTTOM:
Richard Meier, Saltzman House, East Hampton, 1969.

BELOW:
Peter Gluck, Gluck House, West Hampton, 1964. The house, for the architect's parents, launched Gluck's career while he was still in school.

BOTTOM:
Gluck House, living room.

When my mother and father asked me to design their house it was a no-brainer. The idea to do it was incredibly exciting. I wasn't even nervous about it. When you're naive in the best sense of the word, you don't have the same sense of all the pressures. Hopefully you get that way again when you get older, but the transition is a bitch.

—Charles Gwathmey, 1999[10]

CHARLES GWATHMEY WAS only twenty-five years old in 1964 when he began design of a house for his parents in Amagansett. The house made him famous and became a prototype for beach houses all over the East Coast. "The idea originally came from the site," said Gwathmey. "It was a flat site that overviewed the dunes and you could see the ocean on the horizon. Putting the living level up a floor seemed obvious when you stood on the site." This was the point of reference around which the rest of the house would evolve: a living area high enough to see across the dunes.

After finishing his studies at Yale in 1962, Gwathmey traveled through Europe looking at architecture. He was most enchanted by the buildings of Le Corbusier. For him, they confirmed the idea that an architect was an artist and "object maker," not a theorist or businessman. Le Corbusier's Chapel at Ronchamp (1954) made a particularly deep impression, and he went back to visit it twice. "The objectness of Ronchamp was appealing," said Gwathmey. "It was clearly a sculptural object that had presence by its existence on the site. I wondered how you could make a small building establish that same sense of place through its essence, undecorated, unadorned, relying completely on its form and its space and the idea of its single materiality."[11]

Gwathmey cut his teeth in 1964 with a beach house for a crowded site on Fire Island. "The Miller House was sort of a purging, in the best sense," said Gwathmey, "I was still caught up in my Lou Kahn education."[12] Despite the tight lot (75 by 100 feet) and an even tighter budget ($13,000), Gwathmey was able to create interior spaces that still felt expansive. The main floor was raised 6 feet off the ground to gain whatever views of the ocean were attainable between neighboring structures. Four small sun decks ("like pulpits") alternated with four towerlike structures around the perimeter of a central living area. Each of the shed-roofed "towers" contained a separate

friends and all, except Hejduk, in their twenties. Three of the five (Gwathmey, Meier, and Hejduk) designed important projects in the Hamptons. The group was first lumped together in 1969 at a conference sponsored by the Museum of Modern Art.[8] Arthur Drexler, director of MoMA's department of architecture and design, pronounced that their work constituted a new school of architecture. The New York Five name implied not just a school but a radical attitude, like the "Chicago Seven," whose trial was in progress during the same period. The *New York Times* ran a full-page spread about The Five's growing influence, with photographs that made them look like some intense, intellectual rock band, with floppy hair and (except for Gwathmey) wire-rimmed spectacles.

Their work was collected in book form as *Five Architects* (1972) and published with diagrammatic drawings, photographs, and essays by critics Colin Rowe and Kenneth Frampton. *Five Architects* was bound between starkly minimal white covers, reminiscent of the Beatles' *White Album* of 1968. Six of the houses published in the book were built in the Hamptons, and these accounted for almost half of the book's 150-odd illustrations. With all of the pseudo-radical implications that the group's name implied, the work of the New York Five was seemingly devoid of social content, and represented an architecture of pure form, what architectural historian Manfredo Tafuri once referred to as "form without utopia," an architecture of "sublime uselessness." These houses weren't so much about making a better world as they were about making a better weekend. They suggested an updated version of the "country house utopia" that Lewis Mumford once described, the chief aims of which were "possession and passive enjoyment."[9]

ABOVE LEFT:
Paul Goldberger's article about the "New York Five" in the *New York Times*, 26 November 1973.

OPPOSITE, TOP LEFT:
Charles Gwathmey, Miller House, Fire Island, 1964.

OPPOSITE, TOP RIGHT:
Miller House, porch.

OPPOSITE, BOTTOM:
Miller House, interior.

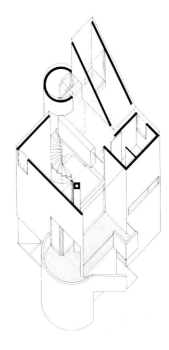

ABOVE LEFT:
Gwathmey House, interior.

ABOVE RIGHT:
**Gwathmey House,
axonometric projection.**

OPPOSITE, TOP:
Gwathmey House, night.

OPPOSITE, BOTTOM LEFT:
**Gwathmey House,
view onto porch.**

OPPOSITE, BOTTOM RIGHT:
Gwathmey House, interior.

function: a master bedroom in one, kitchen, bathroom, and guest bedrooms in the others.[13]

With his parents' house in Amagansett, Gwathmey broke free from the realm of the squat cube and pioneered a new direction for summer houses. After establishing the need for a vertical arrangement, he began to shape his ideas through a rigorous progression of drawings and cardboard models. Originally he had wanted to build the house in concrete and cast it like a sculpture, but that wasn't economically feasible. Instead, he used a conventional wood framework and covered both inside and outside with vertical cedar siding. He still continued to work with ideas of carving and eroding, treating the house as if it were a solid mass to be sculpted. In a sense, the wood framing became the formwork for concrete that was never poured. "If you drive by it fast enough," he said, "you still might mistake it for a concrete house."[14] This effect was enhanced by the slit windows that cut through the outer skin like gunports in a military bunker.

Even though there were only a few other houses in the vicinity, Gwathmey anticipated future development on the adjacent lots and kept the eastern and western facades relatively blank, with only a few selected openings. At the same time, the house developed in a vertical direction toward a loftlike studio for his father's painting. (Another example of architectural innovation in the service of art.) This third-level space was given north light through a clerestory skylight. The sharply

pointed roofline cut a distinctive silhouette against the sky and became one of three elementary shapes that gave the overall composition resonance.

The Gwathmey House was only 1,200 square feet, but it had the presence of a much larger structure. The point of view shifted as one moved around the house in a "continually changing sequence of oblique views."[15] Cubes and cylinders were played against the diagonal fin of the monitor skylight. This interplay was further accentuated by the cylindrical forms of a sun deck and a stairwell that provided circulation to all three levels.

A year after the house was finished, Gwathmey's parents moved out to Amagansett on a year-round basis. At first they thought their son would be able to expand on the original structure, but he made it clear that the house was a self-contained entity and shouldn't be touched. Instead, a smaller building was constructed as a studio for his father. The main house had been set obliquely on the lot; the studio building was rotated at a 45-degree angle from the house. The studio echoed the Euclidean lines of the main house but was less grounded, thereby creating a dynamic dialog between the two structures.

When it was finished, the Gwathmey House created a sensation. Locals thought it looked like a utility building or a power house. Others hailed it as a work of art. It was published extensively and became something of an architectural icon. It also inspired dozens of knockoffs throughout the Hamptons.

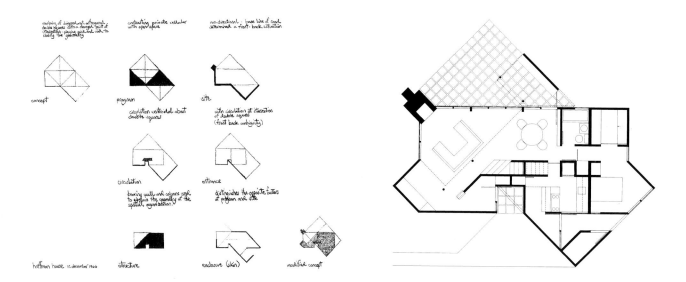

RICHARD MEIER, ANOTHER member of The Five, was the closest adherent to the purism established by Le Corbusier in his early villas. (Meier, like Gwathmey, had begun his professional career with a small beach house on Fire Island.) His first commission on the East End was the Hoffman House in East Hampton. The site was near Georgica Beach but too far away for any significant ocean views. He began by drawing an analytical sequence of diagrams that broke the problem down into "program," "structure," "entry," "circulation," and "enclosure." The result was a pure geometric abstraction, white on white, reminiscent of the minimalist art being made during the same period, in particular the geometric progressions of Sol LeWitt. The house was essentially made up of two intersecting rectangles. One section ran parallel to the road, while the other rotated away at a 45-degree angle. "The spatial interplay of the diagonal and orthogonal organization, centering about the point of intersection of these two systems, is the basis for the design of the house," explained Meier.[16] Indeed, the complexity of the design was a product of the tension between concealing and revealing planes, between privacy and exposure. It was a tension that was at the very heart of the weekend style in both the physical and metaphoric sense.

Designed for a family of five, the Hoffman House presented a blank face to the road but "exploded" open toward the lawn and woods at the rear of the property. The two-and-a-half-story living room was a triangular space surrounded by glass. A freestanding chimney pulled away from the body of the house like part of a three-dimensional puzzle and allowed for views out beyond the fireplace through vertical shafts of glass.

The angular new houses of the Hamptons conveyed a sense of anxious energy. Like the Hoffman House, they alternated between an inward and outward motion, and combined exhibitionist transparency with veils of privacy. Twin houses that Charles Gwathmey designed for the Steel family were further investigations into what was revealed and concealed, in this case on an oceanfront setting in Bridgehampton.[17] One of the houses was built for the Steel parents, the other for one of the couple's sons. The land sides of the two houses were sealed from view with opaque screens of wood siding, while the ocean sides opened generously toward the sea and sky. Architectural elements rotated within a composition of intersecting circles and squares as if parts of a kinetic assemblage. A tall white chimney acted as an armature around which the house progressed vertically. The subliminal impact of synthetic cubism on Gwathmey's work was most explicit in the drawings that he did for these houses. A narrow grid of paving stones suggests the neck of a Juan Gris guitar: a spiral staircase at the center of the plan becomes the sound hole while the double curve of an indoor swimming pool is the body. While they worked beautifully on

ABOVE LEFT:
Hoffman House, diagrammatic drawing.

ABOVE RIGHT:
Hoffman House, floor plan.

OPPOSITE, TOP:
Hoffman House, exterior with freestanding chimney.

OPPOSITE, BOTTOM LEFT:
Hoffman House, living room.

OPPOSITE, BOTTOM RIGHT:
Gwathmey & Henderson, Sedacca House, East Hampton, 1967, interior with freestanding chimney.

TOP LEFT:
**Gwathmey, Henderson &
Siegel, Steel House,
Bridgehampton, plan.**

TOP RIGHT:
**Gwathmey, Siegel, Tolan
House, Amagansett, 1970.**

BELOW:
**Gwathmey, Siegel, Cogan
House, East Hampton, 1971.**

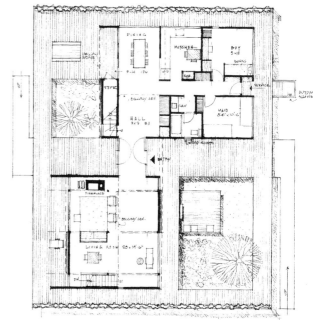

paper, the geometric complexity of the Steel houses didn't translate as effectively to their beachfront setting. Something was lost in the shift in scale from study to structure.

Gwathmey achieved a more successful adjustment of scale with the 1971 Cogan House, built overlooking Hook Pond in East Hampton's estate section. This house was not a freely drifting object. Instead, it was anchored to its spectacular site by a lawn that unrolled like a long narrow carpet to the edge of the pond and then pointed beyond it to the Atlantic Ocean. If the Cogan House suggested a grander scale of architecture that acknowledged the formality of its East Hampton neighborhood, its landscaping made allusions to the great American lawn of affluence that F. Scott Fitzgerald described in *The Great Gatsby*. "The lawn started at the beach," wrote Fitzgerald, "and ran toward the front door for a quarter of a mile, jumping over sun-dials and brick walks and burning gardens-finally when it reached the house drifting up the side in bright vines as though from the momentum of its run."[18] In the case of the Cogan lawn, there were no brick walks or burning gardens. It was just a clean swathe cutting through the marsh reeds to the water's edge.

Julian Neski had first worked on the East End as a partner of Peter Blake, but in the early 1960s he and his wife, Barbara, established their own practice. Together, they designed a series of summer houses that displayed geometric virtuosity and

ABOVE:

Julian and Barbara Neski,
Neski House, Water Mill, 1965.

ABOVE:

Neski House, contact sheet of
photographs by Julian Neski.

BELOW:

Julian and Barbara
Neski, Kaplan House,
East Hampton, 1971.

ABOVE LEFT:
Barbara and Julian Neski.

ABOVE RIGHT:
Kaplan House, interior.

a craftsman's attention to detail. Their first commission in the area was the Chalif House, which was built in East Hampton in 1964, the same year that Gwathmey designed his parents' house. The site was surrounded by large traditional houses and privet hedges. Instead of ignoring this context and creating a purely abstract insertion, the architects made an effort to acknowledge it. "We wanted to match the height of the surrounding mansions without the expense," they said. The house was broken into two opposing forms. Steeply pitched, sloping roofs cut sharply against the sky, opening and closing like scissors blades as one walked around the perimeter of the house. The separate

parts were connected by a narrow, covered breezeway and surrounded by a deck. Inside, the structural bones were revealed in simple post-and-beam construction.[19]

A few years later the Neskis designed a house for Stephen Kaplan in East Hampton that was also divided into separate sections. One area was programmed for adults; a smaller, recessed wing was for the children. It was the way that these two entities intersected, however, that made the Kaplan House such a vivid example of the new weekend dynamic. Spaces were conspicuously interwoven with cutaway walls and parts protruding at nervous angles. The living room was an open well of light that soared two

ABOVE:

Norman Jaffe, 1987.

TOP LEFT:

Norman Jaffe, study for a house at Sam's Creek, 1972.

TOP RIGHT:

Norman Jaffe, Schlachter House, Sam's Creek, Brideghampton, 1970.

OPPOSITE, CLOCKWISE FROM TOP LEFT:

Norman Jaffe, Osofsky House, Shelter Island, 1970, watercolor; Osofsky House, front facade; Jaffe, Siedler House, Shelter Island, 1973, exterior; Sam's Creek development; Siedler House, study.

stories high and was bisected by an upper "adult tree-top retreat" with its own terrace.[20] This area was linked to the master bedroom by a narrow bridge that floated above the living area. The agitated energy of the interior was further expressed on the multifaceted exterior. The masonry form of a chimney penetrated both levels and rose above the roof as a freestanding sculptural entity.

If many architects of this period seemed oblivious to the natural setting, a few tried to acknowledge it. In some of Norman Jaffe's houses there was a sense of "tribute" to the surrounding landscape, a connection to the sublime void of ocean and sky. As Jaffe once observed: "The relentless power of the wave is capable of decomposing any material, and any attempt to resist is humbling. Perhaps oceanfront sites were not meant to be built on. If the decision is so made, then the tribute to the ocean and sky should be the presence of the structure."[21]

Jaffe first visited Eastern Long Island in the 1960s. Inspired by the environment, he moved out to Bridgehampton on a full-time basis and established an architectural practice in 1973. Unlike the floating abstractions of Gwathmey and Meier, Jaffe's houses were grounded in the local landscape. "The site is at once the base," he wrote, "the foreground, and the background." Some of his houses had long sloping roofs that stretched between dune and sky. Others hugged the ground

with boxy shapes and stone foundations. While many of his contemporaries looked to the European modernism of Le Corbusier and Terragni, Jaffe found comfort in the prairie-style horizontality of Frank Lloyd Wright.

The Osofsky House (1970) was designed as the centerpiece in a trio of signature houses on the Shelter Island waterfront. Each house was built in a different style, and each stood apart from the others. The Siedler House (1973) was white stucco and Corbusian. The Jacobs House (1972) was angular and shingled. The Osofsky House was the most noteworthy of the three. It moved toward the water in gradual steps. Blocks of natural fieldstone alternated with voids of glass and planes of cedar that were cantilevered and pushed out toward the bay. Jaffe played heaviness against lightness, transparency against opacity, and thickness against thinness in a forceful composition that shared the influences of Wright's Fallingwater (1937) and the feudal fortresses of Japan.

During the same period, Jaffe designed another sequence of houses for a flat, oceanfront site in Brideghampton called Sam's Creek. This time there were five different structures, and they drifted across the site with more unity of form than the Shelter Island houses. All had low-lying profiles, flat roofs, and shifting planes. The Schlachter House was the first to be built and set the ground rules for the others. It was positioned on the edge of a saltwater creek that

led down to the ocean and had thick granite walls and black slate floors. The horizontality of the Sam's Creek houses was a definitive move away from the verticality of the Gwathmey school. One magazine praised the Schlachter residence for being a "Down-to-Earth House."[22]

Ward Bennett was another designer whose beach houses were grounded in the natural setting. For his own house in the Springs, he created an intimate connection between interior space and the salt-marsh landscape of Accabonac Harbor. For larger commissions like the Hale Allen House in Amagansett (c. 1969) and the Sugarman House in Southampton (1970), Bennett introduced a more ambitious sense of scale and mass. Elementary forms were used, but they were much chunkier than the papery planes of the Gwathmey or Meier houses. In the Allen House, monolithic slabs of reinforced concrete were arranged like so many overscaled Froebel blocks in a manner that suggested the work of Mexican modernist Luis Barragán but drained of color. The bold geometries of the Allen House made a striking contrast to the soft contours of the ocean dunes. Its pale blank walls registered every nuance of changing light and the shadows of passing clouds.

The view to the ocean is dramatically revealed as one moves upward. —Richard Meier, 1984[23]

ABOVE:

Saltzman House, rear facade with pool in foreground.

OPPOSITE, TOP LEFT:

Ward Bennett, Bennett House, the Springs, c. 1968.

OPPOSITE, TOP RIGHT:

Ward Bennett, Allen House, Amagansett, c. 1969.

OPPOSITE, BOTTOM:

Allen House, exterior.

IN THE COMPETITIVE world of Hamptons real estate, a collection of superior views was as important an acquisition as acreage or water frontage. While most of the prime ocean sites were already claimed, with a little slight of hand an architect could still direct the gaze toward a desirable point of interest. Enhancing views could produce odd configurations, however. Houses were angled on their lots in oblique directions or stretched vertically to reach above adjacent hedges, dunes, and other houses. Walls of slatted wood and other screening devices were used to block out prying eyes.[24]

The conventional two- or three-story structure was replaced by a stack of levels that provided a series of constantly changing points-of-view. To achieve the best views, residents ascended various landings, mezzanines, and porches, navigating sequences of surprise turns, sudden openings, and unexpected perspectives. Unlike traditional, nineteenth-century houses, in which views were framed as if they were landscape paintings, these houses produced fragmented montages that were spiritually akin to the multimedia extravaganzas of the sixties.

Richard Meier's 1969 Saltzman House was designed as a "counterpoint to nature," and appeared to drift across its pristine lawn like a cubist ghost ship. Renny Saltzman was a well-known interior designer.

His wife, Ellin, was a fashion consultant. They wanted the house to be a retreat from their hectic life in the city and a place where their two children could "wander off to explore for hours, or help a tree to grow, or run freely in and out of an unlocked front door."[25] But it would also be a showcase and a party place. The Saltzmans wanted to see and be seen.

As with Gwathmey's early work, the Saltzman House gave the illusion of being much bigger than it really was. The beach lay a quarter of a mile to the south and the seaward orientation of the house created a distinct polarity between front and back. The main part was connected to a cabooselike guest house by a bridge elevated on slender *pilotis*. The long facade facing north was almost blank, like the backside of a barn, with only two small windows. On the south side, however, the tautness of the outer skin found release through an eruption of openings, curving walls, projecting sun decks, and receding voids. The ground floor was packed with small, dormlike bedrooms ("so the children would be out and into the sunshine"), and a kitchen/dining area.[26] As it

ascended toward its ultimate goal, the ocean view, the house opened up, space expanded, and expectations grew. The second floor had a two-story living area and master bedroom, and the third floor a sun deck and study. A swimming pool was built in a distant corner of the property, designed as a separate architectural element and corralled by a low white fence so as not to detract from the purity of the main event.

This most photogenic of houses was celebrated in the pages of *House & Garden* magazine as a fusion of architecture and fashion. A photograph by Horst showed Ellin Saltzman dressed in an op-art skirt leaning out from a cantilevered deck. Another had her posing at a rakish angle beside a freestanding spiral staircase. "The house is like a marvelous machine that always works," explained the magazine.[27]

Julian and Barbara Neski's 1972 Simon House in Southampton was another show-stopping performance piece. Both Peter and Merle Simon were in the entertainment business. He starred on a TV soap opera and she was a dancer and singer on Broadway. With its eleven rooms stacked in

ABOVE LEFT:
Ellin Saltzman posing beside spiral starcase. Photo by Horst.

ABOVE RIGHT:
Saltzman House, living room.

OPPOSITE, TOP LEFT:
Julian and Barbara Neski, Simon House, South Hampton, 1968.

OPPOSITE, TOP RIGHT:
Julian and Barbara Neski, Cates House, Amagansett, 1968, floor plan with motel-style arrangement of bedrooms.

OPPOSITE, BOTTOM:
Cates House, exterior.

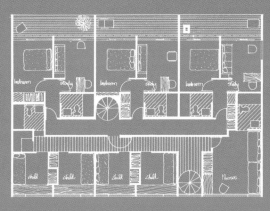

ABOVE LEFT:
Alfredo De Vido, Sheehy House, East Hampton, 1973, living room.

ABOVE RIGHT:
Alfredo De Vido, Garraty House, Sag Harbor, 1973.

spiraling order, the house was conceived as an extension of their whirlwind careers. Each room was on a different level, and each had its own exclusive view. The architects wanted a design that would enable the Simons to experience the trees, water, and sky from constantly shifting planes of reference; in effect, to establish a continuous vertical movement through the different levels, culminating in a final (and most dramatic) view of the sea from the roof deck.[28]

"Julian had this idea of a complete cube," said Barbara Neski, "so we started playing around and broke the cube up into quadrants. Then we decided we would start moving around these quadrants, all the way up to the top." Each level was divided into four parts. As one progressed up the central staircase, the ceilings got higher and the views expanded outward. "It opened up nicely as a stage set," said Neski. "We liked to imagine Merle Simon dancing down those stairs while her husband, Peter, played the piano on a different level."[29]

Another Neski commission during this period demanded more of a psychoanalytical than theatrical treatment of space. The Cates House (1968) was positioned high atop a sandy bluff in Amagansett overlooking Gardiner's Bay.[30] The exterior of the stark white pavilion showed the influence of Marcel Breuer's Tompkins House in Hewlett Harbor, Long Island (1946), but something odd was happening inside its pristine stucco

walls. Internal arrangements were generated by an unusual *ménage à trois* situation: the client, his wife, and her ex-husband—all psychoanalysts—shared the house during the summer months. Each insisted on their own private view of the bay. Each had their own bedroom, bathroom, and terrace, as well as a private study attached for seeing patients. The rooms were strung out in a row—as if the house were a motel for shrinks—with the woman in the middle and the men on either side. Across a narrow hall there were four tiny bedrooms for the children and a nanny room.

At roughly the same time, architect Alfredo De Vido was developing a house with a multiplicity of views and spatial experiences for John A. Garraty, a history professor at Columbia University, and his wife Gail, an artist. Their house was built on a lot overlooking Peconic Bay near Sag Harbor. De Vido gave them a sequence of blocks that appeared to be stacked in a random order—some open, some closed, some pulled out, others pushed in. Deep overhangs, setbacks, and small recessed porches further activated the outer shell. Sloping skylights rose from the roof and brought northern light to Gail Garraty's studio. The narrow, elongated plan of the house provided cross ventilation and allowed every room to have its own water views.

But as one magazine noted, "closeness to the ocean is no guarantee of a good view."[31] As beach areas became more crowded, architects were obliged

ABOVE:
Garraty House.

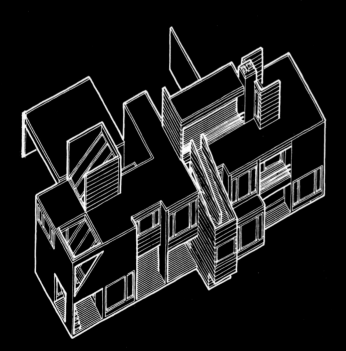

LEFT:
Garraty House, axonometric drawing.

BELOW:
Alfredo De Vido, study for the Koch House, East Hampton, 1970.

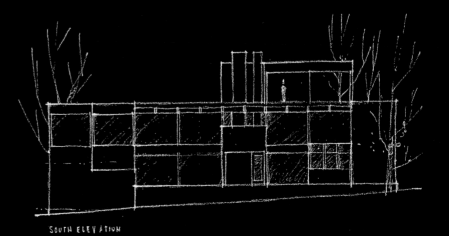

SOUTH ELEVATION

to find increasingly novel strategies for capturing the requisite vista and blossoming sense of space. The 1972 Cohn House, designed by Gwathmey and his new partner Robert Siegel for an oceanfront site in Amagansett, stood at the end of a cul-de-sac with houses crowding in from three sides. For privacy, the architects used a row-house device and closed off the side walls while the southern facade greeted the ocean with floor-to-ceiling glass. Inside, there were three different levels, with bedrooms on the first, a living/dining space on the second, and a master bedroom and private sun deck on the third. A cylindrical shaft contained a spiral staircase that penetrated all three levels.

The Neskis also designed a house in which views were dictated by architectural intervention. The 1970 Sabel House in Bridgehampton was minimal and white with narrow slit windows on one side and an explosion of glass on the other. The flat roof, side wall, and balcony were all extended like architectural blinders so as to direct the views out across the open fields and beyond to the ocean. This created deep overhangs that protected the all-glass facade from the summer sun. The boxy volume of the house was broken by a flying staircase that protruded from its eastern side like a knuckle. This feature provided the client with a separate path from the master

bedroom to the swimming pool so that he could swim laps each morning without disturbing the rest of the household.[32]

The 1972 Lowenstein House was built on a site to the east of Montauk village, just high enough to look out over the ocean. It appeared quite grand on its little acropolis of dirt, but with only 900 square feet of interior space, the house was tiny. The architects, Alan Chimacoff and Steven Peterson, used every trick they knew to achieve the greatest effect with the least amount of money and effort. Interior spaces were stacked vertically as in the Gwathmey and Saltzman houses, but in this case there was a literal transposition from the city: Most of the year the clients lived in a brownstone duplex in Manhattan, and they asked the architects to use the exact same layout to create, as one magazine put it, "a beach house almost like home."[33] Precut sheets of standard plywood were painted white and used for the external skin. The sun deck gave the house another 600 square feet of space and extended the living area outward. Exposed bracing members implied continuity and gave the house a half-built, deconstructed look, similar to Peter Eisenman's 1970 House II in Hardwick, Vermont. Using dirt that was recycled from the excavation, a plateau was built up to the south that further elevated the house on a kind of plinth.

AS THE SHORELINE became more crowded, a different sort of hybrid evolved: the inward-directed beach house, a house with no views at all. This anomaly first appeared in beachfront communities that lay farther to the west, like Fire Island and Westhampton Beach, where small subdivision lots and overdevelopment created a greater need for privacy. In 1967, Bernard A. Marson designed a low-budget adaptation to a crowded oceanfront area in Fair Harbor, Fire Island. The client, Norman Diamond, was a building contractor who wanted his house to combine the freedom of outdoor living with a sense of privacy. The problems with the site were that there were no clear views of the beach and that the neighboring houses were unattractive. As one newspaper reported: "Mr. Marson's solution to the problem of the view was the simplest possible—to provide no view at all."[34]

Like Gwathmey's Miller House of 1964 (that lay just up the beach), there was a squat, medieval-defensive quality to Marson's design. The house was little more than a box on stilts, with the most rudimentary structure of exposed timber framing covered with rough-sawn cedar planks. A long entry ramp sloped down to the beach like a narrow drawbridge. There were no windows except for clerestory slits along the side walls. On the inside, however, Marson created a pleasantly secluded sun court. The rooms wrapped around three sides of this enclosed space as in a Roman villa. The fourth side was screened by a louvered wall that allowed the passage of sea breezes.

The Fire Island aesthetic gradually moved farther east as the Hamptons became more crowded. In the "Beachampton" section of Amagansett many small houses were crowded together on half-acre building lots. The design of the 1968 Gorman House by Julian and Barbara Neski was a result of these conditions. The house sat on a concrete foundation in a way that made it appear to hover a few feet above its sandy site. Standing right at the main entrance, like a household god, was an outdoor shower concealed by a curving white wall. This made a sculptural counterpoint to the rough decking and cedar walls. The house was divided into three separate enclosures, one for the children, one for the parents, and a third for general living purposes. Pavilions with sloping skylights were linked by small courtyards that allowed for outdoor privacy. Even though it was screened from its neighbors, the house had the open, breezy feeling of a bathing pavilion. Internal courtyards drenched the rooms in sea-reflected light.

The Dion House was too far away from the ocean in Amagansett to get a direct view, so architect Peter Hendrickson designed it to be completely inner-directed. The house wrapped itself around an enclosed atrium in staggered sections to provide maximum privacy and good exposure to the morning sun. Another tight situation, not far from the Gorman and Dion houses, guided Franklin D. Israel in his design of the 1972 Snell House, his first commission. With its blank walls, forced perspectives, and selectively placed windows, the house was

ABOVE LEFT:
Bernard A. Marson, Diamond House, Fire Island, 1967.

ABOVE RIGHT:
Diamond House, interior.

OPPOSITE, TOP LEFT:
Julian and Barbara Neski, Gorman House, Amagansett, 1968, boardwalk to entry.

OPPOSITE, TOP RIGHT:
Gorman House, courtyard.

OPPOSITE, BOTTOM:
Peter Hendrickson, Dion House, Amagansett, 1968.

an exercise in negotiating a difficult site. The plan conformed to the oddly angular shape of the building lot. On the ground floor, there was a row of dormitory-style bedrooms. The upper level contained a master bedroom and an overhanging deck that reached just high enough to gain partial views of the ocean.[35]

Not all new houses were being built near the beach. With the costs of waterfront property escalating, people started to move inland. Alfredo De Vido, who had first come out to East Hampton in 1967 to design a house for theatrical producer Hale Matthews, liked the area so much that he decided to build a house for himself. He couldn't afford anything near the water, but was able to buy 17 acres of land in the Northwest Woods, a scrubby forest of pines and oak that stretched from Stephen's Hand Path in East Hampton all the way north to Sag Harbor. This was something of a pioneering venture, as the Northwest Woods were still relatively uninhabited and considered by most to be out of bounds for a summer residence. (Some locals still thought they were haunted by the ghosts of murdered Indians.)

The wooded setting called for a different kind of architecture, one that was more self-contained and enclosed than beach-house design. With its defensive blank walls, De Vido's house had the feeling of a wilderness outpost. It started as a basic cube and then sprouted sheds and small decks on every side. There was no single dramatic view to catch, so the house was directed inwards and upwards with a three-story central atrium

and small upper lofts around the perimeter. Views out were squeezed through openings in the corners of the cube.[36] Over the next decade, De Vido continued to develop his woodsy land. He subdivided his seventeen acres and built more houses. This marked another trend in Hamptons real estate: areas that had once seemed safe from development were now fair game.

BY THE BEGINNING of the 1970s, the beachtopia of Eastern Long Island was corrupting into a dystopia, and residents were upset. While some considered the houses of Gwathmey, the Neskis, and Meier to be masterpieces, others saw them as eyesores. More troubling was the fact that dunes and potato fields were filling up with poorly executed copies of their houses, each trying to outdo its neighbor in expressiveness. New homes were plopped together in seemingly random patterns, fighting against one another for attention. There were few, if any, guidelines. Things got particularly bad in the agricultural flatlands of Sagaponack and Bridgehampton. Subdivision roads and cul-de-sacs spread across the fields with little thought for how their houses would relate to each other or the landscape. A general reaction ensued against what one critic of the period decried as "architectural anarchy."[37] As is often the case, the best work was lumped together with the worst, and all of its was summarily condemned.

Particular scorn was reserved for the later work of Andrew Geller, who had continued to forge his

own path of experimentation throughout the sixties and early seventies, and which, in certain cases, verged on the psychedelic. His 1966 Sagaponack house for fashion photographer Irving Elkin was a wildly pitched succession of angled roofs and skylights. One magazine described it as a "controlled kaleidoscope of color and form." Geller himself referred to it as the "Reclining Picasso," but local citizens and critics compared it to a train wreck, and the area's papers ran satirical cartoons. Another Geller house, also built in Sagaponack, was described as a poor man's version of the Sidney Opera House.[38]

As a style, modernism seemed corrupt. It was now perceived as an enemy, a ruiner of quaint rural places. Those Gwathmeyesque roofs appeared to be so many daggers cutting against bucolic skies. As critic Paul Goldberger lamented: "the sharp, angular structures that occupy some of East Hampton and far more of Brideghampton, Westhampton, and Quogue seem...to be trying to defy the ocean. They do not accept it: they challenge it."[39] The architects were seen as part of a general conspiracy, with their houses being the most noticeable tip of the iceberg.

Between 1960 and 1980, the population of East Hampton grew 27.8 percent. Southampton grew by almost 20 percent during the same period.[40] Thousands of new building permits were issued for single-family homes. Despite such growth, the basic infrastructure was unchanged. Roads were rural—many were still unpaved—and the two-lane Montauk Highway was the only major artery connecting the villages. On summer weekends driving was intolerable, and the traffic worsened every year. Water and sewage systems were also pushed to the limit. The early seventies would bring other benchmarks of creeping suburbanization. In 1974 there was the Hampton Jitney, a deluxe bus line that began express service to Manhattan and brought a closer link to the city. That year also saw the completion of the first shopping mall in the Hamptons, just west of Bridgehampton on Route 27.

Resistance to unchecked growth was first widely manifested in the mid-sixties, when concerned citizens realized that action was needed to preserve the area's rural character. Their growing consciousness about environmental issues was part of a national trend. Out on the East End, there were increased attempts by private citizens and local governments to curb growth before it was too late. A Stop-the-Highway group was formed to prevent a four-lane extension of Route 27 from coming all the way out to Montauk. Both the towns of Southampton and East Hampton adopted limited-growth programs and enacted legislation that was designed to protect the environment. Some of these actions amounted to the closing of barn doors after the horses had already left, but they sent a message. Zoning ordinances were adopted to regulate the size and location of buildings—over the years, a litany of amendments, extensions, and clarifications was added as both townships felt compelled to toughen their standards.[41] Architectural review boards were also established that, to varying degrees, controlled the size, shape, and, in some cases, the style of architecture allowed. Building permits were also limited to an annual number.

East Hampton's first comprehensive plan was adopted in 1968 to "maintain the rural quality of the area."[42] A proposal was made to limit the population to a cap of 63,900, and parts of the township were upzoned to a 5-acre minimum, precluding overdevelopment. Limitations were placed on the size of houses in relationship to the size of their building lots. There were also setback requirements from lot lines and environmentally sensitive areas such as dunes and wetlands. After the influx of the singles scene in the 1970s, a set of "grouper" laws was passed that restricted the number of unrelated individuals who could rent a summer house at any given time. The Village of East Hampton passed a no-group-rental law in 1972—four or more unrelated people were prohibited from renting a single house. Southampton enacted a similar law in 1984.

Several not-for-profit environmental groups were established on the East End to help preserve open land and to resist increased development.[43] In 1972, Suffolk County spent $21 million to buy development rights from farmers. Later, in 1981, Southampton appropriated $6 million to acquire hundreds of acres of land that would have otherwise gone to developers.

A GENERAL SPIRIT of restraint and reaction was also reflected in changing attitudes about architecture. The counter-revolution had started innocently enough. As far back as the 1950s, the flat roofs of the generic modern box already seemed repetitive to some. A few architects, including George Nelson, realized that not all modern roofs had to be flat, and dared to explore new directions. Only five years after Nelson completed work on the Holiday House in 1950, he and his partner Gordon Chadwick designed the Otto Spaeth house in East Hampton. It had a sweeping gable roof that the architects borrowed directly from McKim, Mead & White's 1887 Low House, a famous shingle-style house built overlooking the sea in Bristol, Rhode Island. An article in *House & Garden* asked the question: "What Makes a House Modern?" and showed photographs of the broad Spaeth roof alongside the house's conspicuously modern interiors. In place of the traditional bay windows and covered porches of the Low House, Nelson and Chadwick used undulating overhangs and a semicircular sun deck.

"Is the house shown here really modern? Or is it just the opposite?" asked the editors of *House & Garden*.[44] The article didn't do much to resolve the question. Nelson liked the way that the house's pitched roofline complemented the wind-swept contours of the ocean dunes. He saw the Low House as a protomodernist form, a bold geometric gesture that looked to the future rather than the past. A younger generation of architects read it in a different way, finding in it a crucial touchstone for their own journeys back in time.

Rising above dunes, the house echoes their gently undulating contours.

For the love of the seashore, with its exhilarating impact on the senses,
this Long Island house was designed. Its shingled exterior forms
a sturdy shell against the elements, yet its many window bays admit
the restful sights and sounds of the shore. And, as if to welcome
the surging breakers, a pair of broad sundecks step down toward the beach.

Continued

OPPOSITE:

George Nelson and Gordon Chadwick's Spaeth House (East Hampton, 1955) in *House & Garden*, **July 1958.**

Triangular shape and shingled exterior are reminiscent of 19th century Long Island houses. Yet this house, in plan and purpose, is wholly modern.

What makes a house modern?

Contemporary design can profit,
as this house by the sea proves,
by adapting fine ideas of the past

Main floor plan is oriented for southern exposure and view of ocean, seen through a series of bay windows. A wood bridge (upper right) leads to front entrance and continues around end of house to connect with seaside decks. Fireplace wall screens the front wall of the living room, since it is largely a wall of glass.

Art collection in upstairs hallway is displayed in niches, lit by small square windows that resemble ships' portholes.

Living-dining area is large, the combined room measuring nearly 50' long, and the generous use of glass in the bay windowed wall adds a sense of spaciousness.

LIKE A MURAL, SEA AND SHORE

are framed over and over again by
bays and the wide porch opening

Sheltered porch on second floor makes it possible for the family to catch the breeze without leaving the sun.

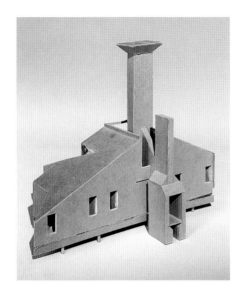

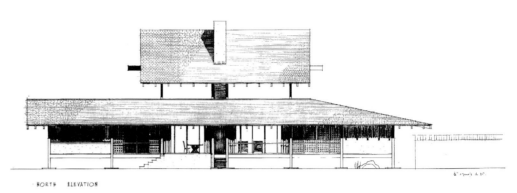

· NORTH ELEVATION ·

More and more designers on the East End began to turn against the strict canon of reductive modernism and to find inspiration in the vernacular forms of historic architecture—especially the colonial saltbox houses and the late-nineteenth-century cottages of the old summer colonies. As Vincent Scully ordained, young American architects were beginning to "dig back down to the roots of American decency."[45] There was a growing appreciation of "vernacular" forms of American architecture, especially the New England shingle style. A revised edition of Scully's *The Shingle Style* appeared in 1971 and had an influence on many younger architects who had either read the book or attended Scully's lectures at Yale. A few years later, Scully published *The Shingle Style Today* to show how the old style was being appropriated by a new generation of designers. The book featured recent projects on Eastern Long Island by Gwathmey, Robert A. M. Stern, Jaquelin T. Robertson, and others.[46]

In 1959, only a few years after the arrival of the Spaeth House, another updated version of the Low House appeared: "Project for a Beach House," designed by a young architect named Robert Venturi, who soon became the best-known proponent of postmodernism in American architecture. Scully himself declared it to be the "first major project of the new shingle style," even though it was never built, even though it was never more than a cardboard model. But it had the power of authority, claimed Scully. It

was thoughtful, literate, and *American* in the way it combined the heroic silhouette of the Low House with an iconic, towering chimney. "Venturi is ferocious," wrote Scully. [47]

However corny it may have looked, here, we were assured, was a new paradigm for domestic architecture. The house would no longer be a celebration of flowing space. Instead, it was to be an evocation of place. "This chimney rises higher, as a signpost of Home facing the Atlantic," wrote Scully, who then compared it to Frank Lloyd Wright's fireplaces "burning in the heart of the house." He also cited the architecture of Edwin Lutyens and even brought in the paintings of Franz Kline, explaining how Venturi's house somehow belonged to the "heroic American abstract expressionism of the fifties," in the way that its chimney thrust through the center of the house like the piers in Kline's *Crosstown* of 1955.[48]

Venturi's house went beyond abstract expressionism, however, to what Scully called the "Signpost Art" of the following decades. Here was one of the early theoretical volleys of postmodernism, the first shot fired against all those glass houses and geometric "preoccupations" that Scully and Venturi now scorned. It was no coincidence that the shot took the form of a beach house and not a more significant type of building—a museum or a corporate skyscraper, for example. The beach house was the sonnet form of American architecture, and an architect would have to

ABOVE:
Vincent Scully's 1974 book
The Shingle Style Today.

TOP LEFT:
**Robert Venturi, Project
for a Beach House, 1959,
cardboard model.**

TOP RIGHT:
**Robert Venturi and
William Short, Miller
House, East Hampton,
1961, north elevation.**

ABOVE:

Jack Lenor Larsen and Robert Rosenberg, the Round House, East Hampton, 1964.

first prove himself there before moving on to bigger challenges. This was where the revolution began.

While his own beach house project was never realized, Venturi did build one of his first commissions (in collaboration with William Short) near Wiborg Beach in East Hampton. The 1962 Miller House, with its tea-house roof and rustic beams, was not based on any American precedent, however, but on another vernacular tradition: that of Japan. Venturi was not the only architect exploring Eastern influences. A distinctly Japanese influence could also be seen in the floating roofs and Zen simplicity of Paul Lester Wiener's houses. Robert Rosenberg, architect of his own glass house in 1952, designed a traditional Japanese house for John O'Toole on a beach site in Quogue in the early sixties. All of the

parts for the O'Toole House were fabricated in Taiwan, shipped to Long Island, and then reassembled on the ocean dunes. Considering the influence that oriental design had on the early modern movement, these imports weren't as radical as they might have seemed; they were still safely within the modernist canon.

More "primitive" forms of architecture were also an influence. Jack Lenor Larsen, weaver and textile designer, returned from a two-month trek through Africa inspired by the architecture and decorations of a N'debele village compound he had seen in the Transvaal. Working with Rosenberg, he developed plans for his own village compound to be built on the 12-acre grounds of an old farm in East Hampton.[49] Instead of one large house, there were

The Round House with
African furnishings.

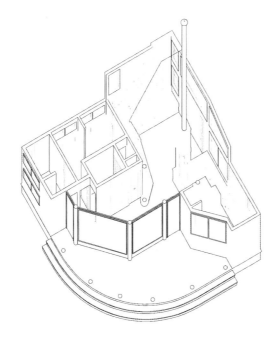

three separate buildings: a main house, a guest pavil-ion, and a studio. All the buildings were round, and their walls were cast in concrete to resemble the mud huts that Larsen had seen in Africa. Buildings and gardens were connected with pathways and circular terraces. Roofs were made from roughly split cedar shakes overlapped in such a way as to simulate the tex-ture of thatch. Inside the main house, Larsen used African furniture, animal skins, and coarsely textured fabrics woven in Swaziland. Exterior walls were painted in a traditional Transvaal pattern. A free-form fireplace was cast by ceramist Karen Karnes.

These cultural crossbreedings were part of a broader reaction against the predictable and machine-like precision of the modernist style. More and more people were buying old barns, moving them to beach-front sites, and remodeling them for summer use. In 1958, Peter Blake converted an Amagansett barn with an exposed post-and-beam structure for the Tobey family. Robert Rosenberg converted an old church that the writer Dorothy Norman moved to her prop-erty in East Hampton in the late fifties. While the exteriors of these projects retained their historic char-acters, interiors were open, modern spaces.

During the early and middle years of the seven-ties, a hybrid style became popular with young New Yorkers who wanted to "blend in" to the local land-scape. The houses they built were far less conspicuous than the abstract showpieces of the Gwathmey-Meier school. Several early variations suggested a sympa-thetic spirit of contextualism. Jaquelin T. Robertson, Alfredo De Vido, Hobart Betts, Norman Jaffe, and some of the other architects who had recently arrived on the East End were all learning to combine vernac-ular elements—sloping roofs and shingled exteri-ors—with doctrinaire modernist interiors. The blocky hybrids they created became another Hamptons "look" in their own right. Some used Venturiesque gestures such as central chimneys and exaggerated gable roofs as domestic signifiers. Julian and Barbara Neski had made early suggestions in this direction with their Chalif House of 1964. While orthodox modern in its geometric starkness, it made subtle references to the past. Thick, rough-cut cedar shakes were used on the roofs in contrast to the smooth gray siding of the outer walls. One magazine called it a "saltbox for all seasons." Another called it a "saltbox split in two." The house's sloping, shed roofs vaguely suggested the vernacular forms of East Hampton's own colonial period.[50]

Robertson's 1967 Seltzer House was small and inexpensive, but it attempted to convey a sense of grandeur and domestic gentility that would soon lead to bigger things. Simple geometric forms and flush windows were all within the vocabulary of the mod-ern beach house. The house shared the same neck-craning-for-views aesthetic that characterized so many houses of the sixties, but Robertson balanced this with white columns and a petticoat porch from which one could watch neighboring lots fill in with houses. Scully singled out the Seltzer House for praise: "[It] embodies a probity, a solemnity even, which seems at once especially awkward, promising, and right," he wrote. "It all feels more like 'tradition' than like 'influence'."[51]

De Vido's 1967 Matthews House had a boxy, shingled shell that one magazine referred to as "cubist Cape Cod."[52] His design for the 1972 Bross House in East Hampton had a soaring diagonal roof, and his 1973 Hammer House in Sagaponack appeared to be several saltbox forms separated and staggered around a central deck. Norman Jaffe used similar combina-tions of sloping roofs and cedar shingles in the 1967 Burland House at Pheasant Walk in Brideghampton and at the 1969 Perlbinder House in Sagaponack. His strongest work of the period came from a different source, however. Jaffe took a trip through Ireland in 1968 and was intrigued by the ruins of an ancient

TOP LEFT:

Norman Jaffe, Becker House, Wainscott, 1970, in *House & Garden*, August 1972.

TOP RIGHT:

Becker House, staircase.

BELOW:

Becker House, exterior.

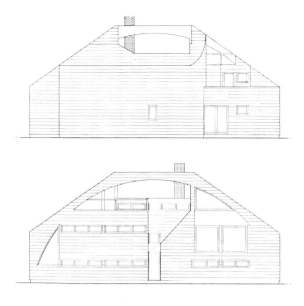 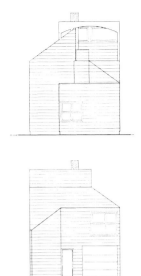 

ABOVE LEFT:

Robert A. M. Stern and John S. Hagman, Wiseman House, Montauk, 1967, elevations.

ABOVE RIGHT:

Robert A. M. Stern & John S. Hagman, Beebe Guest House, Montauk, 1972.

farmhouse he had spotted in the countryside. The stone shell of the building became the inspiration for the Becker House, designed upon his return to the Hamptons in 1969. The house presented a strikingly simple facade of rough stonework running along its western side. This acted like the false front of a Hollywood set. A hyper-extended wall ran 50 feet to the south and helped root the house firmly in its flat, agricultural setting. The borrowed forms of the half-gable with chimney and the extended wall created an imposing sense of scale, but the rugged facade actually concealed a surprisingly small living space on the opposite side. This technique characterized much of Jaffe's later work. A single gestural stroke dominated while the rest of the house evolved beneath it. Inside, Jaffe used exposed beams of rough-sawn Canadian spruce and connected them in a muscular way with thick bolts and steel flitch plates.

Robert A. M. Stern went a few steps further, daring to make direct quotations from historical sources. His dual role as historian and practicing architect made an imprint on his work of this period. Interior spaces of the 1967 Wiseman House in Montauk were multilevel, open modernist spaces, but the exterior made explicit references to the architecture of McKim, Mead & White. The house was built on a wooded site overlooking the ocean beach and could be seen from a distance. Stern made a bold ges-

ture on the side that faced the road. Suggestions of a gable were intercut with layers of shingled wall planes. An arching void evoked the form of a Palladian window. Stern further refined his investigations into the shingle style vocabulary with the 1972 Beebe Residence, also in Montauk. A main house, a guest house, and a beach cabana were planted along a 50-foot cliff and integrated into the surrounding beachscape to "maximize a sense of site, and to take advantage of the prevailing breezes."[53] The main house addressed the ocean with a curving bay, while on the landside it was oriented toward a swimming pool and deck.

The forms of all of these awkwardly transitional houses may have been suggestive of traditional architecture, but they were essentially modern boxes with shingle veneers and a few sloping additions tacked on. The clients who commissioned them still wanted an abundance of glass and open, multilevel interiors. Most of theses houses were still relatively inexpensive to build. They had a feeling of woody comfort while still enjoying the openness and informality of a modern plan. This balance—or often clunky imbalance—between modern form and historical veneer marked them as the first tentative steps away from the modern and toward a more conservative style that would come into its own during the 1980s.

People are looking for roots. They'd all love to be born into a grand old house that had been handed down through the generations.

—Francis Fleetwood, 1998[1]

DURING THE 1980s, new money washed over the Hamptons like a tidal surge. It was a time of gross excess and exaggeration, inflated egos and inflated architecture. The summer crowd was more aggressive, the personalities more abrasive, and the houses more ostentatious. New, 30,000-square-foot mansions went up as fast as prefab Levitts, filling in the last remaining plots of farmland. The weekend utopia of the postwar period was rapidly deteriorating into a high-end suburban nightmare. The Hamptons provided a service to the hordes of new arrivals who were busy creating new identities for themselves. It became a place to show off the achievements and rewards that had come from so much hard work in the city: their cars, their suntanned faces, their fashionable clothes, their furniture, their art, their fit bodies. There was also the emergence of an odd, Thoreau-meets-Gatsby duality between escape and exposure that would characterize the Hamptons scene in the following years: a combination of hiding out and being seen; of wanting to retreat and advance at the same time; of escaping city strife to experience nature firsthand yet having the comforts of the city within easy reach; of enjoying a moment of quiet introspection followed by a flurry of social networking.

A postmodern, neotraditional style evolved that became the preferred means of conveying status and "arrival." The followers of this new style made a concerted effort to imitate the look of old money that previous generations had rebelled so valiantly against. This new/old attitude was perfectly expressed in a 1983 advertisement for Ralph Lauren's line of neotraditional clothing that was shot in the Hamptons. Two WASPy-looking models sat on the veranda of a crusty old shingle-style house, patting a golden retriever. This scene represented "a life long attitude," according to the caption, but an attitude that could be instantly acquired.

New arrivals to the Hamptons embraced the previously suspect symbols of the past as part of their refurbished identities. They, too, wanted to be like the models in the Ralph Lauren ad, with their blond hair and incredibly blue eyes. As one East End realtor of the period put it, "the Hamptons are a good place to secure ready-made charisma. All you need is some money."[2] A big traditional house conferred an instant pedigree on an otherwise insecure owner.

This new approach was decidedly different from the hybrids of the sixties and seventies, which made lighthearted allusions to the past with limited means. The houses of the eighties were big, expensive, and designed as literal appropriations of the past. One new summer resident bought a pricey piece of oceanfront property and instructed her architect to build a house with "nooks and crannies...one that looks like it's been sitting there for a hundred years." Without the slightest hesitation, her architect complied, drawing up plans for a large shingled cottage. The client was delighted. "Modernism doesn't show money," claimed an East End architect who had made an overnight switch from modern to traditional. "If people have a lot of cash to show off, they want something that looks old."[3]

Venerable old estate houses were enveloped and expanded with sprawling "additions" that were often larger than the original houses. Another phenomenon to hit the Hamptons in the 1980s was the million dollar speculative house. "Our goal is to have the houses look as if they had been there since the 1920s," said

OPPOSITE:

Shingle house, Bridgehampton.

one developer who built a series of shingle-style houses complete with turrets, covered porches, and massive brick chimneys. Each house was over 6,000 square feet in size and cost at least $2.5 million.[4] They were by far the largest spec houses ever built on the East End and they sold like hotcakes. Bigger was better. But these mansions were mere garden sheds compared to what came a few years later.

This quest for tradition, for a "sense of place," became an exercise in one-upsmanship. The neotraditional house in the Hamptons grew progressively larger and more literal in its interpretation of the past. Some architects gave up all pretense of creative invention and chose to appropriate directly from the pages of architectural history. Designing could now be defined as copying. Robert A. M. Stern, guru of the "trend-setting traditionalists," explained the finer points of the new attitude. "You learn through imitation," he said, "which is very different from copying. Copying is what a Xerox machine does: imitation is what an artist does." But to the uninitiated it still looked like copying.[5]

Eugene Futterman was one of the first architects on the East End to specialize in the revived shingle style. His design for the 1983 Adler House on the ocean dunes of Southampton was a virtual replica of Whitecaps, an old Southampton cottage. (The original was washed away in the hurricane of 1938.) Futterman had seen the drawing for the house published in an 1897 issue of *Harper's* magazine and thought nothing of presenting it to his clients for their new beach house. There was no hesitation or sense of guilt. There would be a gambrel roof, a *porte cochère* in front, and a turret projecting to the west. The northern side would be wrapped by a quaintly curving porch. The clients loved it.[6]

This was not meant as a clever architectural pun, as Venturi might have played it. The stakes were too high for that. Appropriating the past was now serious business, and architects learned to offer up their latest knockoffs with the straightest of faces. There would be none of the whimsy that had made the beach houses of the fifties such a pleasure. As Peter Blake said, "Most of the stuff that's being built in the Hamptons today is basically showmanship, a display of rich people's bad taste." Barbara Neski was no less blunt, "[Next] they're going to come out in hoop skirts and do their Jane Austen thing."[7]

The move toward conspicuous gentrification came with similar shifts in politics and popular culture. Neoconservatives were already controlling Washington and Wall Street. Newly elected in 1980, Ronald Reagan brought deregulation and "supply-side economics," fueling the general excess of the period. Greed was in the air—greed was good, according to the lords of Wall Street. The most popular shows on television were *Dallas* and *Dynasty*, programs that chronicled the adventures of bitchy millionaires.

The signature design tract of the period was Tom Wolfe's *From Bauhaus to Our House*, which debunked modernist mythology and helped to fuel a growing mistrust of all things avant-garde. Wolfe's 128-page diatribe included a particularly sharp jab at the abstract modernism of the New York Five. "Their buildings were white and baffling," he wrote. "Baffling was *their* contribution."[8] Wolfe became a regular resident of the East End during this period, and he could be found nattily dressed in a white linen suit, propounding his theories at various parties in the area.

By the mid-eighties, Wall Street was reeling from insider-trading scandals. Ivan Boesky was indicted and ordered to pay millions in fines. The brokerage firm of Drexel Burnham Lambert filed for bankruptcy, and Michael Milken, Drexel's top junk-bond dealer, was sentenced to a lengthy prison term. (Both Boesky and Milken had been seasonal pilgrims to the Hamptons.) On screen, this type was embodied by Gordon Gekko, a financial predator played by Michael Douglas in Oliver Stone's 1987 film *Wall Street*. In one memorable scene, Gekko walks down the beach in front of his Hamptons weekend house. It is a summer evening and he is momentarily distracted by the beauty of the setting sun. But he quickly recovers his *sang froid* and barks an order into his portable phone.

As always, the Hamptons made good copy in the press, but the general tenor of the coverage was souring. The stories were now written with either a wistful sense of loss or outright contempt. Fewer journalists and editors could afford summer rentals, and some were starting to feel excluded.[9] The latest extravagance would be reported in a look-what-those-rich-bastards-in-the-Hamptons-are-up-to-now style, outlining the most controversial new house or land

ABOVE:

An aerial photograph of Bridgehampton illustrated a *New York Times Magazine* cover story on the overdevelopment of the Hamptons, 4 September 1983.

grab. Everyone had a favorite moment that signaled the beginning of the end.

In the early 1980s there was Ben Heller, New York art dealer and real-estate prince, with his plan to build four-hundred houses on the Grace Estate, a 667-acre parcel of virgin woods in East Hampton. In 1984 there was Dragon's Head in Southampton, a tasteless medieval castle with turrets and a lagoon built by computer magnate Barry Trupin. To old Social Register types this was particularly sacrilegious, as Trupin's architectural atrocity was built on the site of the DuPont family mansion. Then there was the 1990 Lawrence House in East Hampton, "The House from Hell," according to one magazine, designed by Rafael Viñoly in the style of a soaring airline terminal. This infuriated celebrity neighbors including Lee Radziwill and her husband, Hollywood director Herb Ross, who felt morally justified in taking legal action.[10]

The most telling indicator, however, came in 1985. Signaling a true shift in priorities, Robert Motherwell's experimental Quonset house was torn down by a couple who wanted to replace it with a neocon "Adirondack" cottage (designed by Eugene Futterman). If there were any lingering doubts, this willful act of vandalism made it clear that the Hamptons' experimental legacy was in danger of being systematically erased, as if it had never really happened.[11]

VINCENT SCULLY ARGUED that the original shingle style was a nineteenth-century expression of pluralism "wherein many divergent attitudes and influences are supposed to merge into an integrated but not 'exclusive' whole." The late-twentieth-century version of the style, however, evoked a shockingly singular and unabashed sense of greed.[12]

"I feel comfortable in a house that has rooms where they ought to be," said one neotraditional client. "I get a cold, empty feeling when I walk into a starkly modern house. Old houses, no matter how ratty they are, make me feel comfortable."[13] The big new houses were weighted down with tradition. They did not hover precariously on narrow *pilotis*. They were frontal and had formal entrances and axial plans with none of the odd turnings and obtuse angles that characterized the previous generation of design. The "view" was no longer the primary generator of form. Windows were placed in adherence to a conventional symmetry that sometimes denied the best views. Interiors also returned to the broken-up floor plans of premodern days, with conventional rooms rather than free-flowing spaces. There would be no more multipurpose rooms, sliding glass doors, synthetic materials, or flat roofs. Instead, there were corridors, vestibules, formal dining rooms, maid's rooms, and enclosed kitchens—all conventions that had been cast into outer darkness by the modernists. Everything old was new again.

The new building may have been carried out in the holy name of "contextualism," but it was also just plain boring. The houses got bigger and bigger, and this, in turn, necessitated thicker hedges and higher fences to obscure neighboring houses. This precipitated a craze for earthen berms that were used to separate and screen properties. These further interrupted the flowing lines of the landscape, and caused animosity and litigation between neighbors.

The new/old style offered clients an architectural grab-bag of options. There was so much to choose from, such variety compared to the *sachlichkeit* beach houses of the fifties and sixties. Colonnades, cornices, ogee and ovolo moldings, pilasters, cupolas, dentilling, faux marbling, pendant tracery. The words themselves seemed charged with gentrified significance—pure poetry to a CEO on his way into the corporate stratosphere. It was a style of acquisition and addition, not subtraction. The new style was the physical expression of so many corporate mergers, expanding portfolios, and leveraged buy outs. If postmodernists spoke of "a sense of place," the reality was more about a sense of *having*, a sense of wanting more and more. Every cornice and ogee molding spoke of a deal gone right.

Window treatments took on a specially loaded significance. The new homeowners dreamt of windows in every conceivable shape and size. Custom-design shops fabricated "Gothic heads," elliptical, oval, oriel, trapezoidal, octagonal, and eyebrow shaped windows to meet the demand. National companies like Andersen, Kolbe & Kolbe, and Marvin heard the call and mass-produced a variety of specialized window frames to appease the new traditionalists.

The most ubiquitous of all the fussy new types of fenestration, however, was the Palladian window. Historically, these had three openings, with the central bay arched and wider than its flat-topped pendants. But in the new Long Island vernacular, historical accuracy didn't matter. Anything with a rounded top became known as a Palladian and was seen as an instant evocation of history, status, class, and tradition. In some cases, an oversized Palladian filled an entire facade of a house. But even a tiny, pre-fab version with snap-in plastic mullions suggested, in some submerged way, the grandeur of eighteenth-century estate architecture.[14]

To some, the rounded arch of the Palladian win-dow read as a setting sun or a glaring eye. (To me, it looked suspiciously like a Mercedes-Benz hood orna-ment.) But however you interpreted its shape, the Palladian became as much a signifier as the flat roof had been for the prosperous bohemians of the post-war period. In fact, it became the ultimate antimodern emblem, its curving top and radiating partitions the antithesis of modernism's hard edges.

The wealthy new homeowners insisted on instant gratification. Construction sites were covered with pneumatically inflated domes so that crews could work through the winter months. Fully grown plants were imported to establish grounds that looked as if they had been there since the turn of the century. There would be no waiting around for the privet to fill in or the English ivy to climb up the side of the manor walls. Sweeping beds of high-maintenance perennials were planted by teams of illegal immigrants. Hundred-year-old boxwood plants were ripped by their ancestral roots from plantation estates in the deep south and shipped north. Prefabricated gazebos, pergolas, and greenhouses were brought in from England. A new technique of "ivy-implantation" (something akin to hair-plugs) was developed by a clever horticulturist so that walls could be covered instantly with thick cloaks of ivy.[15] Extrafine mud dredged from a bay in Nova Scotia was rubbed onto shingles to give them a weathered look. Secret mix-tures of buttermilk and yogurt were smeared on stone walls and foundations to encourage the growth of ancient-looking moss. Convoys of flatbed trucks were seen whizzing up the Montauk Highway carrying fully grown trees in a high-speed version of *Macbeth*'s Birnam Wood. If an imported tree had a root ball that exceeded a certain diameter, a toll booth at the George Washington Bridge would be removed to accommo-date its girth. This procedure was carried out in the middle of the night, at great expense. The size of one's root ball was yet another measure of status.[16]

The new/old houses suggested a gentility and breeding that was all too often far from the truth. Who were these weekend men dressing like English polo players, planting privet, and demanding that their houses look timeworn and aristocratic? The roster included some of the most aggressive money grubbers in the history of capitalism—Wall Street sharks, lever-aged-buy-out artists, real-estate tycoons, investment hustlers. All of those turrets and Palladian windows worked together as a kind of money laundering device, but in reverse: they made new money look old and gave it a patina of respectability and entitlement.

SOMETHING ESSENTIAL HAD changed. What had seemed in the 1980s to be another passing phase only escalated in the 1990s. As one magazine gushed, with misplaced enthusiasm, the Hamptons were now the "new, ever-more-turbo-charged Hamptons...a high-profile stage where New York's Type As play out fan-tasy power scenarios deliriously free of the pesky intrusions of the city itself."[17]

It wasn't just high level CEOs and investment bankers who were moving out. Hundreds of lower-level "players" came too, hoping to rub shoulders with the rich and famous. Fresh loads of celebrities poured in from Hollywood and the fashion world. Calvin Klein bought the old estate of Juan Trippe, father of Pan Am Airlines. Ron Perelman, of Revlon fame, bought The Creeks from the Alfonso Ossorio estate. Martha Stewart bought Gordon Bunshaft's sleek travertine house. Ralph Lauren bought the old Carera Beach House that Antonin Raymond had designed for the cliffs of Montauk. Billy Joel and Christie Brinkley built a Palladian villa for themselves on Further Lane in Amagansett. Steven Spielberg built a barnlike house overlooking Georgica Pond. Alec Baldwin and Kim Basinger bought Stony Hill Farm in Amagansett, a former haunt of Jackson Pollock, Arthur Miller, and Marilyn Monroe. Ronald Lauder, son of Estée, created his own villagelike com-pound in Wainscott, with antique houses, barns, and churches imported from all over New England.

And then, in the late 1990s, there came Fair Field, a 100,000- square-foot "villa" built for Ira Rennert in Sagaponack. The house, which reportedly had a $100 million price tag, was designed in the hyperstretched Palladian mode, with twenty-five bedrooms, eleven sitting rooms, three dining rooms, and two libraries. It covered the length of a football field with limestone walls and endless colonnades and pediments. The estate also boasted a 15-acre formal garden, bowling alleys, tennis courts, squash courts, and a hundred-car garage.

In case anyone wondered who's was biggest, *Vanity Fair* published a helpful set of comparisons. The Rennert House was twice as big as the White House, bigger than the main concourse of Grand Central Station, bigger than William Randolph Hearst's San Simeon, and more than twice as big as Bill Gates's compound in Medina, Washington.[18] The magazine also outlined the rags-to-riches tale of Rennert's rise from humble origins in Flatbush, Queens to mastermind of the Renco Group of companies, which, according to *Vanity Fair*, controlled some of the world's worst environmental offenders. Fair Field was not only the biggest house ever built in the Hamptons, but one of the biggest houses ever built in America. Size did matter, after all. More than two-hundred replicas of Peter Blake's Pin Wheel House could have been wedged inside Rennert's megavilla, with plenty of room to spare.

THE HISTORY OF the Hamptons has been an ebb and flow of affluence and assimilation. Each new wave brings a different set of values and perceptions. Some of the early artists imagined themselves in the land-scape of Barbizon, France. Thomas Moran rode his gondola across Hook Pond dreaming of Venice. Brokers and bankers pretended to be English country squires. Carl Fisher saw Montauk as an Arthurian land of make believe. Jackson Pollock was reminded of the Wild West. Modern architects saw a blank slate upon which to conduct their experiments. Something about the place brings out a proprietary instinct. Newcomers develop immediate and strongly personal attachments. Each successive wave, in turn, thumbs its nose at the next.

The slate continues to be open for interpretation, and the Hamptons continue to be celebrated as a kind of promised land. Recent arrivals see a geography of opportunity and networking that is a virtual extension of the city. Weekend utopia has been replaced by an empire of status. Every move is documented and scrutinized, making it "the most self-conscious place on the entire planet," as a foreign journalist recently observed.[19]

One might assume that this luminous landscape has finally reached its saturation point. After enduring so many readings and cultural mood swings, however, the place remains surprisingly unspoiled. Something about it resists change, something in the slanting light and tidal swell renews itself annually. "Flee! Seek otherwise, here is no lasting home," wrote John Hall Wheelock in "Bonac," his ode to Eastern Long Island. Despite so many changes, this sense of imminent departure endures.

INTRODUCTION

1. William K. Zinsser, "Far Out on Long Island," *Horizon*, May 1963, 9.

2. From an advertisement for Techbuilt in *House Beautiful's Vacation Homes*, spring/summer 1968, 18.

3. John Hall Wheelock, "Bonac" in *By Daylight and in Dream: New and Collected Poems, 1904–1970* (New York: Scribner's, 1970), 185.

4. *New Long Island: A Handbook of Summer Travel* (New York: Rogers & Sherwood, 1879).

5. Sigfried Giedion, *Space, Time and Architecture* (Cambridge, MA: Harvard University Press, 1941), 758.

CHAPTER 1

1. William [Mackay] Laffan and Edward Strahan, "The Tile Cub at Play," *Scribner's Monthly* (February 1879), 474–5.

2. Walt Whitman, *Leaves of Grass* (Boston: Small, Maynard, 1897); F. Scott Fitzgerald, *The Great Gatsby* (New York: Scribner's, 1925).

3. *Universal Traveller* (New York, 1835). (Long Island Collection, East Hampton Library); Richard M. Bayles, *Historical and Descriptive Sketches of Suffolk County* (1874); Charles Parsons, "Montauk Point, Long Island," *Harper's New Monthly Magazine*, September 1871.

4. William Cullen Bryant, *Picturesque America* (New York: Appleton, 1874), 248–62.

5. Whitman, *Leaves of Grass*.

6. Ronald G. Pisano, *The Tile Club and the Aesthetic Movement in America* (New York: Abrams, 1999. The group that went to East Hampton included Laffan, William R. O'Donovan, R. Swain Gifford, Walter Paris, Edwin Austin Abbey, Charles S. Reinhart, F. Hopkinson Smith, Arthur Quartley, Edward Wimbridge, Earl Shinn, and William Baird.

7. Laffan and Edward Strahan, "The Tile Cub at Play," 474–5.

8. Charles Burr Todd, "The American Barbison [sic]," *Lippincott's Magazine*, April 1883, 321–8. See also, *East Hampton The American Barbizon: 1850–1900*, (East Hampton: Guild Hall, 1969); Ruth B. Moran, *East Hampton Star*, 24 October, 1935.

9. Laffan and Strahan, "The Tile Cub at Play," 474–5; the story runs from pages 457–78.

10. William Mackay Laffan, *The New Long Island: A Handbook of Summer Travel* (New York: Rogers & Sherwood, 1879), 29.

11. Todd, "The American Barbison," 324.

12. John Gilmer Speed, "An Artist's Summer Vacation," *Harper's New Monthly Magazine*, June 1893, 8.

13. See Moran, *East Hampton Star*.

14. Ronald G. Pisano, *William Merritt Chase* (New York: Watson-Guptill, 1979), 12.

15. John Gilmer Speed, "An Artist's Summer Vacation," *Harper's New Monthly Magazine*, June 1893.

16. Speed, "Summer Vacation," 10.

17. Ibid., 9.

18. Lewis Mumford, *The Story of Utopias* (New York: Boni and Liveright, 1922), 203.

19. Members included Cornelius Agneau, Henry Sanger, Alfred Hoyt, William Andrews, Henry De Forest, and Alexander Orr.

20. Ralph G. Duvall, *The History of Shelter Island, 1652–1952* (Shelter Island Heights, 1952). Self-publication.

21. "Breathing Spots on the South Shore," *Sag Harbor Corrector*, 30 May 1874.

22. Lewis Mumford, *The Story of Utopias* (New York: 1922).

23. See Jeannette Edwards Rattray, *Fifty Years of the Maidstone Club, 1891–1941* (East Hampton: The Maidstone Club, 1941), 129.

24. See: Robert J. Hefner, ed., *East Hampton's Heritage* (New York: Norton, 1982). The first summer home to appear on the ocean dunes in East Hampton was probably a shingled house built in 1888 for Reverend Heber Newton. A few years later, a rambling house was built nearby for Laura Sedgwick.

25. Todd, "The American Barbison," 323.

26. Charles Dekay, "Eastern Long Island: Its Architecture and Art Settlements," *The American Architect* (1 April 1908): 112.

27. Quote from the *Sag Harbor Express*, c. 1895. See Gordon Hendriks, *The Life and Work of Winslow Homer* (New York: Abrams, 1979), 107.

28. Quoted in Rattray, *Fifty Years*, 17.

29. The evolution of the East Hampton colony has been well documented in Hefner, ed., *East Hampton's Heritage*.

30. Cleveland Amory, *The Last Resorts* (New York: Harper & Brothers, 1948), 123.

31. See Alastair Gordon, "Landmark in New Guise," *East Hampton Star*, 27 September 1984.

32. Rattray, *Fifty Years*, 16.

33. Ibid.

34. "Montauk: The Miami Beach of the North: A Carl G. Fisher Development," promotional brochure published by the Montauk Beach Development Corporation, New York, 1927. Long Island Collection, East Hampton Library.

35. See Alastair Gordon, "A New Life for the Montauk Manor," *East Hampton Star*, 11 October 1984; and Gordon, "Fisher's Montauk Legacy Getting a New Look," *New York Times* (Long Island Section), 23 December 1984.

36. *East Hampton Star*, March 19, 26, and April 2, 1926.

37. From "The Miami Beach of the North."

38. Ibid.

39. The master plan for Midhamptons was by the New York firm of Mann & Mac Neiele, Architects and Town Planners.

40. Some of the curving roads that were planned in 1927 were actually built and are used today.

41. "Eastwards to the Sea—The Romance of Beach Hampton," brochure produced by the R. B. Allen Development Corp, New York, 1938.

42. Ibid.

CHAPTER 2

1. Percival Goodman, "A Note on the Modern House," *Architectural Progress* (November 1931): 7.

2. From the first manifesto of the De Stijl group, 1918; Thorstein Veblen, *The Theory of the Leisure Class* (New York: Macmillan Company, 1899).

3. Harriet Sisson Gillespie, "A Modernistic House on the Atlantic Beach," *Arts and Decoration*, January 1930, 52.

4. Ibid., 53.

5. Percival Goodman, interview with the author, New York, 19 February 1986. Goodman was particularly taken by Rue Mallet-Stevens, an entire block of austere white

buildings that Mallet-Stevens designed in Paris's sixteenth arrondissement (1927).

6. Goodman, *Architectural Progress*, 7.

7. Quoted in "Modernity's First Subdivision," *Architectural Forum* (January 1935): 112.

8. Goodman, interview with the author.

9. Quoted in "Modernity's First Subdivision," 112.

10. Quoted in "Week-End House: Architect, Percival Goodman," *Architectural Record* (July 1934): 52.

11. See Alastair Gordon, "A Forerunner of Modern Architecture," *East Hampton Star*, 4 September 1986.

12. See Alan Windsor, *Peter Behrens, Architect and Designer: 1868–1940* (New York: Whitney Library of Design, 1981). The quote is on page 160.

13. See "Color Studies in Remodeling: William Muschenheim Architect," *Architectural Record* (October 1931): 275–8.

14. Anna Lee Arms, interview with the author, New York, 18 January 2000.

15. William Muschenheim, interview with the author, Bridgehampton, 24 August 1986.

16. Quoted in *Creative Art* VII (June 1931): 433–5.

17. "House of Lucien N. Tyng, Southampton, Long Island," *Architectural Record* (November 1931): 365–7; "'The Shallows,' Southampton House of Lucien Hamilton Tyng," *Arts and Decoration* (October 1933): 19–21.

18. "'The Shallows'," 19–21.

19. Frances Miller, *More About Tanty: A Second Growing Up* (Sag Harbor: Sandbox Press, 1980).

20. Miller, *More About Tanty*, 56.

21. Ibid. Holden was best known for designing neo-traditional estates on Long Island.

22. Miller, *More About Tanty*, 56.

23. Frances Miller, *Week-End On the Dunes* (Bridgehampton: 1934). Self-publication.

24. Miller, *More About Tanty*, 56.

25. "A Portfolio of Recent Work by Antonin Raymond, Architect," *Architectural Forum* (November 1941): 341; Antonin Raymond, "Toward True Modernism," *New Pencil Points* (August 1942): 76–85.

26. Raymond, "Toward True Modernism," 79.

CHAPTER 3

1. Harold Rosenberg, "The American Action Painters," *Artnews*, December 1952, 23ff.

2. *Les Etats Genereaux* was first published in the journal *VVV* 4 (February, 1944).

3. Mark Polizzotti, *Revolution of the Mind: The Life of André Breton* (New York: Farrar, Straus and Giroux, 1995), 517. See also: Phyllis Braff, *The Surrealists and their*

Friends on Eastern Long Island at Mid-Century (East Hampton: Guild Hall Museum, 1996).

4. Jeffrey Potter, interview with the author, 18 September 2000.

5. Ruth Nivola, interview with the author, East Hampton, 15 September 1999.

6. Robert Alan Aurthur, "Hitting the Boiling Point, Freakwise, at East Hampton," *Esquire*, June 1972, 204.

7. "Robert Motherwell's Quonset Hut," *Harper's Bazaar*, June 1948.

8. Rosenberg, "Action Painters," 23.

9. Quoted in "An Interview with Jackson Pollock by William Wright," (1950) and "Narration Spoken by Jackson Pollock in Film by Hans Namuth and Paul Falkenberg," (1951) in *Pollock Painting: Photographs by Hans Namuth* (New York: Agrinde Publications, 1978).

10. Peter Blake, *No Place Like Utopia* (New York: Knopf, 1993), 119.

11. Peter Blake, interview with the author, Bridgehampton, August 1999.

12. Ibid.

13. Ibid. For an in-depth analysis of this collaboration see Eric Lum, "Pollock's Promise: Toward an Abstract Expressionist Architecture," *Assemblage* 39 (1999): 62–93.

14. Blake, interview with the author.

15. Arthur Drexler, "Unframed Space: A Museum for Jackson Pollock's Paintings," *Interiors* (January 1950).

16. Robert Motherwell, telephone interview with the author, 22 June 1985.

17. The architect Bruce Goff designed a chapel for Camp Parks, California using three Quonset huts. See Donald Albrecht, ed., *World War II and the American Dream* (Cambridge, MA: MIT Press, 1995), 25–6.

18. Quoted in James Revson, "Razing the Roof Where Motherwell Once Lived," *Newsday*, 6 June 1985.

19. Jeffrey Potter, interview with the author.

20. Robert Motherwell, telephone interview with the author, 22 June 1985.

21. "Motherwell's Quonset Hut."

22. Motherwell, telephone interview with the author.

23. Ibid.

24. Ibid.

25. Revson, "Razing the Roof."

26. Robert Motherwell, "Beyond the Aesthetic," *Design* (April 1946).

27. Ibid.

28. Frank O'Hara, *Robert Motherwell* (New York: The Museum of Modern Art, 1965), 19.

29. Ruth Nivola, interview with the author.

30. Ibid.; Bernard Rudofsky, *Behind the Picture Window* (New York: Oxford University Press, 1955), 163.

31. Bernard Rudofsky, "The Bread Of Architecture," *Arts & Architecture* (October 1952).

32. William K. Zinsser, "Far Out on Long Island," *Horizon*, May 1963, 26.

33. Rudofsky, *Behind the Picture Window*, 163.

34. Ruth Nivola, interview with the author.

35. Ibid.

36. Pietro Nivola, telephone interview with author, 14 May 2000.

37. Charles Jencks, *Le Corbusier and the Tragic View of Architecture* (Cambridge, MA: Harvard University Press, 1973), 149.

38. Ruth Nivola, interview with the author.

39. Quoted in Charles Jencks, *Le Corbusier and the Tragic View of Architecture* (Cambridge, MA: Harvard University Press, 1973), 149.

40. Siegfried Gohr and Gunda Lyken, eds., *Frederick J. Kiesler, Selected Writings*, (Stuttgart: Hatje, 1996), 126.

41. *Progressive Architecture* (July 1961): 105–23.

42. Hohauser was born in New York City in 1933. See Ulrich Conrads and Hans G. Sperlich, *The Architecture of Fantasy* (New York: Praeger, 1960), 78–9.

43. There has been some argument over the nature of this collaboration. See "The Church Project: Pollock's Passion Themes," *Art in America*, (Summer 1982): 110–22; and Rosalind Krauss's tart rebuttal, "Reading Jackson Pollock, Abstractly," in *The Originality of the Avant-Garde and Other Modernist Myths* (Cambridge, MA: MIT Press, 1986), 221–42.

44. Quoted in B. H. Friedman, *Jackson Pollock, Energy Made Visible* (New York: McGraw-Hill, 1972), 174.

45. See correspondence on this subject in the Tony Smith Estate, New York City.

46. "The Pattern of Organic Life in America," unpublished ms., 1943, Tony Smith Estate, New York City. See: Robert Storr, *Tony Smith: Architect, Painter, Sculptor* (New York: The Museum of Modern Art, 1998), 188.

47. Blake, interview with the author.

48. Ibid.

49. Ibid.

50. James Tanner, "The Solid Gold Melting Pot," *Harper's Bazaar*, August 1958, 146.

51. Aurthur, "Hitting the Boiling Point," 206.

52. Ibid.

53. Tanner, "The Solid Gold Melting Pot," 146.

54. Pollock was buried at Green River Cemetery in the Springs, which then became the most desirable resting place for other artists and writers. A. J. Liebling, Frank O'Hara, Ad Reinhardt, and Stuart Davis are buried there.

55. Rosenberg, "The American Action Painters."

CHAPTER 4

1. William K. Zinsser, "Far Out on Long Island," *Horizon*, May 1963, 6.

2. William J. Hennessey, *Vacation Houses* (New York: Harper & Brothers, 1962), 82. My italics.

3. "A House Away from Home," *Life*, 3 August 1959, 78.

4. The house in the *Life* photograph was the Russell House, designed by Peter Blake and Julian Neski for textile designer Jack Russell.

5. "A House Away from Home," 78.

6. It has been said that this showdown was actually orchestrated as a media moment for Nixon who, at the time, was campaigning against John F. Kennedy in the 1960 Presidential race.

7. This according to William Safire, now a columnist for the *New York Times* but then a publicist for Leisurama developer Herbert Sadkin. As quoted in Rhoda Amon, "A Life of Leisurama," *Newsday*, 26 February 1999.

8. Quoted in "Six Thousand Houses That Levitt Built," *Harper's*, September 1948, 54.

9. David Halberstam, *The Fifties* (New York: Villard Books, 1993), 134.

10. See Peter Blake, *No Place Like Utopia* (New York: Knopf, 1993), 136–41.

11. On the growth of Levittown, see Mark Robbins, "Growing Pains," *Metropolis* (October 1987), 72–8.

12. Elizabeth Mock, *If You Want to Build a House* (New York: The Museum of Modern Art, 1946), 5; George Nelson and Henry Wright, *Tomorrow's House* (New York: Simon and Schuster, 1945); *A Total Environment for Living*, publicity brochure for the Techbuilt company of North Dartmouth, Mass., n.d. (circa 1965), author's collection.

13. *Long Island: The Sunrise Homeland*, a brochure produced by The Long Island Association, Inc., New York, 1947, author's collection.

14. See "The Awful Long Island Expressway," *Newsday Magazine*, 13 September 1981 (special issue).

15. Lewis Mumford, *The Highway and the City* (New York: Harcourt, Brace & World, 1963), 235.

16. *The Sunrise Homeland*, 122.

17. Zinsser, "Far Out," 6.

18. "Pinwheel House, Designed by Peter Blake," *Arts and Architecture* (June 1955). Reprinted in Barbara Goldstein (ed.), *Arts & Architecture: The Entenza Years* (Camridge, MA: MIT Press, 1990), 190–1.

19. Zinsser, "Far Out," 6.

20. Carl L. Biemiller, "Holiday House," *Holiday*, May 1951, 102.

21. Nelson and Wright, *Tomorrow's House*, 7.

22. "Holiday House," *Interiors* (May 1951): 86–95.

23. Claire Burch, "The Wind, the Sea and Mr. Burch's Dream House," *Life*, 30 March 1962.

24. "Vacation Headquarters—for 12!," *American Home*, July 1954, 50–1.

25. Karl Kaspar, *Vacation Houses: An International Survey* (New York: Praeger, 1967), 6.

26. "Vacation Headquarters," 51.

27. Le Corbusier and Pierre Jeanneret, *Ouevre Complete de 1910–1929* (Zurich: Ginsberger, 1937), 24. Le Corbusier's unbuilt design for the Errazuris House of 1930 was responsive to the ocean views and breezes of a dramatic site overlooking the Pacific coastline of Chile.

28. Russel Lynes, *The Domesticated Americans* (New York: Harper & Row, 1963), 269.

29. "A House Away from Home," 78; Peter Blake, "Summer Houses," *House & Home*, July 1956, 150.

30. James Tanner, "The Solid Gold Melting Pot," *Harper's Bazaar*, August 1958, 146.

31. Geraldine Trotta, *Dune House: A Story of Summer People in the Long Island Hamptons* (New York: Farrar, Straus and Cudahy, 1960), 4.

32. Ibid., 112.

33. Betty Pepis, "A Window on the Sea," *New York Times Magazine*, 13 July 1952, 30–1.

34. Antonin Raymond, "Toward True Modernism," *New Pencil Points* 23 (August 1942): 76–85.

35. Quoted in Elizabeth Mock, *If You Want to Build A House* (New York: The Museum of Modern Art, 1946), 41; Advertisement for ASG (American Saint Gobain) in *House Beautiful's Vacation Homes*, spring/summer 1968, 12.

36. T. H. Robsjohn-Gibbings, *Homes of the Brave* (New York: Knopf, 1954), 102. The cartoon was by Mary Petty.

37. Cranston Jones, *Architecture Today and Tomorrow* (New York: McGraw-Hill, 1961), 67.

38. Harriet (Rosenberg) Strongin, interview with the author, East Hampton, 18 December 1986; Pepis, "A Window on the Sea," 30–1.

39. Johnson had designed a house for himself in Cambridge, Massachusetts in 1946, while still in the architecture program at Harvard. The Farney House was built three years before Johnson's own Glass House in New Canaan, and four years before Mies van der Rohe had completed the Farnsworth House.

40. Breuer had used this kind of "raised plan" for the Tompkins house and his own house in New Canaan (1947); "A House Away from Home," *Life*, 3 August 1959, 78; Peter Blake, interview with the author, Bridgehampton, August 1999.

40. Blake, interview with the author.

41. Peter Blake, interview with the author, Bridgehampton, September 1999.

42. Ibid.

43. Quote by Wiener in the introduction to *Paul Lester Wiener Collection* (Eugene: University of Oregon Library, 1971), 2.

44. "A Yacht in a Meadow," *Vogue*, May 1963, 150.

45. Glenn Fowler, "Imaginative Use of Plastics Results in Economy of Space in a Beach House," *New York Times*, 5 May 1962.

46. P. Guéguen, "Habitations d'Artistes a Long Island, Etats-Unis," *Aujourd'hui* (June 1960): 66–74; Zinsser, "Far Out," 8. *Aujourd'hui* included stories about the Nivola House and garden, the Rosenberg House in East Hampton, the Lewis House in the Springs, Paul Lester Wiener's house in Amagansett, Peter Blake's Pin Wheel House, and the house of Buffie Johnson and Gerald Sykes in East Hampton. Among others, Zinsser profiled the architects Gordon Bunshaft, Peter Blake, and Edward Durell Stone, and the artists Costantino Nivola, Saul Steinberg, Lee Krasner, and Alexander Brook.

47. Cynthia Kellogg, "Umbrella House," *New York Times Magazine*, 14 June 1959, 40–1; Quoted in "Alexander Knox House," *House & Garden*, July 1959.

48. "Knox House."

49. Blake, interview with the author, August 1999.

50. Bob Smith to Tony Smith, 3 September 1954, Tony Smith Estate, New York City.

51. Zinsser, "Far Out," 7.

52. Blake, interview with the author, August 1999.

CHAPTER 5

1. William K. Zinsser, "Far Out on Long Island," *Horizon*, May 1963.

2. The drawing, c. 1962, was in one of Elizabeth Reese's scrapbooks. Estate of Elizabeth Reese, collection of Richard Moss, Stamford, CT.

3. "Playhouse on a Budget," *New Homes Guide* 41 (1956): 36.

4. "Playhouse on a Budget," 32.

5. Ibid.

6. John P. Callahan, "Year-Round Comfort Provided in Shorefront Summer Homes," *New York Times*, 5 May 1957.

7. Andrew Geller, interview with the author, Amagansett, 19 August 1999.

8. Fred Smith, "Houses that Unsquare the Cube," *Sports Illustrated*, 29 July 1963, 40.

9. Geller, interview with the author. While working for Loewy, Geller developed the interiors and garden scheme for Lever House with Isamu Noguchi.

10. Smith, "Unsquare the Cube," 40.

11. Ibid.

12. The Hunt house was built in Ocean Bay Park, Fire Island, in 1959. See: Stephanie Roth, "OBP's Hunts Build Unconventional House; Narrow Lot Produces Box-Kite Shape," *Fire Island News*, 11 July 1959.

13. Geller, interview with author.

14. Ibid.; "Northport Architect Designs Unusual Westhampton Home," *Long-Islander*, 1959.

15. Geller, interview with author.

16. "$3,000 Week-End House," *Esquire*, May 1958.

17. Terry Pearl, quoted in Alastair Gordon, "In Search of Fun Among the Dunes," *New York Times*, 22 July, 1999.

18. Alice Rogers to Betty Reese, 6 March 1962. From Reese's scrapbook, Estate of Elizabeth Reese, collection of Richard Moss, Stamford, CT.

19. Betty Reese, letter to the editor, *Life*, 30 March 1962.

20. "East Hampton, L.I.: Summer Home Wrecked in Storm," *New York Times*, 3 April 1962.

21. *House Beautiful's Vacation Homes*, spring/summer 1968, 51.

22. "House in the Sky," *Interior Design*, August 1965.

23. "The Second Home Market," *American Builder*, July 1968, 19.

24. Ibid., 20; "The Motivations Toward Homes and Housing," survey prepared for the Project Home Committee by Raymond Loewy/William Snaith Inc., New York, 1967.

25. William Branch Storey, *The World's Fair House: American Contemporary Styling at Its Best* (Cincinnati: Formica Corporation, 1964), 60.

26. "Retirement Living: What to Build Now for Later Leisure," *House Beautiful's Vacation Homes*, spring/summer 1968, 127; "The Motivations Toward Homes and Housing."

27. Richard Bender, letter to the author, 2 August 2000.

28. Only four of the prototype houses were built. See George O'Brien, "Budget Beach House," *New York Times Magazine*, 3 May 1964; and John D. Bloodgood, "Your Plans for A Second Home Start Here!" *Better Homes & Gardens*, July 1965, 102–3.

29. Rhoda Amon, "A Life of Leisurama," *Newsday*, 26 February 1999.

30. Advertisement for Techbuilt in *House Beautiful's Vacation Homes*, spring/summer, 1968, 18.

31. Gropius, Koch's mentor, was committed to the same goal and continued his research while teaching at Harvard. Gropius had proposed the idea for a factory-produced house in 1909. From 1943–48, Gropius and Konrad Wachsmann developed the Packaged House System with the General Panel Corporation. A prototype was built on Long Island. Breuer developed his own scheme for a mass-produced house, the "Yankee Portable."

32. Carl Koch with Andy Lewis, *At Home with Tomorrow* (New York: Rinehart, 1958), 157–9.

33. Ibid., 33.

34. "Kitchen—The Focal Point," *Interior Design*, August 1965; Quote from advertisement for Techbuilt in *House Beautiful's Vacation Homes*.

CHAPTER 6

1. *The Architectural Record Book of Vacation Houses* (New York: American Heritage Press, 1970), 3.

2. J. McCarthy, "Long Island Is Becoming Long City; 118-Mile-Long Metropolis," *New York Times Magazine*, 30 August 1964, 17.

3. See "The Awful Long Island Expressway," *Newsday Magazine*, 13 September 1981 (special issue).

4. "First Person Bliss," *House Beautiful*, January 1962, 96–7; "Seaside Origami," *House & Garden Guide For Young Living*, spring/summer 1969, 68–71; "A House that Sets Us Free," *House & Garden*, December 1969, 78; Ellin Saltzman quoted in "A House that Sets Us Free," 81.

5. Charles Gwathmey, interview with the author, New York City, 16 March 1999; Peter Eisenman, "Cardboard Architecture: House I," *Five Architects* (New York: Wittenborn, 1972), 15–7.

6. Gwathmey, interview with the author; quoted in Richard Meier, *Richard Meier Architect: 1964–1984* (New York: Rizzoli, 1984); Paul Goldberger, "Architecture's '5' Make Their Ideas Felt," *New York Times*, 26 November 1973.

7. Gwathmey, quoted in Paul Goldberger, *The Houses of the Hamptons* (New York: Knopf, 1986), 41.

8. The occasion was a meeting of the Conference of Architects for the Study of the Environment, the Museum of Modern Art, New York, 1969. See Goldberger, "Architecture's '5'."

9. Peter Eisenman, et al, *Five Architects* (New York: Wittenborn, 1972); Manfredo Tafuri, *Architecture and Utopia: Design and Capitalist Development* (Cambridge, MA: MIT Press, 1976); Lewis Mumford, *The Story of Utopias* (New York: Boni and Liveright, 1922).

10. Gwathmey, interview with the author.

11. Ibid.

12. Ibid.

13. See Karl Kaspar, *Vacation Houses* (New York: Praeger, 1967), 126–9.

14. Gwathmey, interview with the author.

15. Kenneth Frampton, "Frontality vs. Rotation," in *Five Architects*, 11.

16. Meier, *Richard Meier Architect*, 35.

17. At the time of the Steel houses, the firm was Gwathmey, Henderson & Siegel Architects.

18. F. Scott Fitzgerald, *The Great Gatsby* (New York: Scribner's, 1925), 6.

19. Julian and Barbara Neski, interview with the author, Bridgehampton, 17 August 1999. See Alastair Gordon, "No Simple Addition: Expanding an Architectural Landmark of the '60s," *Newsday*, 19 May 1991.

20. "Vacation Living Exploits the Sun in the North," *New York Times Magazine*, 26 September 1971.

21. Written statement by Norman Jaffe, Norman Jaffe Estate, Bridgehampton.

22. "Down-to-Earth House," *House & Garden*, July 1975.

23. Meier, *Richard Meier Architect*, 39.

24. Blocking out undesirable views was always an important aspect of beach house design. The radical look of Rudolf Schindler's Lovell Beach House in Newport Beach, California was generated by the need to rise above a public area and to create a private sanctum that would be saturated by sunlight and be as close to the beach as possible.

25. "A House that Sets us Free," *House & Garden*, December 1969, 78–87.

26. Ibid., 78.

27. Ibid.

28. See Norma Skurka, "House of 11 Levels," *New York Times Magazine*, 5 March 1972, 50–1; and "Architectural Record Houses of 1973," *Architectural Record* (May 1973): 46–7.

29. Julian and Barbara Neski, interview with the author.

30. "Summer Home Design Honored," *East Hampton Star*, 18 February 1971.

31. "Record Houses of 1969," *Architectural Record* (May 1969): 55.

32. "Record Houses of 1971," *Architectural Record* (May 1971): 22–4.

33. The house cost $40,000 to build. See Norma Skurka, "A Beach House That's Almost Like Home," *New York Times Magazine*, 27 May 1973.

34. "Fire Island House on Small Lot Gets Privacy on Low Budget," *New York Times*, 22 January 1967.

35. Frank O. Gehry, Thomas S. Hines, and Franklin D. Israel, *Franklin D. Israel: Buildings & Projects* (New York: Rizzoli, 1992), 26–7.

36. Goldberger, *Houses of the Hamptons*, 47.

37. Goldberger, "Great Beach Houses Defer to the Ocean," in *On the Rise: Architecture and Design in a Postmodern Age* (New York: Times Books, 1983), 219–21.

38. "Seaside Origami," 68–71.

39. Goldberger, "Great Beach Houses," 219–21.

40. Town of East Hampton Comprehensive Plan, *A Guide for*

Public Action (East Hampton: 1984). By 1980 the population of Southampton had reached 43,146, while East Hampton had reached 14,029, according to a town-by-town census conducted by the Long Island Lighting Company. *Long Island Population Survey* (Uniondale: Long Island Power Authority, 1999).

41. East Hampton actually passed its first zoning ordinance on 9 September 1957. See, "Notice of Enactment of Building Zone Ordinance of the Town of East Hampton, New York," *East Hampton Star*, 12 September 1957.

42. Town of East Hampton Comprehensive Plan, *A Guide for Public Action* (East Hampton: 1984).

43. These included the Group for the South Fork, the Peconic Land Trust, and an active local chapter of the Nature Conservancy.

44. "What Makes a House Modern?" *House & Garden*, July 1958, 32–5.

45. Vincent Scully, *The Shingle Style Today, or The Historian's Revenge* (New York: George Braziller, 1974), 42.

46. Scully made the not altogether convincing argument for including the Gwathmey House under the shingle umbrella because of its stick-style frame and cedar siding. Scully, *The Shingle Style Today*, 24.

47. Ibid.

48. Ibid., 26.

49. Construction of the main house began in the fall of 1963.

50. "A Saltbox for All Seasons," *Look*, 12 November 1968, 76–7; "Saltbox Split in Two," *Architectural Forum* (September 1965): 58–61.

51. Scully, *The Shingle Style Today*, 25.

52. "A Cubist Cape Cod with Award-Winning Simplicity," *House Beautiful's Vacation Homes & Leisure Living*, fall/winter, 1968, 69.

53. "Beebe Residence Project Description," internal document from the Robert A. M. Stern office, New York.

EPILOGUE

1. Francis Fleetwood, quoted in Tom Connor, "It's Been in the Family for Weeks," *New York Times*, 10 September 1998.

2. Alastair Gordon, "A Place in the Sun, Breaking into Hamptons Real Estate," *On the Avenue*, July–August 1987.

3. Alastair Gordon, "Hamptons Style: Everything Old is New Again," *On the Avenue*, July–August 1987, 22.

4. Alastair Gordon, "Spec on a Grand Scale," *East Hampton Star*, April 1988.

5. Carol Vogel, "The Trend-Setting Traditionalism of Architect Robert A. M. Stern," *New York Times Magazine*, 13 January 1985.

6. For another client who wanted to build a house in Bridgehampton, Futterman created a replica of the W. Chandler House (Tuxedo Park, New York, 1886) designed by Bruce Price.

7. Peter Blake, interview with the author, Bridgehampton, September 1999; Quoted in Philip Nobel, "Footprints in the Sand From the 60s," *New York Times*, 22 July 1999.

8. Tom Wolfe, *From Bauhaus to Our House* (New York: Farrar, Straus & Giroux, 1981), 108.

9. Compare James Tanner's 1958 appraisal in *Harper's Bazaar* to Paul Goldberger's in the *New York Times Magazine*, published twenty-five years later. Tanner, "East Hampton: the Solid Gold Melting Pot," *Harper's Bazaar*, August 1958, 96–8; Goldberger, "The Hamptons: The Strangling of a Resort," *New York Times Magazine*, 4 September 1983, 14–20.

10. Deborah Mitchell, "The House from Hell," *Vanity Fair*, December 1992, 178.

11. See James Revson, "Razing the Roof Where Motherwell Once Lived," *Newsday*, 6 June 1985; "Trend-Setting Quonset Hut is Demolished on L.I.," *New York Times*, 3 August 1985; and Alastair Gordon, "Landmark Destroyed," *The East Hampton Star*, 8 August 1985.

12. Vincent Scully, *The Shingle Style* (New York: Braziller, 1974).

13. Deanna Adler quoted in Alastair Gordon, "In the New-Old Shingle Style," *East Hampton Star*, 31 January 1985.

14. Andrea Palladio (1508–85) had used it in some of his country villas and it later became a standard ingredient for the English Palladian style of the seventeenth and eighteenth centuries. "Palladian window" may be a misnomer since it was Sebastian Serlio, a painter and architect of the Renaissance, who first used an illustration of the arched opening in his book *L'Architettura* in 1537.

15. See Connor, "In the Family for Weeks."

16. Ed Hollander, interview with the author, Bridgehampton, 23 May 1989.

17. "Tales of the Hamptons," *New York*, 5 August 1996, 22.

18. Michael Shnayerson, "Sand Simeon," *Vanity Fair*, August 1998, 80–95.

19. Stephen Bayley "Life in a Luxury Coma," (London) *Observer*, 15 October 2000.

Charles Gwathmey,
Gwathmey House and Studio,
Amagansett, 1965.

"A Guide for Public Action," Town of East Hampton Comprehensive Plan, East Hampton, 1984.

Abercrombie, Stanley. *George Nelson: The Design of Modern Design*. Cambridge, MA: MIT Press, 1995.

Architectural Record. *The Architectural Record Book of Vacation Houses*. New York: McGraw Hill, 1970.

Barry, Joseph. *The House Beautiful Treasury of Contemporary American Homes*. Hawthorn, NY, 1958.

Biemiller, C. L. "Holiday House." *Holiday Magazine*, May 1951, 86–95.

Blake, Peter. *No Place Like Utopia*. New York: Knopf, 1993.

Crosbie, Michael J. *Ten Houses: Alfredo De Vido Architects*. Gloucester, MA: Rockport, 1998.

Dean, John P., and Simon Breines. *The Book of Houses*. New York: Crown, 1946.

Five Architects. New York: Wittenborn, 1972.

Gohr, Siegfried and Gunda Lyken, eds. *Frederick J. Kiesler: Selected Writings*. Stuttgart: Hatje, 1996.

Goldberger, Paul. "The Hamptons: The Strangling of a Resort," *New York Times Magazine*, 4 September 1983, 1420.

———. *The Houses of the Hamptons*. New York: Knopf, 1986.

Gordon, Alastair. *Convergence: The Hamptons Since Pollock*. Roslyn Harbor: Nassau County Museum of Art, 2000.

———. *Long Island Modern: The First Generation of Modernist Architecture on Long Island, 1925–1960*. East Hampton: Guild Hall Museum, 1987.

Group, Harold, E., ed. *The Book of Small Houses*. Garden City, NY: Garden City Publishing, 1946.

Hefner, Robert J., ed. *East Hampton's Heritage*. New York: Norton, 1982.

Hennessey, William. *Vacation Houses*. New York: Harper, 1962.

Kaspar, Karl. *Vacation Houses: An International Survey*. New York: Praeger, 1967.

Kiesler, Frederick. *Inside the Endless House, Art, People, and Architecture: A Journal*. New York: Simon & Schuster, 1966.

Koch, Carl, with Andy Lewis. *At Home with Tomorrow*. New York: Rinehart, 1958.

Krinsky, Carol H. *Gordon Bunshaft of Skidmore, Owings & Merrill*. Cambridge, MA: MIT Press, 1988.

Laffan, William [Mackay] and Edward Strahan. "The Tile Cub at Play." *Scribner's Monthly*, February 1879, 457–78.

Larsen, Jack Lenor. *A Weaver's Memoir*. New York: Abrams, 1998.

MacKay, Robert, Stanley Linvall, and Carol Traynor, eds. *AIA Architectural Guide to Nassau and Suffolk Counties, Long Island*. New York: Dover, 1992.

Meier, Richard. *Richard Meier Architect, 1964–1984*, New York: Rizzoli, 1984.

Miller, Frances. *More About Tanty: A Second Growing Up*. Sag Harbor: Sandbox Press, 1980.

———. "Week-End On the Dunes." (Self-published manuscript, Bridgehampton, 1934).

Mock, Elizabeth. *If You Want to Build A House*. New York: Museum of Modern Art, 1946.

Montauk Beach Development Corporation. "Montauk Beach on Long Island, 'The Miami Beach of the North,' A Carl G. Fisher Development" (Promotional brochure published by the Montauk Beach Development Corporation, New York, 1927).

Muschenheim, William. *Elements of the Art of Architecture*. New York: Viking, 1964.

Nelson, George, and Henry Wright. *Tomorrow's House*. New York: Simon & Schuster, 1945.

O'Hara, Frank. *Robert Motherwell*. New York: Museum of Modern Art, 1965.

Philips, Lisa, ed. *Frederick Kiesler*. New York: Norton and the Whitney Museum of American Art, 1989.

Potter, Jeffrey. *To a Violent Grave: An Oral Biography of Jackson Pollock*. New York: Putnam, 1985.

Progressive Architecture. *Homes*. New York: Reinhold, 1947.

Rattray, Everett T. *The South Fork: The Land and the People of Eastern Long Island*. New York: Random House, 1979.

Raymond, Antonin. *An Autobiography*. Rutland, VT: Tuttle, 1973.

———."Toward True Modernism." *New Pencil Points* 23 (August 1942): 76–85.

Raymond Loewy/William Snaith Inc. "The Motivations Toward Homes and Housing" (Special report prepared for the Project Home Committee, New York, 1967).

Scully, Vincent. *The Shingle Style*. New Haven: Yale University Press, 1955.

———. *The Shingle Style Today: Or the Historian's Revenge*. New York: Braziller, 1974.

Storr, Robert. *Tony Smith, Architect, Painter, Sculptor*. New York: Museum of Modern Art, 1998.

Tuomey, Douglas. *How to Build Your Own House*. New York: Grosset & Dunlap, 1949.

Wolfe, Tom. *From Bauhaus to Our House*. New York: Farrar, Straus & Giroux, 1981.

Zinsser, William K. "Far Out on Long Island." *Horizon*, May 1963, 4–27.

Project architects appear in parentheses

Abercrombie & Fitch, 116–7
Acorn Structures, 119
Adler House (Eugene Futterman), 164
All State Properties, 73
Allen House (Ward Bennett), 142–3
Allvine, Glendon, 27–8
Allvine House (Warren Matthews), 28
Amagansett, history of, 1, 14, 133
Amenity (Richard Bender), 119
American Architect, 15
American Fine Arts Society, 15
American Home, 85
American National Exhibition, Moscow, 72
Architectural League of New York, 28
Architectural Progress, 28
Armstrong House (Peter Blake), 91
Arnstein House (Bernard Rudofsky), 54
Art Village, the, 11–2
Atterbury, Grosvenor, 12, 16
Atterbury House (Stanford White), 12

Barr, Alfred, 34
Bayles, Richard M., 7
Beach Hampton Surf Club, 23
Becker House (Norman Jaffe), 160–1
Beebe Residence (Robert A. M. Stern), 161
Behrens, Peter, 30
Bender, Richard, 93, 119
Bender House (Richard Bender), 119
Bennett, Ward, 142–3
Benson, Arthur W., 13–4
Betty Parsons Gallery, 46, 48

Blake (Second) House (Peter Blake), 89, 90
Blake, Peter, 27, 44, 46–8, 58–59, 62–4, 72, 89–91, 97, 99, 127, 137, 159, 164
Bodanzki, Artur, 33
Bodanzki, Elizabeth, 33
Breese, James Lawrence, 16, 18, 35
Breese Estate, ("The Orchard"; Stanford White), 16, 35
Breuer, Marcel, 30, 75, 89, 121, 146
Bridgehampton, history of, 3, 9, 16, 36, 87
Bross House (Alfredo De Vido), 159
Brouwer House, 12
Brouwer, Theophilus A., 12, 13
Brown, Archibald, 34
Browning, Elisabeth, 11
Browning, Robert, 11
Bryant, William Cullen, 7
Bullard, Roger, 19, 21
Bunshaft, Gordon, 91–2
Bunshaft House (Gordon Bunshaft), 92
Burland House (Norman Jaffe), 159
Butler, Howard Russell, 10, 15

Carera Beach House (Antonin Raymond), 38–9, 166
Cates House (Julian & Barbara Neski), 144, 146
Chadwick, Gordon, 154–5
Chalif House (Julian & Barbara Neski), 137, 139, 159
Chareau Cottage (Pierre Chareau), 49
Chareau, Pierre, 27, 44, 48, 49, 50, 51, 67
Chase, William Merrit, 7, 8, 11, 12, 13
Chimicoff, Alan, 148
Christofanetti, Lucia, 43, 45
Cleveland, Lucy, 11
Cogan House (Gwathmey Siegel), 137

Colen, Arthur, 28, 30
Corbin, Austin, Jr., 16
Crane, Bruce, 10
Creeks, The, (Ossorio Estate), 12, 44, 166

Deck Houses, 119
Diamond House (Bernard Marson), 150–1
Dion House (Peter Hendrickson), 150
Divinity Hill, Shelter Island, 14
Divinity Hill, East Hampton, 14
DeKay, Charles, 15
De Vido, Alfredo, 146, 152, 159
De Vido House (Alfredo De Vido), 152
Devon Colony, 16
Devon Yacht Club, 16, 21
Drew, John, 19
Drexler, Arthur, 48, 130
Dunes, The, (Wiborg Estate), 43
Dune House, 85
Eames, Charles, 72, 79
Eames, Ray, 72
East Hampton, history of, 3, 8, 9–11, 15–6, 33, 43, 45, 53, 67, 87
Eastern Long Island, history of, 3, 7, 9–10, 16, 27, 47, 67, 78, 121, 167
Ecole des Beaux Arts, 28
Eisenman, Peter, 128
Elkin House (Andrew Geller), 153, 169
Endless House, the (Frederick Kiesler), 47, 58–59
Erdman House ("Coxwould"; Harrie T. Lindeberg), 16–7
Ernst, Max, 43
"Excursion," 121

Fair Field, 166–7
Farney House (Philip Johnson), 88–89

Farnsworth House (Mies van der Rohe), 88
Ferguson, Henry, 10
Fisher, Carl Graham, 19, 21–3, 119, 167
Fitzgerald, F. Scott, 7, 43, 137
Five Architects, 130
Ford Foundation, 121
Fowler, George, 10
Frank, Rudolph, 109, 112
Frank, Trudy, 109, 112
Frank House (Andrew Geller), 109
Freetown, East Hampton, 14
Fuller, R. Buckminster, 72
Futterman, Eugene, 164–5

Gardiner's Bay Company, 16
Garraty House (Alfredo De Vido), 146–7
Garraty, Gail, 146
Garraty, John A, 146
Geller, Andrew, 73, 103–4, 107–9, 112, 114–5, 119, 152–3, 169
Georgica Association, 14
Giedion, Sigfried, 3
Glass House (Philip Johnson), 88
Gluck House (Peter Gluck), 128
Gluck, Peter, 128
Goldberger, Paul, 128, 130, 153
Goodman, Percival, 25, 27–8, 30
Gorman House (Julian & Barbara Neski), 150–1
Graves, Michael, 128
Gropius, Walter, 27–8, 30, 121
Guild Hall, 45
Gwathmey, Charles, 34, 128, 130, 133, 136–7, 139, 141–2, 148, 152, 156, 176
Gwathmey House (Charles Gwathmey), 127, 133, 176
Gwathmey Studio (Charles Gwathmey), 133, 176
Hagen House (Peter Blake), 90
Harper's Monthly Magazine, 13

Hejduk, John, 128, 130
Heller, Ben, 165
Hendrickson, Peter, 150
Henry, Edward Lamson, 8
Herter, Albert, 12
Hitchcock, Henry-Russell, 34
Hoffman House, (Richard Meier), 134
Hohauser, Sanford, 59
Holden, Lansing ("Denny"), 36–7
Holiday, 78–9, 81, 83
Holiday House (George Nelson), 78–82, 154
Homer, Winslow, 7
Horst, 144
House on the Dunes (William Muschenheim), 30
House II (Peter Eisenman), 148
Hunt (Eileen) House (Andrew Geller), 106–7
Hunt, Irwin, 109
Hunt (Irwin) House (Andrew Geller), 107–9
Hunt, Joyce, 109

Ideal Museum (Peter Blake and Jackson Pollock), 46–8
Israel, Franklin, 150

Jaffe, Norman, 141, 159, 161
Jeanneret, Charles-Edouard, see Le Corbusier
Jewett, John, H., 19
Johnson House (George Nelson), 81
Johnson, Philip, 34, 54, 88–9

Kaplan House (Julian & Barbara Neski), 138–9
Kaplan, Stephen, 139
Kaprow, Allan, 127
Kent House (Peter Blake), 99
Kiesler, Frederick, 44, 47, 55, 58–9
Kitchen Debate, the, 72, 119
Klee, Paul, 30
Knox, Alexander, 96–7
Knox House (Alexander Knox), 96–7
Koch, Carl, 119–21
Krasner, Lee, 45, 54

Laffan, William Mackay, 5, 9–10
Larsen, Jack Lenor, 157–9
Lauren, Ralph, 163, 166
Lawrence House (Rafael Viñoly), 165

Le Corbusier (Charles-Edouard Jeanneret), 27–8, 55–6, 83, 95, 128, 130, 134, 141
Leisurama (Andew Geller), 72–3, 103, 119
Lever House (Gordon Bunshaft), 91
Levitt, Alfred, 75
Levitt, William, 75
Levittown, 75, 77–8, 121
Lewis House (Robert Rosenberg), 83–5
Lewis, William, 85, 97
L.I.E., see Long Island Expressway
Life, 1, 45, 71–2, 78, 83, 85, 89, 115
Lindeberg, Harrie T., 16
LIRR, see Long Island Rail Road
Loewy, Raymond, 103
Long Island, 3, 7, 28, 30, 44, 47, 48, 71, 115
Long Island Association, 77
Long Island Expressway (L.I.E.), 77–8, 127
Long Island Rail Road (LIRR), 9–10, 16, 22–3, 43, 67, 77
Loos, Adolf, 30
Lord, James Brown, 19
L'Oursin, 127
Low House (McKim, Mead & White), 154, 156
Lowenstein House (Chimacoff & Peterson), 148–9
Lynn House (Andrew Geller) 114–5

Macy's, 73, 107, 119
Maidstone Club, the, (Roger Bullard), 7, 18–21, 43
Maison de Verre (Pierre Chareau), 48–9
Marson, Bernard A., 150
Matthews, Hale, 152
Matthews House (Alfredo De Vido), 159
Matthews, Warren, 27–8
McKim, Mead & White, 154
Meadow Club, the, 21, 35
Meier, Richard, 128–30, 134, 141–3, 152
Midhamptons, 23
Mies van der Rohe, Ludwig, 27, 30, 46–47, 54, 64, 88–9
Miller House (Charles Gwathmey), 130
Miller House (Venturi & Short), 156
Miller Beach House ("The Sandbox"), 36–8, 85, 97, 116
Miller, Frances Breese, 27, 35–9, 97, 103

Mitty's, 127
Montauk, history of, 7, 16, 19, 87
Montauk Association, 13–4, 19
Montauk Beach Development Corporation, 19, 23
Montauk Manor (Schultze and Weaver), 22
Moran, Mary (Nimmo), 10–1
Moran, Thomas, 10–12, 167
Motherwell House (Robert Motherwell and Pierre Chareau), 49–52
Motherwell, Robert, 43–53, 67
Mumford, Lewis, 13, 15, 77, 130
Muschenheim Bathhouses (William Muschenheim), 27, 33–4
Muschenheim, Frederick Augustus, 30, 33
Muschenheim House, (William Muschenheim), 30–2
Muschenheim, William, 27, 30, 34, 39, 97, 119
Museum for a Small City (Mies van der Rohe), 46–7
Museum of Modern Art, New York, 34, 53, 75

Namaganesett Club, the, 21
Namuth, Hans, 45
Nelson, George, 44, 72, 75, 78–82, 127, 154–5
Neski, Julian, 88–9, 128, 137–9, 144–8, 150–2, 159
Neski, Barbara, 88–9, 128, 137–9, 144–8, 150–2, 159, 164
Neski House (Julian & Barbara Neski), 138
Neutra, Richard, 27, 75
New School for Social Research, 34
New York Five, the, (the Five), 128, 130, 134
New York Times, 104, 123, 130
New York Times Magazine, 78, 87, 97, 127
New York World's Fair (1964), 116–7
Nivola, Costantino, 43–5, 53–6
Nivola House and Garden (Costantino Nivola), 43, 54–56
Nivola, Ruth, 45, 53–55

Olmsted, Frederick Law, 14
On the Beach, 71
Orchard, The, see Breese Estate, the
Osofsky House (Norman Jaffe), 141
Ossorio, Alfonso, 43–5, 61, 166

O'Toole House (Robert Rosenberg), 157
O'Toole, John, 157

Parsons House (Tony Smith), 60–1
Peabody, Wilson and Brown, 34–5
Perlbinder House (Norman Jaffe), 159
Peterson, Steven, 148
Picturesque America, 7
Pin Wheel House (Peter Blake), 62–6, 85, 89, 97, 167
Pollock, Jackson 43–8, 53–4, 56, 58–9, 61–2, 64, 67, 167
Pospisil, Edward, 121
Project for a Beach House (Robert Venturi), 156

Quartley, Arthur, 8, 9
Quogue Field Club, 18
Quonset Point Naval Air Station, 49

Raymond, Antonin, 27, 38, 39, 87
Raymond Loewy-William Snaith Corporation, 73, 103, 107, 112
Reese, Elisabeth (Betty), 103–4, 107, 115
Reese House (Andrew Geller) 103–4, 109, 115
Red House, the, 44
Rennert, Ira 166–7
Richards, William Trost, 9
Robertson, Jaquelin T., 159
Rosenberg, Harold, 41, 44, 47, 58, 67, 78
Rosenberg House (Robert Rosenberg), 87–9
Rosenberg, Robert, 44, 83, 85–7, 97, 127, 157, 159
Rothenstein, Guy G., 95
Rothenstein Beach House (Guy G. Rothenstein), 95
Round House, the, (Jack Lenor Larsen and Robert Rosenberg), 157–8
Rudofsky, Bernard, 27, 53, 54
Ruskin, John, 12
Russell House (Peter Blake and Julian Neski), 88

Sabel House (Julian & Barbara Neski), 148–9
Sadkin, Herbert, 73
Sam's Creek Development (Norman Jaffe), 141–2
Saint-Gaudens, Augustus, 7
Saltzman, Ellin, 144

Saltzman House (Richard Meier), 143–4, 148

Sandbox, the, see Miller Beach House

Satterthwaite Villa, 14

Saypol House (Wiener & Bender), 93

Simpson House (Wiener & Bender), 93

Schlachter House (Norman Jaffe), 141–2

Schultze and Weaver, 22

Scribner's Monthly, 10

Scull House (Wiener & Bender), 93

Scully, Vincent, 156, 165

Seltzer House (Jaquelin T. Robertson), 159

Serendipity Homes, 119

Sert, José Luis, 92

Shallows, The, see Tyng House, the

Sheehy House (Alfredo De Vido), 146

Shinnecock Bay, 30, 33–5, 97

Shinnecock Hills, 12–3, 18

Shinnecock Hills Golf Club (Stanford White), 18–21

Shinnecock School of Art, 12

Shute, Nevil, 71

Siedler House (Norman Jaffe), 141

Siegel, Robert, 148

Signa Gallery, 45

Simon, Merle, 144, 146

Simon, Peter, 144, 146

Simon House (Julian and Barbara Neski), 144

Smith, Fred, 107

Smith, Tony, 44, 47, 58–62, 97

Snell House (Franklin Israel), 150

Sokolniki Park, 72

Southampton, history of, 3, 16, 33, 87

Southampton Bath and Tennis Club ("The Bathing Corporation"), 18, 35–6

Spaeth House (George Nelson & Gordon Chadwick), 154–7

Sports Illustrated, 106–7, 115

Sugarman House (Ward Bennett), 142

Sunrise Homeland, The, 77–8

Speed, John Gilmer, 13

Stern, Robert A. M., 161, 164

Stamos House (Tony Smith), 60–62

Stamos, Theodoros, 44, 60–62, 97

Stanmar Homes, 119

Strahan, Edward, 5, 10

Sunrise Highway, 127

Talmage, Rev. T. De Witt, 14–16

Taut, Max, 30

Techbuilt, 1, 3, 119–123

Techbuilt Beach House, 122–3

Tile Club, 7, 9–10, 13, 43

Tillinghast, Stafford, 11

Town Planning Associates, 92

Tompkins House (Marcel Breuer), 146

Trotta, Geraldine, 85

Trupin, Barry, 165

Tyng, Lucien Hamilton, 34

Tyng House ("The Shallows"; Peabody, Wilson, and Brown), 35

United States Information Agency (USIA), 72

Urban, Joseph, 34

Venturi, Robert, 156

Viñoly, Rafael, 165

"What I Did on My Vacation," 127

Wheelock, John Hall, 3, 167

White, Stanford, 7, 12–4, 16, 18, 21

Whitman, Walt, 7

Wiborg Estate ("The Dunes"), 43

Wiener, Paul Lester, 44, 47, 55, 92–5

Williams College, 30

Wiseman House (Robert A. M. Stern), 161

Wolfe, Tom, 164

Wright, Frank Lloyd, 27, 38

Zahn, Anita, 33–4

Zinnser, William K, 1, 69, 95, 99, 101

IMAGE CREDITS: